HOLLOW PROMISES?
Rhetoric and reality in the
inner city

Edited by

Michael Keith
and
Alisdair Rogers

MANSELL

First published 1991 by Mansell Publishing Limited
A Cassell Imprint
Villiers House, 41/47 Strand, London WC2N 5JE, England
125 East 23rd Street, Suite 300, New York 10010, USA

British Library Cataloguing in Publication Data
Hollow promises: rhetoric and reality in the inner city
 1. Great Britain. Cities. Inner areas. Social planning. Policies of
government.
 I. Keith, Michael 1960- II. Rogers, Alisdair
307.120941

 ISBN 0-7201-2036-5
       0-7201-2062-4   pb

Library of Congress Cataloging-in-Publication Data
Hollow promises: rhetoric and reality in the inner city / edited by
 Michael Keith and Alisdair Rogers
      p.   cm.
  Includes bibliographical references and index.
  ISBN 0-7201-2036-5 -- ISBN 0-7201-2062-4 (pbk.)
  1. Inner cities. 2. Urban renewal - Great Britain - Case studies.
 3. Urban renewal - United States - Case studies. I. Keith, Michael,
 1960- . II. Rogers, Alisdair
HT.156.H65 1990
307.3'4216'0942 - - dc20   90-49526
                                                                      CIP

Printed and bound in Great Britain by Biddles Ltd., Guildford and King's Lynn, from
camera-ready copy supplied by the volume editors.

CONTENTS

Contents

PART 3
ALTERNATIVE REALITIES

NOTES ON CONTRIBUTORS

Patrick Bond is a PhD candidate in geography at the Johns Hopkins University, Baltimore and currently a Visiting Research Associate at the University of Zimbabwe analysing the Third World debt crisis. He was a steering committee member of the Maryland Alliance for Responsible Investment from 1986 to 1989, representing student interests. As a Visiting Scholar at the Institute for Policy Studies from 1988 to 1989 he assisted reinvestment coalitions, trade unions, the student movement, farm groups and the anti-apartheid movement across the USA in similar campaigns against financial capital.

Liz Bondi is a lecturer in geography at the Department of Geography, University of Edinburgh and the co-editor with M. H. Matthews of *Education and Society: Studies in the politics, sociology and geography of education* (Routledge, 1988).

Susan Buckingham-Hatfield is currently teaching urban and political geography at Kingston Polytechnic. Her research interests include revitalisation and the role of community groups in the USA (under preparation for a PhD) and the orientation of student project work to community needs from which *Community Enterprise in Higher Education* was published in 1989.

Bob Colenutt works for the Docklands Consultative Committee. He is the co-author with Peter Ambrose of *The Property Machine* (Penguin, 1975) and a councillor in the London Borough of Lambeth.

Jon Dawson works at the Centre for Urban Studies at the University of Liverpool. **Michael Parkinson** is Director of the Centre for Urban Studies at the University of Liverpool. He is is the author of *Liverpool on the Brink* (Hermitage, 1985) and the co-editor of *Regenerating the Cities: the UK crisis and the US experience* (Manchester: Manchester University Press). He has also worked as an adviser to the Merseyside Development Corporation.

Michael Keith is a lecturer in the Department of Geography at QMW, University of London. He has written mostly on racism and policing in the 1980s although his current research is concerned with the relationship between racism and urban policy and he is also co-editor with Malcolm Cross of *Racism, the City and the State* (Unwin Hyman, 1991).

Contributors

Sarah Ladbury and Clive Mira-Smith currently run the City Research Unit, an independent consultancy on urban issues. They were both formerly Research Fellows with the Urban Change Group at University College, London.

Patrick Le Gales is a research officer at the Observatoire Sociologique du Changement, Paris. He has written about comparative urban policy in Europe, and is currently involved in a project comparing social change and the role of the lower middle classes in Italian, British and French cities.

Alisdair Rogers is a Demonstrator at the Department of Geography, Oxford University. His research has focused on the social geography of the USA and race and racism.

Neil Smith is a Professor of Geography at Rutgers University and the author of *Uneven Development*, (Basil Blackwell, 1984). He is also the co-editor of *Gentrification of the City* with Peter Williams (Allen and Unwin, 1986).

Mel Thompson is a Research Fellow at the Centre for Research in Ethnic Relations at the University of Warwick. Her main research interests are in the locating oral histories of migrants within a wider theoretical framework of migration. Her present research involves the comparative experience of Caribbean migrants in Canada, the USA and Britain. She also has a wide experience of anti-racist and equal opportunity policy in the educational field.

ACKNOWLEDGEMENTS

This volume began as a co-operative venture between the Urban Geography and Social and Cultural Geography Study Groups of the Institute of British Geographers and we would like to acknowledge the support given by both groups. It also greatly benefited from the advice of friends and colleagues at the Centre for Research in Ethnic Relations, at the University of Warwick, particularly in the Urban Change team under the direction of Malcolm Cross. Penny Beck was a great help at Mansell. We are also very grateful to Jenn Page and Ed Oliver at QMW, University of London for their secretarial and cartographic expertise. There are many other colleagues we would particularly want to acknowledge for their support, although Harbhajan Brar, David Gilbert, Stephen Pile, Gillian Rose and John Solomos all deserve special mention and Charlotte Wellington, to whom the book is dedicated, deserves far more than that.

CHAPTER 1

HOLLOW PROMISES ?
Policy, theory and practice in the inner city

Michael Keith and Alisdair Rogers

It is tempting at times to ask 'where is the inner city?' One can run to a map, locate examples, even indulge in exercises of cartographic explicitness, but eventually the answer, at first so obvious, can become progressively more confusing on closer inspection. Everybody knows about the clustering of certain social and economic problems in some parts of some of the older metropolitan areas of post-industrial economies. But do these places have a great deal else in common? Or is *the inner city problem* no more than an exercise in name-calling? Is this nothing more than the perennial appearance of uneven development, one of the principal diagnostic phenomena of capitalism, only this time at the intra-urban rather than a regional or national scale?

More worryingly, what are the implications of tying manifestations of urban crisis to these places that we call inner cities, thus characterising a social problem as a spatial expression? In other words, does the very notion of the inner city serve to site the blame for poverty on a location, a variation on the invidious rhetoric of blaming the victim? By dressing up deprivation in this spatial vocabulary it is possible to hide the more unpalatable realities of economic restructuring, redundancy and exploitation.

In this volume we have tried to bring together a collection that will go some way to answering these questions without losing sight of either city experience in a welter of academic abstraction or powerful analysis in a stream of political rhetoric. We have tried to build on the uncertainty that surrounds the very definition of the inner city, firstly to examine the utility of particular cases of state intervention (Part 1 of the book), then to highlight some of the misconceptions that have informed political initiatives in the inner city (Part 2) and finally to present alternative perspectives on community mobilisation, entrepreneurship and urban crisis in the inner city (Part 3).

With one exception (chapter 10) the essays in this volume focus on Britain and the USA. These two countries share a political culture, a conservative strategy of managing the social and economic changes of the post-1980 period by re-establishing the conditions for successful capital accumulation and 'de-integrating' society (Krieger, 1986). For Krieger this involves increased racial polarization and poverty, and a corresponding erosion of some of the social rights instituted under the welfare state. Both Reagan and Thatcher administrations, he argues, have reversed post-war consensual and integrative politics in favour of the fragmentation and competition of the market. In the case of Britain at least, we shall argue that this strategy is grounded most recently in the imaginary space of the inner city.

Further points of similarity include the exchange of policies and ideas (Barnekov, Boyle and Rich, 1989; Parkinson, Foley and Judd, 1988). Although the exchange was never exclusively one-way (e.g. Butler, 1981 on enterprise zones), the American experience initially served as a model for British efforts to regenerate cities on the part of both the state (Urban Development Corporations, the stream-lining of urban grants) and private capital (e.g. the Rouse Corporation's festival market places, which have inspired developments in Glasgow, Manchester and Newcastle). Following the Reagan administration's retreat from urban policy, President Bush's appointment of Jack Kemp as head of the Department of Housing and Urban Development and the announcement in June 1989 of the formation of a Presidential Task Force on the Inner City signalled a possible return flow of ideas. Given the task of reviving urban policy at low cost, Kemp is considering such Thatcherite innovations as housing vouchers, tenant management and tenant purchase of public housing. On both sides of the Atlantic, a more privatised mode of housing consumption is being encouraged.

Finally, given the internationalization of financing, property development and construction, prestige regeneration projects in Britain and North America involve the participation of a small number of firms. The most notable are Rouse's own Development Corporation and the Canadian-based Olympia and York, behind both the Battery Park City (New York) and Canary Wharf (London) projects. Cesar Pelli is the architect of both schemes.

2

It is therefore the connections of political culture, policy formation and property capital as much as those of urban experience that have prompted us to focus principally on these two nations in this volume. An American model of 'privatism' (see Barnekov, Boyle and Rich, 1989) has in recent times been deemed as *exportable*. Here again policy and practice in the *inner city* are as much about the way we chose to conceptualise social problems as they are about the experiences of *inner city* communities themselves. A particular theoretical diagnosis of American urban crisis achieves a certain respectability and is assumed to generate policy templates that are universally useful in all post-industrial societies, as applicable in Newcastle as in New York.

If it is difficult to define inner cities in terms of some geometric configuration of urban morphology, it is even less easy to identify the inner city within any national political economy. Are inner cities only found as pockets of deprivation within an area of relative prosperity, as has been the case in London, Birmingham and New York, where the East End, Handsworth, and select sections of Manhattan and Long Island are traditionally contrasted with the rest of the city? Or do cities trapped in declining regional economies such as Pittsburgh in the USA or Newcastle in Britain also display distinctively *inner city problems*?

Given such ambiguity, perhaps the notion of the inner city should be dropped altogether from academic analysis. After all, flawed basic concepts should not form the starting point for rigorous analytical investigation. Yet such cynicism begs important questions and detaches objective academic research from the common sense categories of everyday language in a suspiciously elitist manner. It is not as though academic social science has yet found a language that can address these problems that is not contentious. *All* academic paradigms, from the Chicago school onwards, that have tried to capture theoretically the essence of 'the city' have come to grief (Saunders, 1981) and so the concepts that are used to describe and analyse the nature of contemporary urban life may be *necessarily* flawed. Hence, a political economy of *the urban* is scarcely more plausible now than it has ever been in the past. In these circumstances to talk of *the inner city* may be to accept a vocabulary which we might prefer not to endorse but it might also use the only language in which we can be heard. Beside this, the very persistence of the term is itself worthy of interest and on academic, moral and political grounds any resolution of the uncertainty that surrounds the value of the concept of the inner city must surely start by taking on this vocabulary for what it is.

So it is against a background of almost two decades of popular acceptance of the *urban problem*, a crisis of the cities, that this text is set. In two decades remarkably

3

little has been done to alleviate the conditions of some of the poorest city citizens, who personified the unacceptable face of the urban crisis, even if the terms of the debate itself have changed dramatically. Any book about the inner city in 1990 cannot ignore this failure and must surely look at both the reality on the ground today and at the manner in which academic analysis has conceptualised these problems in ways that have facilitated this persistence. It is imperative not to accept the subjects of popular interest as the objects of theoretical scrutiny, not to reify a concept of dubious historical provenance, but instead to unpack the powerful rhetoric that hides behind the notion of *the inner city*, to outline the contours of alternative urban realities and to place this empirical evidence in the political and economic context that will determine the life chances of those people that live in real places in real urban locations today.

There are moral and political implications that follow on such a stance. For there is a sense in which the ready and correct dismissal of essentialist definitions of any legitimate inner city problematic has characterised literature of the left. Typically, the call has been to go *'Beyond the inner city'* (Byrne, 1989). This has had political and analytical ramifications, with the inner city debate frequently lacking a left perspective, leaving the field to a contest between liberal assertions of the case for sympathy (ESRC, 1986; Robson, 1988; MacGregor and Pimlott, 1990; Wilson, 1987) and more recent and robust demands on the right for a faith in strategies of benign neglect based on market led regeneration and tempered by occasional state facilitation of the private sector (Savas, 1983; Trippier, 1989). In contrast, the contributors to this book, whilst differing between themselves in many respects, share both a critical refutation of the manner in which *the inner city* has commonly been taken as unproblematic and a belief in the need to use the vocabulary of popular debates to propose alternative conceptualisations of urban crisis and to subject current policy to critical examination.

So there is an important strategic point here. From a purist point of view if the terms of debate set by the study of an inner city problematic are illegitimate then perhaps they should not be addressed at all. However, we believe that not only is such a stance disingenuous, but it also promotes a fundamentally flawed political strategy and reproduces naive notions of academic objectivity. In this volume we are in part trying to draw out the links that tie the assumptions involved in policy debates to some of the grim realities that affect local communities in contemporary city life. This has certain implications for the kind of research on the inner city that we are interested in. The questions that are asked in academic texts are as significant as the results that are produced. For in defining any research agenda two pitfalls have to be avoided. One is that academic research should pluck the fruits of the contemporary political agenda and lend credibility to vogue and vague notions that may fleetingly assume a high profile, reify concepts that are of the moment and endow them with the status of real analytical phenomena.

The second, equally flawed strategy, particularly relevant here, is to ignore the realities of contemporary life in which state policy and popular practice are informed as much, if not more, by the common sense construction of a neat array of *social problems* as by the theoretical wisdom of the ivory tower. The social construction of an inner city problem echoes through the political world, structures the vocabulary of policy formulation and has ramifications in the realms of political economy. The politics of the inner city problem are not just the surface manifestation of economic imperatives; here there is no straightforward linear determination of superstructure by base. Instead we are talking about a series of complex configurations of politics, economics and ideology that recursively interact to guarantee that it is not possible to understand what is happening in the local economies of Glasgow, Liverpool or Birmingham in the UK or Baltimore, New York or Toronto in North America without reference to inner city policies wedded to a particular form of symbolic, frequently spectacular, regeneration. Policy formulation takes place in a theoretical, social, economic and political context. We cannot divorce economic change from esoteric architectural style, state intervention from community immiseration, new wealth from recurrent poverty; all encapsulated in the notion of the inner city. One issue here centres on the notion of novelty. The urban crisis or the *inner city* problem conflates a number of quite different economic, political and social issues. The urban ramifications of massive economic restructuring in the 1980s did not produce the same effects as the legitimacy crisis of welfare state capitalism in the cities of the 1960s and 1970s. But by hiding in the term 'inner city' the novel appears as perennial, the strange appears to be familiar.

In the political process that structures the future of cities professionals talk at politicians who leak to journalists who are lectured by academics who scrutinise any policy pronouncement. Just occasionally somebody may even listen to the urban citizens whose city and whose fate is being discussed. In this Babel like context the apparent exchange of information between different interest groups may commonly founder. Each in turn speaks their own language of jargonistic expertise and coded euphemism. It is in this context that even the barest skeleton of a common vocabulary that captures the different forms of urban life may be welcomed and it is in this search for cogent communication that the notion of the inner city, so commonly discredited analytically, remains so powerful descriptively. The term 'the inner city' may tell us much more about the manner in which an agenda of social problems is set by the combined and unequal influences of a variety of interest groups than about the political economy of cities but its very reproduction in a set of discourses about 'the urban' guarantees it a status of its own.

Academic theorisation conventionally attempts to find a language that *represents* reality. The theoretical project attempts to represent an accurate abstraction of the empirical diversity of the social world, in this case, the urban world. In this text we are in part challenging this straightforward relation. There is no essential definition of the inner city; it is now a truism to note that *the inner city* is theoretically chaotic. It cannot serve as a term that describes objectively a specific set of conditions. Conceptually, it is a term that is linked not to one social problem but to a host of economic, social and political issues. Linguistically, it is a signifier with no referent and a multiplicity of significations.

But it is precisely this problematic relationship between language and reality that instead of rendering the term theoretically redundant exemplifies one of the problems implicit in *all* urban social theory but addressed only occasionally. We want to say quite explicitly that the language with which the problems of contemporary urban life are addressed is necessarily problematic. It is not just that the academic protocols of putative objectivity, cross referencing and theoretical vocabulary sit uneasily beside political polemic which reads so differently from the equally strict conventions of focused brevity in the local government or consultant's report, although these issues of *style* are themselves not minor. It is also that the perspectives necessarily adopted by very different interest groups, some of which we have tried to reproduce here, will contain a degree of indeterminacy of translation between themselves. But this indeterminacy should not, and ultimately cannot, be hidden or brought together under a single overarching account.

In this sense we are arguing that all accounts, including those that aspire to academic objectivity, are structured by the social contexts in which they are generated. Academic, or theoretical, discourse is not privileged but is instead a form of accounting which uses abstraction to illuminate. Our task as editors of this book is to make these social contexts explicit and our own intentions to contribute to a critical discussion of the inner city issue, which challenges the meanings of the powerful, as open as possible. Authorship counts.

Politicians and academics, policy makers and local communities, all have their own, understandably distinct agendas and commonly, it would seem, their own languages. But these agendas overlap, subtly borrow concepts and ideas from each other. It is the attempt to examine some of these interdisciplinary intersections that lies at the heart of this text.

In this book we have tried to bring together practitioners from different fields as well as from four different academic disciplines. Half the chapters are written by people involved at first hand with the initiatives that they discuss. This has important ramifications for both the style in which they are written and the claims to truth that they are making. In this sense we are not concerned to produce a book by academics for a purely academic audience. Yet neither are we attempting to understate the value of theoretical abstraction. Indeed we want to examine the ways in which a concept which appears to be logically fraudulent, the inner city, has sustained its central position in both popular and academic discussion of the urban. This is why this volume is concerned with an attempt to tie together policy, theory and practice.

FROM A *SOCIAL PROBLEM* TO A *SUITABLE CASE FOR TREATMENT*

It is not the intention to rehearse here the history of the evolution of an *inner city problem* from an academic vogue of the 1960s and 1970s, to part of the vocabulary of common sense understandings of contemporary urban life, to a major and recurrent item on the political agenda of two nations (for such information see Barnekov, Boyle and Rich, 1989; Peterson, 1985; Robson, 1988; Sills, Taylor and Golding, 1988).

We are concerned here with the more recent debates that have used the inner city as a central organising theme, debates that have grown out of the economic boom years of the second half of the 1980s in many of the richest economies in the world. It is in these countries, particularly in the United States and the United Kingdom, that significant upturns in the economy have done little to relieve a sense of urban crisis reminiscent of the 1960s, although the political terms of debates that address urban problems have changed dramatically over this time.

The most crucial change in emphasis over the past twenty years, and particularly over the past ten, has been the common rejection of any suggestion that poverty alone warranted social policy intervention based on state amelioration. Whereas urban policy on both sides of the Atlantic was originally justified as a form of welfare initiative, it is now presented in functional economic terms aiming to introduce growth to areas of depression or industrial decline. Recently produced

7

figures on British Urban Development Corporation expenditure highlight precisely what a small fraction of budgets are currently spent on community projects as opposed to economic initiatives.

	1988/89	*1989/90*
Black Country	1.3	1.8
Bristol	0	1.0
Central Manchester	1.4	1.6
Leeds	0.9	0.1
London Docklands Development Corporation	3.3	6.5
Merseyside	4.5	3.1
Sheffield	0.4	0.7
Teesside	2.4	0.3
Trafford Park	0.1	0.3
Tyne and Wear	0.3	0.9

Source: Hansard 24/5/89

Figure 1.1: Percentage of UDC budgets used for community projects and voluntary sector initiatives

Put crudely, state intervention in contemporary urban Britain (and America) is justifiable only to facilitate market led growth.

Under this rubric there have been several locations which in the 1980s, at least at a particular, symbolic level, have lent a rhetorical credibility to the notion of an urban renaissance in many parts of the First World. The list of cities that have 'refused to die', 'come back' or 'turned around' increases steadily. Some, like New York, have restored their economies after a decade or so of decline, while others, such as Baltimore or the London Docklands, have focused optimism on high prestige, frequently waterfront, projects. How much longer such presentation remains credible in the light of trends in cities such as New York, where there are at least 90,000 people sleeping on the streets and an annual budget deficit of around $500 million is itself a significant issue. Moreover, these successes have to be set beside the less successful regeneration projects attempting to replicate the well known formula in cities such as Richmond (Virginia), Toledo (Ohio) and Flint (Michigan), all of which are faltering (Guskind, 1989).

This focus on a particular strategy of growth-based survival on both sides of the Atlantic has been lent a credibility by the apparent successes of these high profile city projects. In Britain, American experience is commonly cited as setting a precedent both for what can be done and for the policy strategies necessary for success.

It is in this context that a new future role for inner cities finds favour with Robson, who justifies the need for an inner city policy on the potential of the city to become a place of consumption linked with business services: "the role of cities in production is no longer that of access to labour, but of access to information" (p16). These observations may reflect what is already happening, yet their implicit optimism needs to be tempered by the realities of this kind of economic growth (see also Kasarda, 1985 for a similar assessment of the US context).

In work looking at the labour markets of Los Angeles and New York, Sassen (1989) has argued that economic growth creates both wealth and poverty. Two new forms of poverty arise from the bifurcated wage and occupational structure of the producer services sector (businesses dealing in information) and through the development of a semi-skilled or deskilled labour force in personal services such as restaurants, hotels and domestic service. Evidence from both cities supports the contention that the informal sector in services and labour intensive manufacturing is growing alongside the higher status sectors of the economy. In this context the fallacy of any straightforward equivalence between economic boom and social wellbeing is exposed. Poverty is a constitutive element of a particular form of economic growth as much as it is a product of economic recession.

It is not necessarily the case that similar patterns are being repeated in the quite different social context of the UK. As Pahl (1988) points out, it is not possible to accept uncritically the idea that an underclass has emerged in British society. But the view that poverty is the consequence not of the failure of growth but of its very success is one that needs to be taken seriously. In short, what we understand as the persistence of poverty may in fact be more complex, a function of new social relations tied to new forms of economic development. By focusing principally on spatial variation and concentration of deprivation it is easy to overlook the processes that underscore these recurrent areal patterns.

By 1987 the revolutionary restructuring of the British economy in the 1980s had, so it appeared, left residual pools of localised recession and left wing politics. The economic miracle of the decade seemed to have passed the inner city by, leaving a few localities outside the new society. The agenda here had changed by the time of Margaret Thatcher's election victory promise to do something about 'those inner cities'. In contrast, by the late 1980s, the inner city appeared to be less prominent on the American political agenda. The most evident shift in the terms of debate in Britain concerns the focus and nature of growth. Consequently, the whole vocabulary of political debate has changed. These changes are inextricably linked to the new social context of the 1980s in which the parameters of the social problem that is the inner city have changed. Conceptually, the inner city is a space outside society which has shown, for whatever reasons, a marked recalcitrance in responding to the macro-economic revival that surrounded it on all sides (Massey and Meegan, 1989). In short, the inner city appeared in 1987 to be a suitable case for treatment.

The language of parliamentary debate in Britain has reflected this change. Rhetorically, the central organising theme of the debates on the inner city in Britain over the last three years has been the problem of exporting the *successes* of the rest of the nation to this extraordinary conceptual space. The debates take on an almost sacramental nature as speakers resort to the most basic metaphors of reproduction and renewal in a search for the rites of an inner city spring (Goldberg, 1990). The key word becomes *regeneration*. Typically, in one of the first debates about inner cities of the third Thatcher term, Nicholas Ridley, then Secretary of State for the Environment, justified his aggressively business led strategy, introducing more Urban Development Corporations:

"They will have the same powers as the larger UDCs, but above all they will create the business-friendly environment and single minded approach which are the necessary preconditions for regeneration." (Nicholas Ridley, Hansard Vol 117 ; 1 July 1987, 534)

This language permeates policy making discussion. To take just one example, the British House of Commons Employment Committee report on the effects of urban development corporations mentions the concept of regeneration eight times in the opening eleven paragraphs, stating that

"we do not see Urban Development Corporations as being primarily and immediately concerned with employment; they are about regeneration." (1988, p3)

Their report returns again and again to this unproblematic notion of regeneration in spite of their own rather plaintive recommendation that "the remit for UDCs should be altered to provide a more precise definition of 'regeneration' " (1988, p4)

Yet there remain some continuities, echoes of the past pathologies of urban life. Economic degeneration taints those who are associated with it. This is more than blaming the victim, it involves making the victim part of the problem. One minister for the inner cities in Britain has made this quite clear:

"[W]e must ensure that those who live in derelict inner-city areas are not people who are there because they have no choice and who would leave the moment they were given an alternative." (Kenneth Clarke, Hansard Vol 129; 7 March 1988, 35)

Instead, as ministers are quick to suggest, there is something essentially specific about the nature of the inner city, a political echo of a spatial fetish:

"I do not agree with the proposition that the only problem in inner cities is poverty and that all that we need to do is to alleviate poverty, there being no need for other policies. I do not accept either the Right-wing proposition that we need only to make the country better off as a whole without making any special effort in the inner cities." (Kenneth Clarke, Hansard Vol 129; 7 March 1988, 37)

"The inner cities will succeed in solving their problems only through their own strength and determination." (Timothy Raison, Hansard Vol 117; 1 July 1987, 543)

American rhetoric on the city shares some of these themes, notably those of enterprise and the liberating influence of the market, although there have also been distinct differences embedded in US political culture. Carter's federally aided approach to help cities adjust to changing economic realities gave way to Reagan's sink-or-swim philosophy.

"States and cities, properly unfettered, can manage themselves more wisely than the Federal Government can." (US Department of Housing and Urban Development, 1982, p1)

11

However, while "[t]he Administration does not believe that any city is condemned to inevitable decline" (US Department of Housing and Urban Development 1984, p27), the emphasis on comparative advantage and entrepreneurialism carried an inevitable warning.

> "Improving the national economy is the single most important program the federal government can take to help urban America; because our economy is predominantly an urban one, what's good for the nation's economy is good for the economies of our cities, although not all cities will benefit equally, and some may not benefit at all." (Savas, 1983, p447)

Wolman (1986) argues that what informed Reagan's urban policy was the misplaced notion of a national and urban dichotomy, economies engaged in a zero-sum game; the federal government could assist the one but not the other, since the costs of doing so would detract from national economic recovery. What lay behind the urban strategy of the 1980s therefore was the discipline of the frontier, that most American of archetypes.

> "History shows us that the inherent strength of American communities and institutions can be attributed in large part to the freedom Americans had to experiment without the deadening hand of capital control. Frontier communities were left alone to devise ways of dealing with unusual crises and opportunities without having to conform to rules that bore no relation to local conditions. The enterprise zone concept sees inner cities, in effect, as 'urban frontiers' constrained by regulations and a tax code that is irrelevant to the problems and opportunities that exist. By reducing these suffocating barriers, the aim would be to simulate frontier creativity in urban neighbourhoods." (Butler, 1984, pp 141-2)

Like Savas, Butler was another expert from the Heritage Foundation who sought to influence urban policy with ideas. The contrast with Britain's lingering commitment to active intervention is revealed more clearly by Kemp himself.

> "The British just wanted to move whole industrial sites, whereas I did not want to force people to move from the South Bronx. The idea was to try to bring back the spirit of entrepreneurship that I thought people in these neighbourhoods would be inclined towards if the right environment were established." (in Guskind, 1989, p1358)

Thus, the spirit of regeneration, derived from the frontier experience, is an innate quality of Americans, even in the South Bronx.

SO WHERE ARE THOSE INNER CITIES?

In spite of our concern with the dubious provenance of the term itself there remains a need to research 'the inner city problem', evaluate existing policies and propose new ones. Robson's volume, *Those Inner Cities'* (1988), although an authoritative contribution to this debate, in accepting common sense constructions of social problems (e.g. the section in Chapter 1 on 'Crime and unrest') stubbornly ignores the reality of politics and uncritically reproduces the inner city as a space outside society.

We are not trying to ignore the material traumas of contemporary cities. A cursory look at the experience of late capitalist economies across the world suggests that changes in the labour process are closely linked to highly demarcated differentiations in the labour force; socially constructed identities that describe the division of labour, differential incorporation into the economy tied to cultural (ideological) constructions of gender, skill, age and race. The degree to which deprivation is reproduced across successive generations of oppressed and minority groups will largely depend on the interaction between such divisions of the labour force and the regional economies of the localities in which such minorities are concentrated.

In this sense we want to tie the structural changes in political economy that have marked most nations in the last decade and have commonly had their most profound consequences in cities, to attempts to demarcate a space that corresponds to the political, social and academic construction of a traumatised inner city. Inherently, these attempts have been doomed. Similar and perennial manifestations of urban crisis at the empirical level are not attributable to a consistently repeated set of causal processes that would justify a conventionally theorised problematic of *the inner city*. Poverty has many different roots but only one public face. But it is in the tension between conceptual confusion and social reality that it is possible to expose some of the assumptions that inform policy and some of the hidden agendas that are currently structuring the life chances of subordinated communities. A case in point can be taken from recent British experience.

LEGITIMATION AND THE NEW AGENDA IN BRITAIN

It is a commonplace now to acknowledge the difficulties involved in drawing a boundary around the inner city. Across the political spectrum there are always those quick to proclaim the injustice of specific circumscriptions. The reasons for this are obvious. In the United States in the 1960s the political will to get to the trough of federal aid resulted in the Model Cities programme rapidly expanding from a focus on 66 metropolitan centres to a total of almost 140 cities spread across the nation (Levine, 1989). Similar competition multiplied the areas receiving urban programme funding in Britain at roughly the same time. Enterprise zones altered arbitrarily the relative locational advantage of firms inside and outside their perimeter. And, of course, relative spatial concentrations of deprivation do not involve absolute absence of deprivation from other areas. In the words of a suburban Conservative party member in one of the British parliamentary debates on the inner city,

> "Will my right hon. Friend not lose sight of the fact that need does not always exist only in the inner areas of a city." (Jill Knight, Hansard Vol 117; 1 July 1987, 535)

The number of 'unemployed' is never on its own an adequate description of the forms of economic restructuring that are occurring, even when such figures are calculated with integrity.

Once it is accepted that the inner city is an idea rather than a place it is tempting to ask which interests really do benefit from the recurrence on the political agenda of the urban crisis. We wish to suggest here not a conspiracy theory but a coincidence of interests that embodies these beneficiaries. It consists of a fortuitous, almost accidental, alliance between a particular fraction of development capital and New Right political reformers, not always particularly clearly articulated, which has in the last few years managed to don the cloak of inner city concern. The social reformers who staffed the think tanks that fed into the right wing of the Conservative Party and who advocated the restructuring of education, the dismantling of the welfare state and the restriction of local government power, needed a theme through which to proselytise their views. The forces of property development always wanted to structure the terms by which the city became again a safe investment location for capital. An understanding of an economic project, distinct from, but complementary to, an exercise in political legitimation, helps to decode the most recent expressions of concern for the ever ailing inner city. The inner city provides a medium through which the political project may be legitimated and the site on which new forces of economic change may be played out.

It is in the very nature of democratic politics that policy change must be rationalised in a vocabulary that both appeals to popular understandings of the social problems that are being tackled and yet does not disturb certain common sense understandings of the workings of the economic system. In the British context of the 1980s the political project that has come to be identified as 'Thatcherism' has commonly been seen as an attempt to legitimate both the reintegration of a restructured British economy into the global economy and the revision of the relationship between the state and civil society that the preferred version of restructuring required. Most neatly captured by the notion of the free economy and the strong state (Miliband and Saville, 1979; Gamble, 1988), the project has involved both the disciplinary reaction to those who have come out worst from this restructuring in the handling of uprisings among British Black communities and a series of confrontations with the Trade Union movement and the need to present massive cuts in welfare service delivery as essential for economic prosperity.

In the post 1987 era this logic has underscored urban policy interventions which incorporate two key themes, one a straightforward exercise in symbolic amelioration and social control of racial injustice, the other the manipulation of the raw social context by which the Thatcherite ideology of privatism can be extended in housing, education and local government finance through the particular representation of contemporary urban life that the term inner city evokes. As long as new measures of social policy in these areas could be presented as *solutions* to an inner city problem they stood a greater chance of popular acceptance than if they were seen as no more than further attempts to rid the nation of the welfare state legacy of the post-war era and the dependency mentality that went along with it. Third term Thatcherism became grounded in the imaginary place that was called the inner city.

There can be no area in which the distance between the pretence and practice of British inner city policy has been greater than that of racist injustice and racial deprivation. Regularly presented as the principal policy medium for the resolution of these two problems, the impact of urban policy on either has been as minor as the significance they have had for the formulation and legitimation of policy has been major. Dating back to the late 1960s when the announcement of the Wilson government Urban Aid programme followed swiftly on the heels of Enoch Powell's predictions of rivers of blood flowing through British cities as a result of racial conflict, there has regularly been a connection between the fear of (racially based) civil unrest and the implementation of high profile symbolic palliatives for inner city malaise (Sills, Taylor and Golding, 1988; Solomos, 1988).

Yet at the same time urban policy in Britain has provided an escape clause that allows British politicians to avoid the implementation of race specific policies aimed at redressing racial inequity. As Rex (1988, p58) has pointed out, the 1977 White Paper 'A Policy for the Inner Cities' stated that it was not concerned with the problems of Black communities as these were the responsibility of the Home Office and the Commission for Racial Equality. Nevertheless, it was presented by the minister responsible (Peter Shore) as a way of fighting the National Front, an integral part of government race relations policy. Similar ambivalence has continued to characterise much of the thinking behind British urban policy. Typically, in the wake of the uprisings of 1985 in Britain the government announced the advent of a new policy measure, the introduction of eight Inner City Task Forces to Moss Side (Manchester), Chapeltown (Leeds), Notting Hill (London), North Peckham (London), North Central (Middlesbrough), Highfields (Leicester), St Paul's (Bristol) and Handsworth (Birmingham). Seven of the eight are well known Black communities and the sites read like a civil servant's check list of those places where the state expected an uprising (excluding those with Inner City Partnerships already present), yet no race specific dimension was added to their brief. Moreover, the self-defined small scale nature of these projects placed them in marked contrast to the first seven Urban Development Corporations announced in Britain in the 1980s in London Docklands, Merseyside (see chapters 2 and 3), Sheffield, the Black Country, Teesside, Tyne and Wear and Greater Manchester, all of which received over £100 million in financial support. The suspicion that a two tier urban policy has developed, high profile symbolic initiatives for the Black poor and a particular (American) model of urban regeneration for the decayed white heartlands, is not readily dismissed. This is in marked contrast with US federal urban policy where racial deprivation has provided an explicit and recurrent theme.

In Britain the inner city provides an analytical empty vessel which serves well rhetorically to provide a rationale for a disparate set of political projects, not only those of racial subordination but also far fetching social reforms. It is within this conceptual framework that a government minister at the Department of the Environment can, with seemingly irrefutable common sense, conceptualise inner cities as the places where "those living there have not been able to participate in the economic miracle of the Thatcher years" (Trippier, 1989, p7) and which require a strong police presence because "the future prosperity of the inner cities depends directly on how safe they are in which to live and work" (ibid, p22). It is in this context that the Conservative party presented its new programme for the third term, following the Queen's speech; a set of policies lent a coherence by the inner city problem:

"Today's debate is about those parts of the Gracious Speech related to the inner cities - local services and education. In choosing to link the issues for debate, the Opposition at least seem to recognise that they go together as part of a coherent strategy." (Nicholas Ridley, Hansard Vol 117 ; 1 July 1987, 536)

"A partnership between local and central Government on inner city policy must be one between partners who believe in attracting private enterprise and capital through a constructive attitude to the private sector, low rates, sensible planning and the pursuit of excellence in education, housing and many other essential services. Partnership where there is no consensus seldom seems to work. But with compatible partners, much can be done, and I believe increasingly that there will be more compatibility when the practice of local accountability conforms with the theory.
The present rating system gives neither accountability to residents nor effective control over local authority spending to Government." (Nicholas Ridley, Hansard Vol 117; 1 July 1987, 534)

Approximately two-thirds of the minister's speech comprised an attack on the inefficiency of local government, more specifically socialist local government, and a trenchant defence of the value of the proposed community charge as a key factor in promoting the regeneration of British cities.

"Profligate spending has not only driven employers and would-be employers away and thus lost jobs, but resources have been taken away from other areas by the rate support grant formula as the spiral of inner city decline causes the rate base in inner city areas to diminish, while their needs ... grow"

"There must be an incentive for councils to control their costs. The community charge provides that incentive, and our new local government Bill that was published last Friday provides local authorities with a way of so doing." (Nicholas Ridley, Hansard Vol 117 ; 1 July 1987, 536, 538)

A whole legislative package - the Educational Reform Act, the new Housing Act, and the revolution in local government finance - is framed by the immiserated inner cities, borrows its evangelical force from the language of philanthropy.

There are two important points to note about the economic project that has run alongside the exercises in political legitimation in the imagined space of the inner city. The first is the old truism that the beneficiaries of urban policy in both Britain and the United States have not always been those for whom the policy was apparently designed. In 1960s America urban renewal was angrily equated with 'nigger removal' (Friedland, 1982). Likewise, in the British experience the act of pumping money into a particular spatially defined area has never guaranteed that those most in need in that area will benefit. As Bob Colenutt describes in this volume (chapter 2), state financed property speculation can be represented as inner city benevolence when the government hands over rich tracts of real estate to an unaccountable Urban Development Corporation in London. There are self-evidently interests other than those of social concern in the spatial revitalisation of urban economic activity and there is no need to descend into a dogmatic public v. private sector debate on the efficiency of urban renewal to suggest that these interests stand to benefit when state intervention, so discredited in the early Thatcher years as creeping socialism, can be represented as a free market solution to urban crisis.

The second point is best captured in Peter Hall's 1982 defence of the enterprise zone model of urban policy, when, perhaps inadvertently, he called for the state to facilitate multinational corporations, "doing in Liverpool what they already do in Singapore or Mexican border cities" (1982, p418). Again there are echoes from across the Atlantic. In the early 1980s Jack Kemp drew on Puerto Rico's *Operation Bootstrap* as an inspiration for his support of the Enterprise Zone model in the United States (Guskind, 1989). In short, the strategic choice in British and American urban policy has not been simply about the encouragement of economic development, it is also about the changing nature of that development itself, more specifically the changing nature of the labour process in an economy designed for the post-Fordist era (Lash and Urry, 1987; Murray, 1989). On one level this is self-evident within the ascendant economic rhetoric.

> "Our policies are based on the proposition that we need to bring the enterprise economy into the inner cities. That has been successful in reviving the national economy as a whole. It can be a success in the inner cities if the same principles are applied consistently by the Government and by leading people in business throughout Britain." (Kenneth Clarke, Hansard Vol 129; 7 March 1988, 43)

The diagnosis is a chronic case of socialism, the prognosis pessimistic and the prescription an evangelical dose of Thatcherite economics. A conscious strategy has been adopted to promote a low skill, low cost, numerically flexible and compliant labour force as preferred to alternative models of a high skill high wage economy. In part this complements the manner in which cities are increasingly economic actors competing against each other in the new global economy (Hill, 1984). In this vein, the spectacular presentations of the postmodern city should not be divorced from the ubiquitous role of spatial competition in capitalist societies:

"the way in which particular localities must engage in a bitter and divisive struggle to sell themselves to capitals as the most desirable location for their activities in an attempt to defend the right to live, learn and work in their place." (Hudson and Sadler, 1986, p188)

This is invariably as true of urban locations selling cultural capital with voodoo economics as it is of declining industrial regions of manufacturing industry (Harvey, 1989).

But at another level it is significant that almost every new initiative in British urban policy in the last decade has involved a 'freeing up' of the labour market. Deregulation of health and safety legislation and 'training initiatives' which are bracketed with inner city policy, as with Employment Training in the UK, enforce labour discipline as an integral part of urban regeneration (Trippier, 1989) and share many of the same assumptions as the 'workfare' models of welfare/labour market regulation in the USA. In this context the rhetorical commitment to the free market begins to look contradictory not only in terms of the feather-bedding of urban redevelopment but also in the imposition of a particular new economic order, a specific choice about the form of economic change that will occur. We are not arguing that either is necessarily an illegitimate exercise, only that it is significant that these things are done in the name of urban regeneration.

THE CITY AS SPECTACLE

Once the inner city is defined as a suitable case for treatment it becomes the logical social laboratory for any and all political, economic and social projects which can be presented as palliatives for the urban crisis.

So we have two key themes, both fallacies, but both as profound in their consequences as they are specious in their origin. One is the definition of a distinctive social problem, demarcated in space - *the inner city*. The other is a political ethos which has structured the vocabulary with which economic distress can be addressed around the archetypal notion of *regeneration*.

This is the perfect marriage: a disease and a cure, both geographically specific. In the 1970s in America 'urban renewal' was discredited as President Nixon unilaterally proclaimed an end to the urban crisis, in Britain as part of the grand failures of state social engineering against which Thatcherism was set. But the tawdry image of urban renewal has been given a facelift and can now return, again with all the metaphoric power of seasonal fecundity. To make the return more palatable what is needed is symbolic reassurance that changes draw on the life blood that epitomises the regenerative power of the city.

After all, in the postmodern city presentation is all. The inner city provides the perfect site to be the playground of post-industrial capital, and what a sight this can be! A new identity is to be as important as new social relations, part of the forging of cultural capital through which the city is to be sold. Image is all and those who refuse to play the game will be damned. In the words of *The Economist*, the British city of Liverpool is

"a museum to the depression, failing to hype itself back to prosperity in the fashion of Glasgow and Newcastle ... stuck in the past, in a time-warp of Beatlemania and class solidarity." (*The Economist*, 12 August 1989, p25)

Spatially circumscribed definitions of an inner city problem can, we have seen, focus on the patterns of economic depression and social injustice rather than the processes at work behind them. The inner city becomes a problem of space rather than a problem in space. But this does not mean that the reality of these concentrations is irrelevant. After Lefebvre, we still wish to see space as an object commodified, but in late twentieth century Britain this commodity has not one but a multiplicity of identities. Networks of production and consumption relations, ossified in fixed capital and anachronistic infrastructure, share the same geographical location as the places mediated by the rich political symbolism invested in the notion of *the inner city*. Spatially shifting, but perennial, concentrations of (frequently exacerbated) poverty share urban landscapes with the sites of regeneration, which by their very presence offer powerful ideological testament to the life forces of renewal retained by late capitalist growth.

It is here that the contradictory character of the inner city assumes such significance. Sills *et al*. (1988) contrast the political projection of the inner city as a place of hopelessness and blight and a residuum of crime and disorder with 'The Action for Cities' connoted vision of British values embodied in policy prescriptions extolling stability, partnership and self-help. This contrast is served by a dual locational identity, defined negatively and positively. The imported imagery of the ghetto (American, conflict-riven, Black, crime, decay, neglect, dependence) contrasts with a local vocabulary of urban tradition (English, community, white, stable, work, self-help, renewal, care).

This chameleon-like character of the inner city lends the concept its remarkable potency. The cumulative effect of the language of the British inner city has been to give it a contradictory definition, as a conceptual space both inside and outside of society. It is inside in the sense of geography, its supposedly stable working-class past implying the moral obligation of society to do something about the fundamental causes of the problems. But in the political language of the right in the 1980s it is outside in the sense of being cast as alien, normally via the stigmata of race or socialism, the locus of criminal delinquency, the site of disorder. The conception of the inner city as internal demands a policy response; external conceptions provide a rationale, even an excuse, for inactivity, a justification of neglect and hostility. On one level it is hard to see how we can avoid reproducing this contradictory space when speaking of the inner city as a place, a fusion of social problems. But at another level it is imperative that we do so because it is here that policy, theory and practice intersect. The contradictions that are built into the term 'inner city' have to be seen not as the root of analytical uncertainty but as the source of rhetorical utility. Contradictions can be subsumed in something so unproblematic as the designation of places.

In this context the rhetorical power of spectacular redevelopment should not be underestimated. What does it matter if the prestige presentation of another shopping mall in Albert Docks, Canary Wharf, Riverwalk or Seaport produces effects which are of marginal relevance to metropolitan political economy? They lend a credibility to powerful, primordial tales of rebirth, as important for their pomp as for their pump-priming of the local economy.

It is not really necessary to locate the degree of premeditated dishonesty involved in the politics of policy formulation. As Edelman (1971, 1985) has pointed out, political discourse is itself routinely structured by the symbolic presentation of social problems and policy solutions. *Social problems* are discursively constructed and demand policy resolutions that must be first and foremost valuable in the context of this discourse. In plain English it is more important, in an administrative context, *to be seen* to be doing something about a politically generated agenda of problems than it is to examine critically the agenda itself.

It should therefore be of little surprise if the expenditure on inner city regeneration turns out to be a risible fraction of that necessary to have a major impact on the level of urban immiseration as long as it can still produce the sort of photogenic spectacle so clearly embodied in Birmingham's super-prix or Phoenix's grand prix, Boston and New York's marathons or Liverpool's Tall Ships Race. This line of argument does not demand an exercise in conspiracy theory sociology, or even a belief in premeditated state malice, only an acceptance of the realities of the world of policy formulation in which both issues and policy prescriptions are not structured solely by empirical reality. The spectacle of inner city regeneration offers a powerful medium for a political commitment to a strategy based on what is superficially market led growth.

GROUNDING THE INNER CITY

It is not just that politicians speak with forked tongues. Admittedly, there is commonly a manifest purpose and a hidden agenda in almost all urban policy (Sills, Taylor and Golding, 1988, p36). But, equally significantly, surface appearance draws meaning from its own context. This is where the spectacular forms of regeneration that characterised the 1980s (Harvey, 1989) were not so much a postmodern discontinuity as a logical extension of the tradition of symbolically rich, effectively marginal, policy palliatives that were offered to the urban crisis from the 1960s onwards. It is also where writing about urban immiseration takes its significance from the context in which it is placed. There is much in recent British government pronouncement which on its own is unobjectionable or even highly laudable. After all, we all do want to live in 'safer cities', we (mostly) all do want employment and material affluence, and do not want to discourage enterprising individuals. But where the inoffensive becomes disingenuous is when policies that are irrelevant are proffered as solutions, whether as fostering an entrepreneurial culture, minor training initiatives or financing property speculation.

And the disingenuous becomes invidious when this is set against an attempt to locate blame for economic dislocation on its victims, cast inner city residents as "a poor social mix" (Trippier, 1989, p19), and offer instead a radical recasting of multi-national capital as the means of saving the inner cities.

Yet these contexts are set by the parameters of political discourse in exactly the same manner as the conceptual vocabulary of academics and practitioners structures their own treatment of the same issues. In exactly the same way as it is essential to deconstruct the rhetoric of Hansard by examining the context which structures Parliamentary debate, what we want to do here is to reveal this grounding of other contributions to this volume.

Four themes recur throughout this volume. None provides easy answers to the problems raised here but all relate to the difficulties of tying together policy, theory and practice in the contemporary city.

The spatial fetish

One of the powerful motivating forces behind any spatially focused social or economic policy is that a degree of political consensus can be reached in identifying economic dislocation and poverty with particular *places*. This is the heart of the notion of the inner city; at the very moment that policy draws the boundaries of the inner city a place takes on the qualities of coherence that it does not possess, embodies all the contradictions that are part of the original concept. There is a danger that a concentration on spatial manifestation masks the realities of social processes, that space itself is fetishised. By defining the object of policy in spatial terms the contradictory interests represented may be understandably subsumed in a real or imagined community identity which stems from or reproduces the notion of shared interests (see Sue Buckingham-Hatfield's case study in Chapter 4). Neither is it the case that this is a facet of capitalistic conspiratorial machinations, a spatial rubric of the principles of divide and rule. Territorially based affinities are the very stuff of popular mobilisation, social movements and the rights by which the left have historically based political demands.

Yet the focus of urban policy on specific areas has regularly reproduced these contradictions in microcosm. Gentrification benefits selectively, takes away with one hand as it gives with another, bestowing respectability at a cost of displacement (chapters 5 and 6). The inner city is transformed, but for whom? In a very different sense London Docklands was an invented place, a series of disparate communities which were united by the imperatives of a specific form of development chosen for them by an imposed Urban Development Corporation (chapter 2).

We are not proposing here any simple remedy to this problem, only restating the point that spatially realised problems do not always have spatially constrained solutions. The problems of the city can be conceptualised as much in terms of service delivery and collective consumption as about a particular representation of the inner city (see Patricke Le Gales in chapter 10 on France). The inner city is a social problem of an imaginary space, realised incoherently, though no less brutally for this incoherence. The way to resolve this necessary dilemma is surely not to discredit spatial policy altogether but to contextualise it, to draw out the links between the locally specific and the internationally ubiquitous, as Patrick Bond describes in his description of the campaign for the community control of capital in Baltimore (chapter 8).

Engagement

At times urban policy debates take place in a context where almost all agree that the wrong answers are being offered to the wrong questions. Yet there is no simple point of either pure detached observation or committed involvement from which this can be made. And here there are marked differences in the way the contributors to this volume see the inner city problem. The fraudulence of many of the basic policy tools implemented in the inner city immediately raises questions about the nature of either constructive engagement with flawed institutions, as seen in the consultancy work of Ladbury and Mira-Smith in chapter 7, or about the monitoring role adopted by the Docklands Consultative Committee, which has aided the campaigns of those whose interests the London Docklands Development Corporation has consistently ignored (see chapter 2). In contrast, the local circumstances are such that for Parkinson the Merseyside experience is one that he may disapprove of in principle but lives with far more readily in practice.

Following on from this, the superficial certainties of theoretical abstraction do not lend themselves easily to neat policy prescription, theoretical writing is necessarily partial, of limited value in helping people to see urban crisis from a different

24

perspective. This is the lesson from Patrick Bond's chapter on the nature of possible mobilisation illustrated from the experiences of inner city Baltimore (chapter 8). It also suggests that caution that must be exercised in reading the chapters by Neil Smith (chapter 5) and Liz Bondi (chapter 6).

What we have tried to avoid here is a sterile debate on the preferred ideologies of urban regeneration cast in terms of the relative merits of private and public sector involvement. It is certainly the case that urban areas such as inner Liverpool would benefit from private sector involvement and a stronger economic base but as Barnekov, Boyle and Rich (1989) point out this is little more than a truism.

In this sense it would be naive to make 'policy recommendations', given that a central tenet of this work is that 'policy' is more the product of a particular set of vested interests than a technocratic implementation of neutral measures. Yet the prospects for the people who live in blighted cities are bleak unless as a bare minimum there is a recognition across the political spectrum of the specificity and the extent of racial inequity in both the UK and the USA, a reconsideration of democratic involvement at both the local state and national state levels, and an attempt made to locate urban policy within local economic strategy; urban policy needs to be conceptually disentangled from regional policy.

The manufacture of expertise

We are trying to suggest here that academic enterprise may be useful as long as it is placed in its proper social context. This social context is not one where a body of intellectuals think up resolutions to an objectively defined urban crisis and then make this knowledge available to the wide church of policy makers and practitioners in the best enlightenment spirit. Things do not work like this at all. Expertise is contingent, socially manufactured. In the British and the American cases it is as necessary to contextualise the production of knowledges about the inner city as it is to unpack the glossary of terms of urban regeneration used in contemporary political discourse. The Ford Foundation was interested in a specific agenda in funding philanthropically inclined research into urban crisis in the USA in the late 1950s and early 1960s.

In the early 1980s in Britain, the Economic and Social Research Council funded a major research project which lent an official academic seal to the work of individuals concerned. Some used this expertise to work in the private sector as consultants advising on urban policy; in one case a firm that employed no Black people was selected for its 'inner city expertise' to evaluate the Handsworth Task Force in inner Birmingham which it had previously also been paid to advise but which was now being shut down to make room for a newly fashionable Urban Development Corporation, this time in the Birmingham Heartlands (*sic*). And as inner city expertise readily becomes transformed into a supplementary expertise on Black people, within months the same company was awarded a contract by the Department of Trade and Industry to evaluate the effects of inner city policy on British Black communities. Whilst individuals in the company privately admit to knowing little about 'race and racism', a major research contract which did not go out to open tender is safely located in an institution which can only with a degree of implausibility don the cloak of academic neutrality. The oppression of Black communities which justifies policy intervention but barely touches on policy implementation may be mirrored rather than challenged in the nebulous realm of academic research.

In contrast, the style of some of the chapters of this book does not pretend to be *academic*. Chapter 2 by Bob Colenutt is written from within the political processes that structure the work of the Docklands Consultative Committee in monitoring the London Docklands Development Corporation (DCC, 1990). Chapter 7, which is written by Sara Ladbury and Clive Mira-Smith, is a piece of work by the Cities Research Unit, a private consultant, and accordingly reflects the style and the medium in which it is rooted, whilst similarly Jon Dawson and Michael Parkinson's chapter is written from a perspective that is able to take on board their own personal involvement with the Merseyside Development Corporation. These differences are important, just as it is important to highlight the political position taken by the editors of the volume and the empirically based nature of some of the chapters (chapters 8 and 9) compared with the more abstract nature of others (chapters 5 and 6).

The importance of language

There is no suggestion here that any academic work is pristine pure in this regard. Instead we are arguing that all academic texts are effectively working with a particular brief and it is important that this be either spelled out in the production of academic texts or taken apart systematically by the readership. This is no different from an examination of the political and practical frame within which the work of policy analysts (e.g. chapters 3 and 7 here) or those more ostentatiously 'involved' (e.g. chapters 2 and 8 here) is placed.

We have already flagged the very language used to address a set of urban issues as a central problem. This key theme crops up repeatedly throughout the book in all the contributions because it is through language that the hidden assumptions that make up the common sense of both theoretical and empirical discussions are revealed.

One of the rewarding products of placing language under the microscope is the abolition of many of the categoric certainties that often inform rhetorical discussion of the inner city. Several examples come to mind here. The dichotomy between private and public sector is not so clear cut as it may appear. In London Docklands state subsidies have hidden under different names, disguising state intervention on a massive scale as Bob Colenutt describes in chapter 2. Conversely, Dawson and Parkinson (chapter 3) argue that in Liverpool the unaccountable work of Merseyside Development Corporation has to be set beside the ineffectual work of the putatively democratic local state. As Barnekov, Boyle and Rich (1989) have pointed out, 'privatism' in urban policy is as much a cultural tradition or ideology as a coherent set of practices.

Similarly, the notion of fostering a local enterprise culture has been suggested both inside and outside Parliament (Trippier, 1989) as a potential source of urban renewal and in Britain is officially inscribed as a goal of all Inner City Task Forces. Yet it is a peculiar use of the term that confines the concept of entrepreneurial ability to the realm of material affluence.

This is surely where academic research can be used as a useful corrective by examining the power of some of the central terms which are used in day to day discussion to make sense of the urban present. Typically, the notion of *ethnic enterprise* may be useful or dangerous, depending on the context in which it is used.

When used by certain political interests on both sides of the Atlantic to reproduce the myth of migrant mobility it can be extremely misleading. Mel Thompson (chapter 9) goes some way towards rescuing the term, arguing that whilst the trumpeting of particular forms of entrepreneurial success is dangerous because it can be used to locate the blame for economic distress on the victims of economic disruptions, it is equally worthwhile not disparaging a broad set of practices that qualify under a more conventional definition of this term. This balance, which celebrates the survival of Black communities in situations of great hardship, whilst not losing sight of the economic circumstances in which urban poverty is generated, needs to be emphasised because it undermines the pernicious popularity of cultural stereotypes. Afro-Caribbean communities in the UK are stereotyped as economic underachievers whilst the same 'ethnic group' in the USA are often described by the dangerous caricature of 'Black Jews' because of their economic successes, with attempts made in both cases to trace the success/failure to the cultural proclivities of the group itself.

The offensive becomes particularly unpleasant in the British case when used by certain interest groups to highlight a supposed dichotomy between a stereotypical notion of Afro-Caribbean business failure and an equally flawed representation of 'Asian' success.

Secondly, an emphasis on the complexity of the issues at hand prohibits the portrayal of the Black community as either problem or victim, a recurrent feature of much race relations discourse and popular debate, and a recurrent feature also of much discussion of inner city communities generally.

Likewise, concepts which are used in abstract glossaries of urban regeneration good practice need to be examined in practice before they can be accepted as universally applicable. Here, Sara Ladbury and Clive Mira-Smith highlight the central fallacy underpinning the complex relationship between training and labour markets (chapter 4), Sue Buckingham-Hatfield demonstrates the dangers of crude measures of the leveraging of private capital with government investment and she, Neil Smith (chapter 5) and Liz Bondi (chapter 6) all focus on the downsides that may be involved in the visible expression of residential urban regeneration that is often conveniently tucked away in the concept of gentrification. On each occasion a common sense category tied to urban renewal often hides a set of social processes which does little for those whose poverty provided the central rationale for urban policy in the first place.

All of these categories are necessarily in constant flux. It is not necessary to purge the political and academic language which we use to think about the inner city, only to be aware of its contingent value. This is why we do not want to abandon the term inner city, either analytically or politically, only to ground it in the academic debates which have reproduced it conceptually, the political debates that have refashioned it discursively and, most significantly, the social injustices and inequalities that lend the term its emotive power and mobilising force.

PART ONE
POLICIES: MAKING SENSE OF THE INNER CITY

Once placed in their political context, it is difficult to imagine a set of guidelines of good practice in urban policy precisely because of the interaction of policy, theory and practice that this volume attempts to emphasise. Yet this begs the question of how policy initiatives should be assessed, given that they regularly embody flawed conceptualisations of urban crisis, were created in contentious circumstances and reflect spatial realisations of a political agenda as much as objectively circumscribed *social problems.*

This section attempts to highlight some of the ambiguities involved in just two of the criteria by which the success of urban policy is commonly measured. The first is that of leverage. A notion common to much contemporary urban policy is that state capital pump-primes local economic development. On one level, whilst the rhetoric of such intervention is often that of the free market, the logic seems to differ little from that of social engineering and regional policy which was commonly thought out of fashion and eschewed in such circles over ten years ago. At another level all three chapters here demonstrate that the notion of private investment following public is far from simple; in both London's Docklands at the grand scale, and in Pittsburgh, in finer detail, urban policy initiatives amplified social polarisation and benefited the local communities, which had provided the rationale for policy intervention, far less than might be expected. Merseyside, in contrast, has continued to reflect as much its disadvantaged structural and geographical position within the UK economy as any set of generic urban problems.

From a different perspective such repeated defects of urban policy might be expected to be overcome through local community involvement, yet again the three contributions here demonstrate a complexity which belies naive aspirations. In London, the community, Bob Colenutt suggests, was never even considered, yet even when, as in the case of Pittsburgh, community involvement is statutory, the outcomes may be only to amplify those within the community (or coming into the community) with the greatest resources and power to exploit the local political system. The Merseyside experience reinforces this with its particular history of conflict between the local and central state.

CHAPTER 2

THE LONDON DOCKLANDS DEVELOPMENT CORPORATION
Has the community benefited?

Bob Colenutt

It is no longer fashionable to say anything nice about the London Docklands Development Corporation (LDDC). After almost seven years, when the press were unwilling to print an unkind word about the LDDC, everything has now changed. The 'flagship' of the government's inner city 'regeneration' is on the defensive. It is not in danger of sinking, but it is no longer leading the way. The 'success' of the LDDC is now suspect and its operations under closer scrutiny. In the other parts of the country where UDCs have been set up, prominent UDC Board members are quick to reassure local people that 'we don't want a Docklands here'.

But what do they mean by this? Why is it so important for them to say such things? Has the LDDC, in spite of all the hype and political prominence, been in some sense a failure? And if so, why?

This chapter examines four questions about the LDDC which help to explain both the predicament faced by the government today and also the contradictions thrown up by tying the salvation of the inner cities to property-led regeneration agencies such as the LDDC.

(1) Why has so little of the development in Docklands 'trickled down' to benefit the people of the East End of London?

(2) Why has the LDDC changed the presentation of itself from that of a *'yuppie' development agency* to an inner city concern *'working for the community'*?
(3) Why has the government decided that no new UDCs will be announced, at least until after the next general election?
(4) What are the alternatives to UDC style 'regeneration' from the perspective of the political left?

TRICKLE DOWN?

Nearly £1 billion of public money and over £4 billion of private money has gone into Docklands since 1981. The official figures produced by the LDDC itself that describe the results of this investment are superficially very impressive:

> "20,000 jobs had been created by 1988. This total was predicted to rise to a projection of 150,000 jobs by 1995
> 15,000 homes had been built by 1988, with a projection of 30,000 by 1995" (Source: LDDC estimates)

Already, the development activity has had a massive physical and economic impact, especially in the western part of Docklands and on the Isle of Dogs in particular, with spillovers into surrounding areas such as Greenwich and North Southwark (Figure 1). Yet in spite of this physical transformation, the statistics of unemployment and homelessness, which of course are not cited by the LDDC, show that LDDC-led 'regeneration' has not trickled down very far into the working class communities of East London.

To take one example, in October 1988 male unemployment in East London was at the highest levels in the South-East: 21 per cent in Tower Hamlets; 18 per cent in Southwark and 14 per cent in Newham, reflecting the acute poverty and low levels of education in these areas. Homelessness in these three boroughs rose almost fourfold between 1981 and 1987 (from 1308 to 4394). Incomes, as shown by the Family Expenditure Survey and the Docklands Housing Needs Survey in 1986 show very low incomes among the majority of the populations of these three boroughs. Thus, only 10 per cent of the population of Newham, Tower Hamlets and Southwark can afford a new house in the LDDC area.

Moreover, in spite of massive changes on the key development sites, the environment of the East End, where most ordinary mortals live on council estates

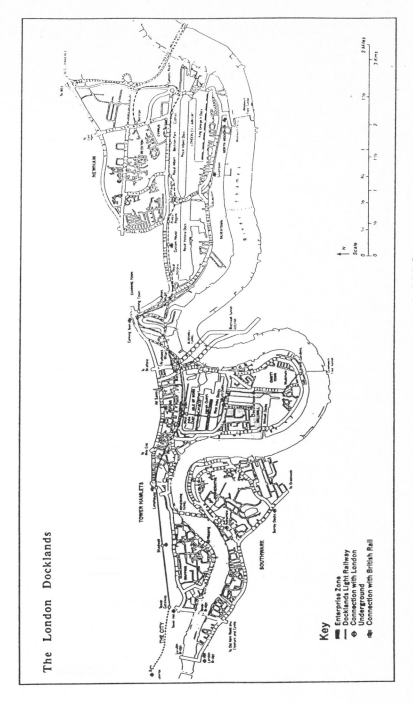

Figure 3.1: Inventing a new place. The area covered by the LDDC

and streets in and around the busy A13, or in Canning Town or in North Southwark, has changed little if at all. There have been dramatic changes to the environment of Surrey Docks, Wapping, the Isle of Dogs and Beckton, where extensive housing and commercial developments have taken place. But whether one walks through these parts of Docklands or through surrounding areas where the 'ripple effect' is supposed to be taking place, there remain run-down estates crying out for funding, for modernisation and for improvement.

New development sits beside old poverty. In Wapping there are poorly maintained public spaces adjoining expensive new developments with their own private courtyards and river terraces. Docklands is far from being a Garden City, or a New Town for most people. The activities of the LDDC and Developers are no compensation for cuts in local authority services.

It is therefore no surprise that local opposition to the LDDC has continued for over eight years now, even though the first chairman of the LDDC, Nigel Broackes of Trafalgar House, predicted that within a few years local opposition "will not exist". Even where there is no overt campaign against LDDC schemes, there is widespread cynicism and suspicion about the aims and effectiveness of the Corporation. Those in the new housing may feel the area is improving, but the thousands in bad housing or without jobs see no benefit at all. Even some in new houses now want to move out because of the construction works, traffic congestion, and a general decline in the image and attractiveness of Docklands over the past three years.

It is not easy to measure with any accuracy the trickle down effect of the sort of redevelopment seen in Docklands, particularly the more indirect benefits. But it is the considered view of local authorities monitoring Docklands development that the residents of the East End are getting "little more than crumbs from Docklands". On occasions larger pieces fall from the table, but given the vast size of the investment cake, the East End has got very little.

WHY HAS THERE BEEN SO LITTLE COMMUNITY BENEFIT?

There were clear political reasons for setting up the LDDC and other Urban Development Corporations, and for deciding the way in which they conduct their affairs. Part of this strategy involved local authorities being bypassed and a reliance on the regenerative power of private capital in the form of property developers. But in addition, the strategy LDDC chose to adopt has itself contributed to the problems they now face:

Bricks and mortar

The LDDC is concerned largely with physical development of land and buildings. Government grants to Docklands are a subsidy to property development, most particularly in the Isle of Dogs Enterprise Zone, but also elsewhere. Moreover, because the LDDC approach is led by the market, the development process was driven by the property boom in London and the South-East throughout most of the 1980s. Reg Ward, the former Chief Executive of the LDDC, wrote in the Annual Report 1984/85 that land values were "the most accurate barometer of physical and economic regeneration".

By letting the property market lead, the industrial sector has been ignored and on many occasions existing industry has been driven out or left to die. This experience is not confined to the LDDC: several of the other UDC areas are experiencing the same problems. The significant point is that the LDDC has intervened to help out developers of retail, housing and office projects, but has done little for existing local firms and businesses. Nor has it made building up the industrial base an objective.

The free market solution?

Secondly, the development of Docklands has been 'unplanned' in the sense that the Corporation has not followed or adhered to statutory plans of the Boroughs nor followed normal planning and consultation procedure. Reg Ward argued that planning was an obstacle to 'regeneration'. There never have been any economic or social targets, but given the attitude of government over the first seven years of the LDDC this is hardly surprising. But more recently, as criticism of 'non-planning' and piecemeal development has grown, the LDDC, along with the other UDCs, is introducing some social programmes and is trying to be reasonable and cooperative with local communities and 'host' local authorities.

The House of Commons Employment Committee 1988 report, 'The Employment Effects of Urban Development Corporations', concluded that

"UDCs cannot be regarded as a success if buildings and land are regenerated but the local community are by-passed and do not benefit from regeneration". (Para 89).

Hollow promises

The committee went on to recommend that the remit for UDCs should be altered to provide a more precise definition of 'regeneration'. The government, in its written response to the committee, refused to change the remit, but nevertheless the point is now well taken in most studies of urban regeneration.

Labour recruitment

The third reason why local people have not benefited is that Dockland development draws in workers from a very wide area across London and the South-East. Residents of the East London boroughs make up only a fraction of those working in Docklands or seeking jobs in the area. Moreover, around two-thirds of the jobs 'created' by LDDC are in fact transfers from the City of London financial district and Fleet Street's newspaper printing and publishing centre. We also know that the construction industry offers few 'local jobs': it brings in contractors and sub-contractors from all over the country. Quite apart from that, LDDC figures show 13,000 jobs were *lost* from Docklands between 1981 and 1988, of which quite a large proportion were jobs held by residents of the Docklands boroughs. Because the types of jobs lost are quite different from the 'new' jobs, the proportion of Docklands residents in the new jobs is much lower (about 15 per cent) than the percentage in the 'old' jobs (about 40 per cent).

Housing

Just as those benefiting from new jobs have come mostly from outside the Docklands the markets for private housing in Docklands are not local either. In the first phase of development in the early 1980s around 30 per cent of changes were bought by former council house tenants, but as prices have rocketed this percentage is now below 10 per cent. New residents are coming in from a wider and wider catchment area. Local people also lose out because, even on LDDC owned land, 85 per cent of the 15,000 houses are for sale, so ruling out local people needing to rent in precisely those London boroughs with notoriously long waiting lists for council accommodation.

'Skills' for local people

Lastly, where the LDDC has belatedly entered into 'agreements' with local authorities, such as with Newham and Tower Hamlets, and helped to set up training schemes like SKILLNET, designed to improve the skill levels of local communities, it has had little impact so far on getting local people into Docklands jobs. This is because such schemes are taking a long time to get off the ground and because employers generally recruit from non-local networks (see also Ladbury and Mira-Smith in this volume). There is also a political cost to pay for such ostensibly benevolent reforms. / In the Royal Docks the London Borough of Newham in 1987 agreed to support the broad pattern of land use in three consortia schemes and co-operate with LDDC plans on land development and transport change in the area in return for the provision of 1,500 rented houses, a minimum of £60 million of social facilities and training measures to ensure maximum local employment. But now this much vaunted initiative has foundered because there is little or no market interest in redevelopment.

To be fair, there is a significant Construction Training Programme in association with Canary Wharf which is beginning to make some local impact. Yet on the other hand, new employers in offices on the Isle of Dogs are not required to take on any local people or train people for the jobs that are on offer.

WHY HAS LDDC CHANGED ITS PRESENTATION?

The public relations exercises of the LDDC have undergone a marked change over the past two years. The Corporation now claims that it is 'working for the community'. Although this message is unlikely to be one that LDDC highlights when it approaches Whitehall for money, there is no doubting it has shifted its public relations away from targeting solely yuppies and City businessmen.

In the LDDC Annual Reports published since 1981, the images and the language have altered dramatically. The 1986/87 Annual Report showed windsurfers with the subtitle 'The Emerging City'; but the following year, in 1987/88, the cover showed local kids milking cows at the Mudchute Farm. The sub-title was 'Working for the Community'. The then Chairman, Christopher Benson (Chairman of MEPC property company), said that there would be

"increased emphasis on the social and community aspects of regeneration - not purely the physical provision of buildings." (LDDC, 1988)

The interesting question to ask is 'why has this happened?'. There are several possible answers, all of which contain some truth. One view is that the Corporation can now afford to do this. After all, with so much physical development now on the ground it can be generous to 'the community'.

37

Moreover, having engineered physical development, social engineering is the next challenge, to tie in with the expectations and requirements of new residents - and also to those of the developers. The developers now need social facilities and infrastructure, such as schools, open space and leisure facilities to support their own schemes.

A third view is that these changes, at long last, are a concession to the ever widening criticism of the LDDC. Not only troublesome 'action groups', but the House of Commons Employment Committee, the National Audit Office, and the media are criticizing the LDDC.

The end of the property boom is another salient factor: with developers in trouble, this is not the time to present Docklands as a paradise for 'yuppies', especially since so many of them are also now criticising the environment of Docklands.

Finally, perhaps this change of mood can only be explained in the wider context of gradual changes in government policy on the inner city and UDCs - the emergence of a 'new realism' tempering the policies and rhetoric of the radical right.

NEW REALISM IN GOVERNMENT POLICIES FOR THE INNER CITY

David Trippier, who in 1988 was the Environment Minister responsible for Inner Cities, announced in December of that year that it was unlikely that the government would create any more UDCs : why?

One of the reasons is almost certainly the very high cost of UDCs to the public purse. UDCs were intended to be merely pump-primers to bring in the private sector, which after a time would be reduced as private sector finance took over. The LDDC is sometimes cited as a success story because it is has attracted in so much private investment. The LDDC claims a 'leverage ratio' of 12 : 1, private : public investment. Do these figures prove the government's case that the LDDC is good value for money?

LDDC leverage ratios are in fact highly misleading. Public investment is defined solely as LDDC grant, thus excluding equally important Enterprise Zone allowances and Department of Transport funding for roads and new railways. LDDC figures also omit the £400 million or so that was spent by local authorities and government in the area prior to the inauguration of the LDDC. If these are taken into account the ratio falls to 4:1, and will fall further, as new rail lines like the £1 billion Jubilee Line are largely paid for by government, and as government foots the bill for the £600 million Docklands Highway, a four lane motorway from East to West Docklands.

Thus, pump-priming has turned into a bottomless pit for the Treasury, in spite of the reinvestment of large receipts from land sales. Even this latter source of funds is now drying up as the property market slides into an ever deeper slump. It was in these circumstances that the LDDC had to go to the Treasury for more money in 1989/90, and again in 1990/91, and was very successful in getting what it wanted.

The financial reality of Docklands reveals the systematic confusion that surrounds the government's claim that the Docklands is an example of the market regenerating the inner cities. The development of Docklands is anything but *laissez-faire* economics. It is dependent upon massive government intervention in land assembly and reclamation, in transport costs, and in education provision. Moreover, it is anything but unplanned since it depends on considerable state involvement, promotion, and subsidy.

A further factor tempering government enthusiasm for LDDC relates to what can be called the 'Prince Charles' Factor. Three years ago, there was hardly an architect who would criticise the new townscape of Docklands or the Isle of Dogs. The giant Canary Wharf office centre, its largest tower reaching 860 feet, went through without a public inquiry, amazingly with no comment from the Royal Fine Arts Commission or the media as a whole. Now all has changed. The Prince does not like Canary Wharf. Nor do many others. The President of the Royal Town Planning Institute, in a speech in December 1988, said about the Isle of Dogs:

> "Did you not come away thinking that the urban development challenge of the century adds to little more than opportunistic chaos - an architectural circus - with a sprinkling of postmodern gimmicks, the ghastly mega-lumps of Canary Wharf and a fairground train to get you there?"

Similarly, the media treatment of Docklands and inner city challenges elsewhere has changed dramatically. The changing image of 'yuppies' and spiralling costs and congestion have seen to that. It is open season for criticising UDCs for lack of planning, lack of strategic thinking and short termism. The government in 1989 had to appoint a special transport minister for Docklands (Mr Portillo) to keep the lid on the widespread anger of developers about the lack of transport to Docklands.

In addition, there are undercurrents of 'nastiness' about Docklands development which are doing its image no good at all. From being a much sought-after residential area, it has lost its fashionable air. The media have weighed in. For example, the TV drama 'Thin Air' in 1988 brought out some of the unpleasantness about the 'wheeler-dealing' that has been going on during the Docklands boom years.

Other interventions have reinforced the feeling that all is not well with the ethics of Docklands. For example, the Bishop of Durham was widely quoted in December 1988 as saying that UDCs and Housing Action Trusts were "vast dispensers of patronage". The sleaze factor has been highlighted by the revelation that large chunks of the Brinks-Mat bullion robbery money were laundered via Switzerland into luxury flats on the Isle of Dogs.

The political currency that underpinned the spread of UDCs is no longer so clearly in the government's control as it was a few years ago. In other UDC areas local authorities and UDC Boards are working together to ensure that there is some balance to redevelopment, and officials are making great efforts to reassure residents and distance themselves from the LDDC experience.

Perhaps more importantly, the government has backed away from declaring more UDCs partly because of the costs and adverse publicity but also because it can achieve its aim of driving local authorities into the arms of the private sector by other means. Cuts in capital budgets, use of the land dispersal register, and the mere threat of UDCs achieve the same political goals without incurring the political problems and contradictions of UDCs.

CONCLUSIONS

There is now a major question mark in policy-making over the meaning of 'regeneration' and particularly over who benefits from *regenerative* policies. There is a new consensus that purely physical developments based on property-led solutions are not enough. Moreover, land use planning, which in the early 1980s was alleged to be an obstacle to investment, is very much back on the agenda. It is now recognised in the business community that infrastructure provision is vitally important. Ironically, the property market now wants more certainty about the future. Even in the prosperous South-East there are demands for direct subsidy and state assistance. From a different political quarter, the Green movement is resurrecting environmental issues which again tie back into a possible new vogue for planning.

A further change is that Michael Heseltine's original idea that UDCs should be 'single purpose agencies' has backfired. Given the complexities and plural nature of urban development other agencies must be closely involved. Specifically, this points to the necessity of local authority involvement, just as the Audit Commission Report on Urban Regeneration 1989 concluded. Yet a crucial side-effect of the UDC programme has been to push hard-pressed local authorities into the arms of the private sector without the problems and costs of UDCs rebounding on the government.

Finally, the UDC experience, and particularly that of the LDDC, has now brought into focus alternative strategies for urban regeneration. The lessons of UDCs are being learned by local authorities and political parties. The most important of these lessons is that 'regeneration' must be linked to local needs and the local economy. The second lesson is that the property market cannot and must not be allowed to dictate the form, pace and content of urban change. This direction and control must come from local democratic structures, both in local government and in the community. The third lesson is that local economic development cannot take place without an overall strategy for national and regional development.

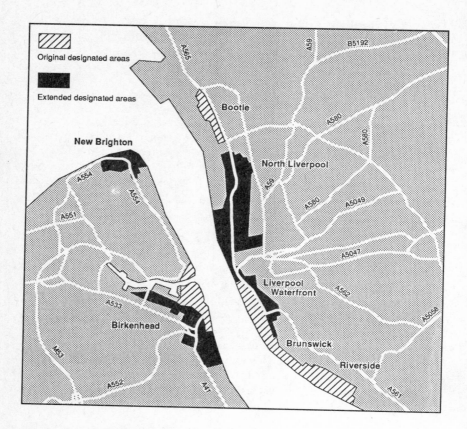

Figure 3.1: Merseyside Development Corporation

CHAPTER 3

MERSEYSIDE DEVELOPMENT CORPORATION 1981-1989
Physical regeneration, accountability and economic challenge

Jon Dawson and Michael Parkinson

URBAN DEVELOPMENT CORPORATIONS AND URBAN REGENERATION

Urban Development Corporations, the centrepiece of Mrs Thatcher's urban policy, articulate most dramatically the current British government's vision of city regeneration. Designated in 1980 but launched in the immediate aftermath of the 1981 urban riots, the first UDCs were introduced into the London and Liverpool docklands. After the 1987 election the government introduced a second wave of UDCs in Cardiff, Bristol, Manchester, Trafford Park, Sheffield, Leeds, Tyneside and Wearside, Teesside and the Black Country. Development Corporations are the foremost example of the government's antipathy to local authorities: they are designated, empowered, financed by, and directly accountable to, central government.

With their statutory origins in the 1980 Local Government Planning and Land Act, UDCs are designed to bring land and buildings into effective use, encourage the development of new and existing commerce, create an attractive environment and ensure that housing and social facilities are available to encourage people to live and work in the area. To enable them to fulfil these tasks UDCs have been granted extensive financial, planning and land acquisition powers. They are able to acquire land by compulsory purchase, by voluntary agreement or by the Secretary of State vesting it in them. Planning powers also rest firmly with UDCs which are responsible for development control policy and decisions within their area. Moreover, UDCs have powers to operate outside their immediate boundaries, if they think it necessary to secure regeneration. By supplanting local authority planning powers in this way, UDCs are intended to remove the political uncertainty and restraints of local democracy which, in the government's view at least, represent a significant hindrance to the development process and a deterrent to private investment (House of Lords Select Committee, 1981).

Underpinning government faith in UDCs is the belief that a single-minded agency with limited objectives, using streamlined administrative procedures and free from political ambiguity is better placed than local authorities to turn round a closely defined area (Adcock, 1984). In the government's mind its single-minded agency approach assumes an entrepreneurial ability that contrasts with the alleged inflexibility and bureaucratic ethos of local authorities. UDCs are designed to create the conditions and confidence necessary to attract private capital. Government financial support is, therefore, primarily tailored to providing incentives to the private sector by reducing the costs and risks of inner city investment. In practice, UDCs place heavy emphasis on quickly realised and highly visible results - 'flagship' projects that will materially improve the local environment and its image. Inevitably, therefore, and despite the broad range of goals allocated to them, UDCs tend to stress property-led regeneration and thereby dilute wider urban policy goals.

Each UDC is governed by a board commonly comprising local businessmen, senior local politicians and the Corporation's Chief Officer. They have three major revenue sources. They receive a substantial annual budget from central government coffers, they may borrow from the national loan fund for commercial purposes and they can make use of the proceeds from land sales.

In many ways the first two UDCs could not have possessed more diverse characteristics nor could they have differed more greatly in their potential to transform their respective areas from derelict urban landscapes to localities resonant with dynamic private sector activity. The London Docklands Development Corporation (LDDC) was faced with the opportunity of regenerating an area, which no matter how physically derelict, had an unfulfilled development potential the equal of any piece of real estate anywhere in the world. Lying within a mile of one of the leading financial centres of the modern capitalist economy which was about to reap the economic benefits flowing from the deregulation of the domestic financial market and the internationalisation of world financial markets in the 1980s (Parkinson and Evans, 1990), London Docklands was ripe for development.

In sharp contrast, the circumstances faced by Merseyside Development Corporation (MDC) could hardly have been less propitious. Its designated area lay at the heart of one of the most economically depressed cities in Western Europe which had suffered a massive withdrawal of private capital during the previous three decades and endured a series of political traumas in the process (Parkinson, 1985, Figure 3.1).

Despite these important differences, the original dockland areas shared similar economic histories. Both had been, in their prime, booming and prosperous ports. But shifting patterns of international trade, the development of alternative transportation, containerisation, inter-port competition nationally and internationally and growing industrial disputes all contributed to their rapid decline in the 1960s. Related manufacturing industries such as food processing, chemicals and engineering suffered keenly from the ports' decline and the surrounding areas endured massive job losses and an exodus of their people. The dock closures inevitably led to the visible scars of acute environmental deterioration and abject physical dereliction.

The first two UDCs were thrust into these circumstances in 1981. The MDC was initially given control over a limited area of 865 acres of derelict and fragmented dockland which was geographically isolated from the rest of the city with little indigenous population or economic activity. Redevelopment had been frustrated by poor communications, disparate land ownership patterns and the fanciful 'hope' values sought by many landowners. Moreover, despite the efforts of Liverpool City Council and Merseyside County Council during the 1970s, no realistic development plans existed for the area. LDDC on the other hand was charged with the regeneration of a massive eight square miles where entire communities lived and worked and which was the focus of a well-advanced redevelopment strategy - the London Docklands Strategic Plan - approved by the GLC, loc i authorities and the Department of the Environment.

At the end of the decade, the government continues to make great play of the success fermented by the private sector in physically regenerating the docklands - especially the phenomenal development activity engendered in London. However, despite launching the second wave of UDCs amidst government promotional hype proclaiming LDDC and MDC a success story, there has been scant attention paid in government circles to any rigorous analysis of the London and Liverpool experience. To help redress this imbalance, this chapter seeks to evaluate the MDC's policy and practice and will complement Colenutt's contribution on London in this volume.

EVALUATING THE MERSEYSIDE DEVELOPMENT CORPORATION

Essentially there are two important phases in MDC's history which, for any meaningful evaluation, require different criteria of analysis. In the first phase from 1981 until November 1988 MDC's remit was confined to regenerating an area with little indigenous population or employment. The second phase began in November 1988 when MDC's boundaries were extended to localities embracing economic activity, entire communities and active local authorities.

However, assessing UDC achievements is not without its problems. First, the indicators of 'success' are clearly critical, yet there are no uniformly agreed objectives. The government, for example, emphasises physical renewal and the extent to which public expenditure has levered private sector investment. Yet whilst this may be an adequate instrument of analysis for derelict and deserted areas, it is less convincing as the sole criterion of success in areas which have indigenous communities and economies and active local authorities. Moreover, the lack of adequate data collected by UDCs compounds problems in assessing even the government's preferred narrow determinants of success and frustrates the systematic monitoring of the impact of their programmes. Finally, as other commentators have observed (eg. Church, 1988), any evaluation of the impact of the UDCs has to be viewed in the light of co-existing initiatives, boundary definitions and the fact that any assessment is unavoidably interim. Despite these complications this assessment of the MDC experience will focus on three broad themes.

(1) *Efficiency* - how successful has MDC been in terms of the physical regeneration of its area and in promoting private sector confidence and investment?
(2) *Accountability* - how responsive has MDC been to the local authorities and communities in its area and how has it worked with other agencies.
(3) *Equity* - what have been the consequences of regeneration for job creation for local people and for social housing provision?

These themes can be applied to MDC, both before and after 1988, and for comparative purposes the assessment will also reflect on LDDC's experience. Firstly, we will consider the 'efficiency' theme and the question of physical renewal and private investment. Whilst these criteria will be an important element in future analyses of regeneration in the post-1988 area, at this stage any meaningful evaluation is essentially confined to the initial designated area. Moreover, the characteristics of the initial area suggest that the 'success' of its regeneration can be best assessed in these terms.

MDC PHASE 1: PHYSICAL REGENERATION AND INVESTMENT

There is little dispute that in terms of physical regeneration both MDC, in its initial area, and LDDC have been visibly successful. Whilst their ability to lever private sector investment has varied widely, both have transformed once derelict landscapes and upgraded impoverished environments. In these terms LDDC has clearly outshone MDC. Given its inherent advantages however, this is not altogether surprising and the commercial and residential property markets have responded quickly and emphatically to LDDC's pump-priming activities. Pursuing an entrepreneurial and demand-led strategy, LDDC claim to have leveraged over £4.4 billion of private investment for an outlay of £440 million of public money predominantly applied to land reclamation and infrastructural provision - a gearing ratio of 10 : 1.

By contrast MDC's land reclamation and infrastructural provisions have demonstrated a markedly weaker propensity for attracting private capital. Despite expenditure of £170 million, by 1988 private investment totalled a relatively meagre £25 million. The reluctance of private capital to commit itself to a still depressed regional economy must be viewed in the context of MDC's changing development strategies. At the outset, emphasis was placed on stimulating industrial demand. MDC's initial development strategy earmarked 55 per cent of its land for industrial development, 40 per cent for commercial residential and recreational use, with 5 per cent left for port related activity. However, by 1984 it was clear that significant industrial investment was simply not forthcoming. The absence of demand for industrial development forced MDC to abandon its original strategy and opt instead for a tourist and leisure based strategy. Whilst the National Audit Office's 1987 report subsequently criticised MDC for its initial policy failures there is some validity in its argument that the economic climate in the early 1980s, not MDC's internal failings, was primarily responsible for curbing industrial growth on Merseyside.

Notwithstanding these criticisms, MDC's change of strategy direction has been broadly justified. Whereas industrial demand fell below expectations, demand in the tourism and leisure sectors has exceeded them. Three high profile initiatives testify to Merseyside Dockland's tourist potential: the rehabilitation of the Albert Dock, the International Garden Festival in 1984 and the International Tall Ships Race. The Albert Dock is MDC's 'flagship'. It is Britain's largest Grade 1 listed building and, after extensive redevelopment costing £25 million, now accommodates the Tate Gallery, a Maritime Museum, Granada Television's news studio and upmarket offices, shops and flats. As a tourist spectacle it welcomed over 3.5 million visitors in 1988 alone and now ranks as the North West's premier tourist attraction.

The waterfront's leisure potential received a further boost with proposals for a major transfusion of private investment on the adjacent Kings Docks site, in the shape of a retail centre, ice arena and multi-screen cinema. However, it has yet to be realised. Indeed, the proposed development has been thrown into doubt with the Secretary of State's decision to call it in for a public inquiry following representations from environmental pressure groups objecting to the scheme's architectural quality. Regardless of the Minister's decision on this particular case, heightened developer interest is evidence that substantial public expenditure in declining areas will attract future private investment. Moreover, there have been other successes. Ninety small firms are operating in the Brunswick Industrial Park, a marina now graces the once derelict docks and about 100 low income houses for rent have been built and over 200 flats for sale at the top end of the Merseyside housing market developed and sold.

A number of issues, however, remain unresolved. Many of the shops and restaurants in the Albert Dock operate with below market rents and service charges and their future remains uncertain as outgoings rise to market levels. Equally, the International Garden Festival site, which successfully attracted visitors in the initial year on a subsidised basis, has since remained problematic (Parkinson and Evans, 1990). Bankruptcy hit a private operator in 1985 and MDC continues to have difficulty attracting further developers to manage the site. In the meantime it remains unused and sealed off for much of the year. Despite these reservations MDC has enjoyed major successes in physically regenerating its area, which looks dramatically different than at its initial designation.

Indeed, by 1987, when the government was reviewing the future of UDCs and their boundaries, MDC's initial land use strategy seemed broadly complete. Developments had either been realised or were at least in the advanced stages of negotiation in the bulk of its area. The government was essentially faced with the option of winding down MDC's operations or extending its boundaries. Clearly, MDC's initial boundaries had been too tightly drawn - a fact recognised at the time - and much work remained to be tackled in surrounding areas. The Department of the

Environment commissioned consultants to prepare a detailed boundary extension report. The Secretary of State took on board the consultants' recommendations and, in November 1988, sanctioned the extension of MDC's boundaries.

MDC PHASE 2: NEW BOUNDARIES, NEW CHALLENGES

The wider geographical remit fundamentally altered the nature and characteristics of MDC's area and accordingly the challenge and tasks the Corporation faces. The newly designated area incorporates substantial parts of Liverpool's North Docks and areas of mixed commercial and some residential uses inland, together with industrial and commercial areas adjoining the initial designated area in South Liverpool. On the south side of the River Mersey the extension takes in the commercial heart of Birkenhead with a mixed housing/industrial dock hinterland and also housing and leisure areas in New Brighton. The designation almost trebled its original area by adding over 1500 acres to the Corporation's responsibilities and increasing the number of its residents from 1000 to 6700.

The new remit brings to the fore locally many of the larger issues about the UDCs that in its original form had been relatively irrelevant to the operation of MDC. In contrast to its initial responsibilities, MDC is now operating in localities with a significant indigenous population where local authorities play a major role. These characteristics clearly add extra dimensions to MDC's urban regeneration strategy, raise central questions about local accountability and highlight the thorny problem of uneven development.

MDC's success or failure will inevitably be judged on its ability to develop quite different approaches to urban development than the physical regeneration process that has been the hallmark of its achievements to date. Its more complex area - socially, economically and politically - bringing with it a new and more complex set of issues, calls for a more sophisticated policy response. MDC's performance must in future be assessed in terms of its ability to work with local authorities and community groups and its achievements in bringing jobs and prosperity not only to its area but also to its indigenous population. In other words, community development comes onto the agenda and distributional issues become more significant.

Whilst national debate has shifted the focus of urban regeneration policy away from the narrowly defined goals of physical development, the extension of its boundaries has forced MDC to confront the issues of jobs, training and social housing provision, although MDC would argue that these objectives were always part of its long-term agenda. Indeed, aware of the harsh criticisms made of its sister Corporation in London Docklands, concerning the distribution of employment opportunities (Peat, Marwick, McLintock, 1987), affordable housing for local people (National Audit Office, 1988) and democratic accountability (Nicholson, 1989) the local regeneration lobby is united in a consensus that the acutely uneven development characteristic of London Docklands should not be replicated on Merseyside. In fact, experience so far suggests that MDC's approach to urban regeneration has been less cavalier than LDDC's, reflecting its concern to minimise the social costs of development to its residents and to avoid projects likely to prejudice other areas of the city. For instance, MDC resisted retail proposals for Princes Dock considered prejudicial to Liverpool city centre (MDC, 1989). Whilst this approach has opened MDC up to the *laissez-faire* criticism of market interference, it creates a policy flexibility within which there is potential to engage with local authority and community imperatives.

MDC's new responsibilities pose difficult questions about the Corporation's legitimacy and its capacity to handle its wider remit. Its organizational form - a small core staff and extensive sub-contracting to consultants - together with the advantages of political stability, administrative simplicity and speed of implementation offered by an agency rationale, have proved well suited to redeveloping a derelict dockland estate. It remains to be seen, however, whether the UDC model can effectively and efficiently adapt itself to its broader goals. Furthermore, MDC's capacity to meet the new challenges has to be questioned, since it has been granted limited additional resources and has recruited no extra staff to meet its wider remit.

The remainder of this chapter, taking into account these uncertainties and the changing nature of MDC's development role, will discuss the consequences of its past and future policy and practice on the central - and controversial - themes of accountability, housing and economic development.

ACCOUNTABILITY

The primary objection to UDCs has been that they are not directly accountable to local authorities or local people in their areas. Government policy for the UDCs - part of its growing disenchantment with, and undermining of, local authority activities - emphasises their ability to act entrepreneurially, free from the constraints under which local authorities operate. But it also questions the extent to which this freedom creates a loss of democratic control.

The UDCs are financed by, and report to, central government. They are the local planning authority for their designated areas. Their boards operate behind a shroud of secrecy - MDC does not even publish its corporate strategy. In their defence, UDCs claim that they are politically accountable to Parliament, administratively accountable to the Department of the Environment and financially accountable to the Treasury. Nevertheless, the fact remains that the extent to which they are genuinely accountable locally is entirely within their own discretion.

In London Docklands, the intense pressure for development has produced bitter conflicts between LDDC and the surrounding local authorities and community. However, accountability has been a less controversial political issue on Merseyside. The slow pace of development and the lack of residents in the initial local area has produced less charged relations between MDC and local organisations (Parkinson and Evans, 1990). Despite original opposition to the principle of the MDC all three local authorities have taken a place on the board. Liverpool City Council did withdraw when Labour took control in 1983, but even then political relations were never as strained as in London. Rather, the city became preoccupied by its budgetary dispute with Mrs Thatcher's government and virtually ignored the MDC. Relations took on a more positive tone in 1989 when the leader of the City Council returned to the Board, reflecting the reconstituted Labour group's more pragmatic policy of forming alliances with government and the private sector.

Throughout the period, officials of MDC and the local authority have maintained good working relations, which is hardly surprising since many of MDC's plans and personnel were drawn from local authorities. There have been few disagreements over major planning issues and there has been surprisingly little explicit community opposition to MDC - except from the Black community in Toxteth. Moreover, the obvious success of MDC in opening up the docklands for mass market consumption has also effectively restrained local opposition. Public access to an environmentally attractive waterfront has received a favourable response in the city and has undoubtedly muted political debate.

Since the boundary extension however, accountability has become a much more pressing and pertinent issue. Not only did the boundary extension encompass local authorities with active development policies and programmes, it also brought within

MDC's remit one of the strongest community groups, organisationally and politically, in Britain. With influential links to central government the Eldonian Community in Vauxhall has developed the largest new-build housing co-operative in the country. In the process, it succeeded in enlisting financial and political support from central government. It has received international recognition and a long and impressive list of visitors - including the Prime Minister - have lauded its achievements. Actively pursuing further ideas for community development and local economic regeneration it presents a challenge to conventional development rationale which focuses upon maximising the leverage of private sector investment for the minimum necessary public expense.

Adapting to these new circumstances, MDC's initial policy approach signifies a concern to adopt a co-operative rather than confrontational stance. In particular it has attempted to take on board community aspirations and local authority plans rather than ride roughshod over local wishes. This co-operation has gained practical expression in the formulation of Area Strategies for most parts of the extended area, notably New Brighton, Stanley, Vauxhall and Birkenhead. Reminiscent of conventional municipal statutory local plan-making, the preparation of the Area Strategies - ' informal ' local plans - have enabled MDC to create a forum in which local authorities, residents and the private sector alike can contribute as consultees to the local urban renewal process. In practice, public participation in land use proposals emerges in MDC's liaisons with local authorities, landowners, residents and interested developers, both in the preparation of draft Area Strategies and through opportunities for public consultation on the published drafts. For instance, the draft Area Strategy for New Brighton (MDC, 1989b) acknowledges local authority commitment to a major housing improvement programme and an ongoing policy of coastal protection and beach enhancement.

Similar consultation procedures were adopted for the Vauxhall Area Strategy, which in its draft form (MDC, 1989c) reflects community concerns for affordable housing and at least provides space for community based economic development plans. The community element of the strategy marks what is in many ways a unique experiment in physical and economic regeneration. It suggests a partnership between 'bottom-upwards' community controlled organisations and a 'top-down' central government-led area based initiative. However, although the 'informal' local plan makes provision for community development, the lack of effective mechanisms, particularly in the economic sphere, to counter an impoverished community's inherent lack of financial, managerial and skilled resources must inevitably make project fulfilment, with the significant exception of community housing initiatives, far from certain.

Whether MDC's co-operative outlook would survive market-led development pressures that contravene local authority or community wishes has not yet been tested. Nevertheless, so far as policy and plan formulation is concerned, recent practice indicates a willingness to reflect both local wishes and concerns for policies elsewhere in the city. The broadly favourable response from all quarters to the New Brighton and Vauxhall draft area strategies suggests MDC has succeeded in allaying local fears of inappropriate development and has responded to local aspirations in a way that will promote co-operation with the private sector. Indeed, the formulation of 'informal' local plans itself suggests that unfettered free market development, reminiscent of London Docklands, is unacceptable to MDC. Rather, it sees development proceeding within a tightly controlled land use strategy. For all the government's anti-planning rhetoric, it is ironic that land use planning should re-emerge so strongly within the context of a privatised urban regeneration agenda.

HOUSING

In the London docklands housing has been the most politically controversial issue since LDDC assumed control over virtually the entire housing land reserve of three local authorities in its area. However, on Merseyside, at least until November 1988, housing remained a low-key issue. Not only were Liverpool's original docklands essentially non-residential but the Merseyside housing market in the early 1980s was less buoyant, creating less pressure upon MDC to provide housing. Moreover, MDC's relatively modest housing programme for the initial area, its mixture of public and private provision and the fact that it has not displaced existing residents prevented housing becoming the political minefield for MDC that it was for LDDC. The extended boundaries, however, place the housing debate on Merseyside at the centre of the regeneration agenda. If MDC is to avoid the hostile criticism endured by LDDC it must avoid re-enacting their unpopular approach.

In contrast to existing local authority plans, LDDC explicitly encouraged mainly private housing to diversify the existing housing stock which was 80 per cent council housing. Fuelling the top end of the market in this way caused resentment. Furthermore, efforts by LDDC to provide affordable housing for sale proved inadequate in the face of intense demand pressures. As a result only 5 per cent of intended affordable housing satisfied affordability criteria for a local community where 75 per cent earn less than £10,000 per annum (National Audit Office, 1988; House of Commons Employment Committee, 1988).

Continued criticism of LDDC policy led it to introduce a belated social housing initiative in 1986 aimed at providing new and refurbished housing for rent and shared ownership. But the image of highly paid newcomers benefiting from a rapidly inflated housing market at the expense of low income natives is a broadly accurate assessment of LDDC's record. The experiences of London Docklands housing development clearly raises critical policy issues for MDC if it is to nurture more equitable development in its extended area.

MDC's approach to housing development in its extended area acknowledges the need for social housing provision. Moreover, it displays a political sensitivity to local authority and community plans. For instance, the New Brighton Area Strategy (MDC, 1989b) acknowledges the borough council's housing role and commits MDC to undertaking environmental improvement schemes to complement the authority's existing policy programme. Equally, MDC's strategy for Vauxhall reflects Eldonian community proposals for an extensive mixed tenure housing development. Aware of the interest in low cost housing for rent and purchase in the area, sparked by the Eldonian housing development activities, the Corporation's Draft Area Strategy (MDC, 1989c) incorporated consultant's findings and earmarked land for a balance of housing type and tenure.

More importantly, the strategies provide the basis for effective partnerships to reconcile MDC's imperatives with local authority and community proposals. In the case of the Eldonian's housing developments, the partnership would comprise several key actors. The Eldonians themselves are originators of the scheme. MDC as planning authority will determine planning permission and perform land assembly and reclamation works to bring land up to development standard. A housing association will co-ordinate and supervise development activity. Finally, the funding agencies - predominantly the Housing Corporation, in the case of housing co-operative and housing association stock development, and the private sector in the case of housing for sale - will provide the necessary finance.

Whilst this partnership should ensure that social housing provision does not simply remain a well-intentioned plan, two cautionary notes about social housing provision generally need sounding. First, the advent of the 1988 Housing Act and the limiting of Housing Association Grant to an average 75 per cent of development costs forces housing association and housing co-operative developments to secure the balance of funding from private sources. Government policy assumes that increasing the ratio of private sector funding into the social housing process will enable more houses to be developed from available public funds. There is, however, a trade-off. Obtaining private funds is not likely to create an insurmountable hurdle in itself. But the burden of satisfying private sector returns on loans and investments will fall upon tenants, through increasing rental levels risking the exclusion of those most in need of social housing provision or at least further enmeshing them in the poverty trap. Moreover, if the housing market were to weaken, withdrawal of private funds could restrict development.

Secondly, if this partnership and private sector-led developments elsewhere in the MDC succeed, conflicts are likely to arise. The realisation of community-led and private sector housing schemes, the improvement of the local environment, amenities and infrastructure and an emerging demand for new housing in the area will translate into increasing private developer interest and higher land prices. Without firm planning control from MDC these developments could again exclude the local community and jeopardise further social housing provision. MDC will have to balance realising market values against local wishes and community input to the development process. The pressure to revert to maximising leverage ratios and suppress local authority and community-led development would be intense. Although hypothetical at this stage, the degree to which MDC upholds the publicly consulted 'informal' local plans, in the face of pronounced market pressures challenging its land use provisions, could prove crucial in future.

ECONOMIC DEVELOPMENT

MDC insists that, in the short term, most of its expenditure has not been intended to create but to regenerate physically derelict dockland areas and create confidence in a depressed local economy. The Corporation would argue that attracting future private sector-led employment is a long term aim and that, given the nature of the task it is too soon to assess the success of its strategy. There is some truth to this claim. But equally, MDC in its first eight years was not a major generator of jobs - and the individual cost of those created was extremely high.

In job creation terms its return on the £170 million so far invested has been small. It has created 1,900 jobs but during the same period over 800 existing jobs have been lost in an area which lies at the heart of three parliamentary constituencies with some of the highest unemployment rates in Britain. In 1981, there were only 1,800 jobs within MDC's boundaries. By 1989, there were 3,000 - a net gain of 1,200 in office functions, retailing and small firms in nursery workshops. In addition, MDC estimate construction projects generate over 700 jobs annually. MDC also operates a grants programme which provides support to 93 firms, allegedly creating 300 jobs and safeguarding 600 existing ones. MDC has also supported training programmes which provided 7,100 places in 1988 (MDC, 1989a).

Even though much of the training was short term, MDC's record in this respect compares rather favourably with LDDC's unimpressive training programme. Moreover, it can be argued that MDC's revised strategy, focusing upon leisure and tourism, supplies jobs better suited to the skills of the local population than the London Docklands emphasis on service sector growth. MDC has also been more sympathetic than LDDC to the interests of existing firms in the area. Its refurbishment of industrial units in the docks has been successful and well received (Parkinson and Evans, 1990). Equally, the lack of pressure for land has meant, in contrast to LDDC, that MDC has not had to decide whether existing firms should be forced to quit the area.

Whilst it can be argued that physical regeneration, not job creation, was MDC's original priority, the extension of the boundaries removes this premise. In future, job creation will inevitably become one of the main indicators of success. MDC's broad emphasis in its draft area strategies, on less prestigious physical projects and on commercial and industrial development suggests it now views its primary task in business development and employment creation terms.

However, despite this shift in emphasis, MDC policy reaffirms conventional economic development rationale as the central plank of its regeneration strategy. Land acquisition, site assembly, land reclamation, infrastructural improvement and environmental enhancement are the means through which it engages with local authorities, the Department of Environment and most importantly, the private sector to lever investment that will lead to economic growth.

At the same time, reflecting community representations, notional support is given to 'bottom-up' initiatives. However, unlike housing co-operative and housing association development, the targeted mechanisms to ensure community led economic development are less formalised and fail systematically to bridge critical funding and support gaps in the economic development process. Community led economic initiatives remain a badly organised feature of urban policy targets. The lack of effective mechanisms, tailored to community needs, makes community led economic development, even for the influential Eldonians, an uphill task with forbidding obstacles to overcome.

As one way of ensuring that local people share the benefits of any resurgence in local economic fortunes, MDC places considerable emphasis on the role of skills training. However, whilst the extended area incorporates 30,000 jobs, an unemployment rate of 30 per cent stubbornly persists. MDC, with matching European Social Fund contributions, finances its training programme through METEL (Merseyside Education Training Enterprise Ltd.) - an independent agency established by the now abolished Merseyside County Council. By equipping local people with marketable skills MDC hopes to improve their chances of securing employment when vacancies arise (although see Ladbury and Mira-Smith, Chapter 7). Although targeting employment through the labour market is inevitably uncertain, skills training certainly improves the job prospects of local people. Nevertheless, training *per se* does not create jobs and, at the end of the day, local employment opportunities will depend on combining an appropriately skilled population with success in stimulating private sector investment.

As we have observed, MDC seeks to use pump-priming measures to promote regeneration. The renewed emphasis on industrial and commercial development assumes that the local economic environment is in good health and that the private sector will respond to such techniques. MDC's chairman claims "... there is a significant difference in 1989. The economic climate on Merseyside is now very conducive to development ... enabling us to define preferred strategies with greater flexibility than hitherto." However, with the UK economy teetering on the edge of recession, the mere provision of reclaimed land, infrastructure and renovated buildings - the core of MDC's economic activities - may be an inadequate investment incentive. It must therefore remain an open question as to whether the local economy is sufficiently robust to attract private sector capital.

CONCLUSION

Government rhetoric and the proliferation of development corporations around the country assumes that the UDC model provides a winning formula for regeneration. However, as we have observed, regeneration can attract diverse interpretations. Any judgement of the UDCs record will depend upon the meaning of regeneration, urban policy objectives and the criteria employed to measure them. The pioneering UDCs in Liverpool and London have demonstrated a capability to mobilise the property development process and achieve high profile and visibly impressive physical renewal. At the same time, their capacity to leverage private capital in support of these developments has varied considerably. In London, substantial pump-priming, from public funds, by extensive infrastructural provision and aggressive marketing combined with a more buoyant and dynamic economy has induced far higher leverage ratios and inspired a prolific construction boom that dwarfs the Merseyside renewal.

Nevertheless, despite the weaker Merseyside economy, MDC has undoubtedly succeeded in transforming the docklands' image from that of a decaying twilight zone into a popular and fashionable urban environment. The Liverpool waterfront has become a magnet for tourists from near and far. Moreover, despite setbacks due to intervention from the environmental and conservation lobby which have been sustained by the Secretary of State for the Environment, retail and office development interest remains strong.

However, successful regeneration cannot be adequately defined in solely physical terms. Other crucial factors are the distribution of social and economic benefits and issues of accountability. These issues have been important from the outset in London Docklands and acquired increasing currency on Merseyside following MDC's boundary extension. As Colenutt makes clear (Chapter 2), LDDC's record in these respects is less than impressive. The indigenous community has borne the brunt of the costs of regeneration but has enjoyed few of its rewards. Newly built houses, newly created jobs and environmental improvements have not significantly benefited the original population. Private sector led regeneration has profoundly increased the inequality of access to both private and public goods in the area. Lacking the direct accountability mechanisms and the power to engage with LDDC, local authorities and communities have been neglected in favour of private sector interests.

In contrast MDC's record on equity and accountability has been less controversial. This was the case before the boundary extension but it is also so after 1988, despite its move into areas with active local authorities and residents. Whilst MDC's employment creation record has so far been marginal, the service sector jobs generated by the policy focus on tourism and leisure based industries may be more appropriate to the skills of the local community. Moreover, in its initial area, unlike in London, there were few original residents to displace and environmental improvements succeeded in granting access to large stretches of the waterfront formerly sealed off from the public. As we have seen, however, the boundary extension raised the profile of local accountability and equity issues and the potential for conflict between MDC and local authorities and communities.

However, the broad local consensus on MDC's recent area based development strategies indicates that the Corporation is attempting a co-operative approach. It has engaged local authorities and local communities as participants and consultees in the strategy making process and as joint actors in regeneration projects. This approach is markedly different from LDDC's practice and, indeed, from MDC's accountability concerns in its initial phase. At the outset, the introduction of the MDC was opposed by local authorities. However, pragmatic working relationships have since developed. Nevertheless, the durability of these politically negotiated relationships is uncertain and they may prove fragile in the face of competing development pressures. Moreover, the fact remains that despite its recent record on public participation, MDC's accountability to elected authorities and local communities continues to be at its own discretion. This raises the question of how effectively MDC's 'informal' local plans, incorporating local authority and community concerns, will be sustained when the market prefers a different course.

Several further assessments of the UDC policy can be drawn out of MDC's experience. First, there is evidence to support the thesis that investing substantial public expenditure into declining areas will attract future private investment. Second, despite the assertions of government ministers to the contrary, public intervention into the local development process, through the UDC programme, has been significant. This interventionist approach stands uneasily alongside the free-market rationale. Whilst MDC aims to stimulate private sector activity, it is clearly public sector led and financed. Not only has MDC produced land use strategy documents to direct the course of development - central government has also intervened directly against market, and indeed MDC's, wishes to counter environmental and conservation criticisms of the plans for Kings Dock. The calling of public inquiries is significant. It undermines certainty in the development process - one of the central rationales underpinning the creation of the UDCs.

Assessing or predicting the economic performance of UDCs cannot be viewed in isolation from the area's market potential. Indeed, there is little doubt that UDC success and economic advantage go hand in hand. The varied success of LDDC and MDC in stimulating private sector activity powerfully demonstrates the critical nature of the local economy's strength. If a locality lacks a dynamic economy, merely introducing a UDC into its area is no guarantee of economic revival. Whereas LDDC enjoyed substantial private sector growth due to its close proximity to the City of London, the less buoyant Liverpool economy has witnessed less dramatic 'inner city' regeneration.

It is also important to recognise that throughout the 1980s, whilst MDC has received access to substantial financial resources, the government has simultaneously squeezed local authority budgets, particularly Liverpool City

Council's (Liverpool City Council, 1987). The retraction of finances from city coffers calls into question the government's real commitment to urban regeneration. Although the waterfront areas, under the auspices of MDC, have clearly benefited from government expenditure, the physical and social infrastructure of the wider city has been neglected.

MDC's wider remit inevitably brings with it a broader strategy and will encourage it to form more elaborate working relations with other agencies in the field. This is particularly apparent in MDC's efforts to forge alliances with local authorities in its extended area and to complement their regeneration efforts. However, the modest additional resources granted to MDC to cope with its new challenges cast doubt on its ability to transform its single purpose agency practice. Clearly, if MDC does not possess the institutional resources to meet its new challenges it will not succeed. Equally, however, if they are essentially operating as traditional institutions and if it does succeed as a multi-purpose agency, it begs the question whether UDCs were necessary in the first place.

MDC has clearly demonstrated a capacity to realise physical renewal of its initial area and has operated effectively as a single-purpose agency. It has essentially used its very extensive powers and privileges - direct access to central government resources and influence, relative autonomy and freedom from local political accountability - to achieve what the government required. However its ability to carry through the wider social and economic issues that are now central to its agenda has yet to be proven.

CHAPTER 4

THE ROLE OF COMMUNITY GROUPS IN GOVERNMENT INVESTMENT IN PITTSBURGH'S NORTH SIDE

Sue Buckingham-Hatfield

A common theme of urban redevelopment in both the USA and UK is that of leverage, or the use of small amounts of public funding to attract larger sums of private investment. The success of such strategies is therefore usually expressed in terms of the ratio between public and private investment. Such evaluations are frequently made at the aggregate scale, for a city or designated redevelopment area as a whole. There is less monitoring of such programmes at the micro-scale, that of the neighbourhood or census tract. Given that urban districts may be subject to geographically uneven patterns of investment and disinvestment, the question arises as to whether urban redevelopment funds are targeted to those neighbourhoods most lacking in capital or those where private revitalisation is already well established. In other words, does public investment follow private, and thereby exacerbate such unevenness, or does it act to compensate for the lack of private capital ?

This chapter seeks to examine at a small-scale the variations in deprivation and investment in an urban area of Pittsburgh. It asks whether there is any clear spatial relationship between need and public investment. Secondly, it explores the creation and institutionalisation of community groups as part of the processes of channelling state funds into revitalising neighbourhoods. It is argued that geographically constituted groups such as community organisations are not necessarily representative of socially diverse populations. The targeting of investment to areas rather than people, and the creation of a layer of bureaucracy to 'represent' such areas, is, in other words, a critical process in the delivery of urban policy initiatives.

PITTSBURGH'S NORTH SIDE

Although Pittsburgh was severely hit by the decline in the steel industry, its tertiary and quaternary sectors were thriving and there were demands on the city to respond to and cater for the large number of firms locating and expanding their professional and managerial activities there.

One of the areas that was targeted for local government investment lies on the north side of the Allegheny river, directly across from the 'Golden Triangle' which forms the heart of Pittsburgh's downtown. Originally an independent city, Allegheny City was incorporated into an expanding Pittsburgh in the early twentieth century. Through its development as a neighbouring city to Pittsburgh, Allegheny City had a self contained identity and a variety of housing provision. For the Carnegies, Mellons and Heinzs were built substantial brick mansions up the slope from the river whilst the clapboard terraced houses on the riverside were occupied by mostly Eastern European immigrants drawn by work in the steel mills.

As Pittsburgh expanded during the twentieth century and out-of-town residential locations became feasible, the population profile of the North Side changed. The area became marginalised, cut off from the hub of business activity across the river. Its architectural and social heritage was no obstacle to the deterioration of the erstwhile mansions in Manchester, Allegheny West and the Mexican War Streets area. These neighbourhoods were increasingly occupied by a poor population living in crumbling apartments and rooming houses.

In 1967 the once impressive Manchester neighbourhood was declared an Urban Renewal Area by the federal government, in 1968 a Redevelopment Area by the City Commission and in 1971 a Title I Federal Urban Renewal Project. Lobbying efforts from the local (predominantly African-American) activist population secured a large Urban Development Action Grant (UDAG) in 1979 which the Pittsburgh Urban

Renewal Authority (URA) used as a springboard to launch a broader improvement programme in the North Side.

The URA targeted six North Side neighbourhoods by selected criteria of decline. The UDAG supported an initial city bond issue that was designed to underwrite a home buying programme in the neighbourhoods. Initially this was given to both individual home buyers and investors, although this policy was later reviewed to exclude investors. In 1982 the programme area was extended to cover an adjoining neighbourhood, California Kirkbride, which registered similarly high rates of deprivation to the original six neighbourhoods (Allegheny West, Central North Side, East Allegheny, Fineview, Manchester and Perry South).

The stated objective of the City of Pittsburgh in launching the North Side Revitalisation Program was:

"to improve physical conditions without causing displacement of the low and moderate income residents and to stabilise the housing market." (An Evaluation of the North Side Revitalisation Program October 1979 - October 1983, prepared by the Urban Renewal Authority, City of Pittsburgh.)

While there were quite clearly areas of acute deprivation in the North Side, this was by no means ubiquitous. During the time of the programme there were marked variations in deprivation and revitalisation indicators. Marked also was the apparent increase in the discrepancy between revitalising and deprived areas both between and within North Side neighbourhoods. Although leveraging was a stated principle of local government investment policy, no particular relationship could be established between government 'seed funding' and private investment. Public money followed private as often as it led.

The legal requirement for local government to consult with the local community over spending federal money created a potentially critical role for community groups, and raised the question of their role in the decision making process. The Pittsburgh Planning Office interpreted community in geographically distinct terms and liaised with only one group per designated neighbourhood. The neighbourhoods were by no means socially or economically homogeneous, yet the active membership of the representative groups were.

The rest of this chapter will outline the variations in deprivation and investment in the North Side and then explore the disparities between need and investment through the activities of community representatives.

DEPRIVATION AND INVESTMENT IN THE NORTH SIDE

The neighbourhood unit was the focus of much of Pittsburgh's development under the citywide 'Renaissance II' programme. This was inspired by the first Renaissance programme in 1943 in which leading business interests in Pittsburgh took the initiative to forge a partnership with city government to address three critical problems of the time: air pollution, flooding, physical dereliction. Out of this partnership the Urban Renewal Authority (URA) was born in 1979. Between 1979 and 1985, $482 million was spent on neighbourhood improvement projects and programmes. On average this represented around 35 per cent of the annual operating budget available to the city. The agency chiefly concerned with neighbourhood liaison was the City Planning Office, which employed a number of community planners responsible for consulting with their allocation of neighbourhood groups. The role of the community planner was responsive and informative rather than proactive.

Housing had been the responsibility of the Urban Renewal Authority (URA) since the early 1970s when it achieved independent recognition through federal legislation. The URA commanded a large budget share (just over half of citywide neighbourhood expenditure) during the Renaissance II programme. Funding was broadly divided between federal programmes and locally raised bond issue finance. The majority of housing expenditure (almost 70 per cent) made by the URA was committed to home improvement loans and equity participation units (the latter designed for owner-occupiers on low to moderate incomes). Although rental accommodation comprised more than a third of Pittsburgh's housing only 5 per cent of URA housing expenditure was expressly devoted to this sector. This was consistent with the philosophy of local government, in which owner-occupation was seen as the most efficient way of stabilising a neighbourhood. The URA also had a responsibility for allocating a large share of the Community Development Block Grant (CDBG).

The North Side, recipient of substantial government investment through the URA, exhibited a strongly differentiated housing market. The level of owner-occupancy did not correspond with house prices, as Table 4.1 quite clearly shows.

Other variations can be observed and are given in full in Tables 4.2a and 4.2b: the rise in median income earned in the North Side was markedly low, but concealed a degree of polarisation. The average income in Allegheny West, for example, in 1980 was 35 per cent of the city average (and this represented a decline on 1970), yet house prices at sale were the highest in the city in 1983-84. The percentage of households earning more than $50,000 in 1980 was about 80 per cent of the city average. This, together with house price rises since 1980, indicated that houses were being sold to buyers on incomes substantially higher than the average in Allegheny West. Gentrification activity was indicated by a substantial reduction in properties without exclusive plumbing between 1970 and 1980 and by a disproportionate allocation of Historic Preservation Grants. The neighbourhood housed 3.5 per cent of the North Side's population but received 17 per cent of the North Side's Historic Preservation Grants.

Table 4.1: Average Property Sale Price Relative to City and to Local Owner Occupancy Rates.

N'hood	Two Year Weighted Rank in City (70 neighbourhoods)	5 Year Change 1980-85 (%)	Average House Price 1983-84 ($)	% Owner Occ.
Allegheny West	1	193	125,340	11.5
Manchester	20	278	40,681	29.0
Central N. Side	39	10	26,105	25.0
Perry South	46	15	22,351	56.0
California-Kirkbride	49	25	19,633	40.0
East Allegheny	49	25	19,633	26.0

Source: URA Housing Dept; Residential Trend Report 1985

Manchester was the other neighbourhood that experienced high house price rises while maintaining low owner occupancy rates (29 per cent compared with a city average of 64 per cent). Despite these house price rises, housing conditions in Manchester remained poor with almost 30 per cent lacking exclusive plumbing facilities.

The variations in prosperity in the North Side become more acute when observed on the smaller scale of the census tract. Within Central North Side between 1970 and 1980, the census tract containing the Mexican War Streets historic area experienced the most drastic drop in dwellings lacking exclusive plumbing arrangements, the highest property price increases, the sharpest rise in owner occupancy, a decrease in the proportion of elderly people and a slower than city average population decline. Its neighbouring census tract to the north exhibited diametrically opposite trends, suggesting that whilst one area improved another declined. Similar intra-neighbourhood imbalances were observed in Manchester, California Kirkbride and East Allegheny.

In considering indicators of revitalisation and gentrification, the percentage increase was above the city average in several areas (Tables 4.2a and 4.2b): above average rises in professional and managerial jobs and owner occupancy in Allegheny West, California Kirkbride, Fineview, Manchester and Perry South. Manchester was the only neighbourhood not to witness conversion of buildings to single occupancy above the city average. The above average increases in 20-45 year olds and college-educated residents were evident in Allegheny West, Central North Side and Manchester, whilst East Allegheny experienced the latter. Allegheny West, the highly polarised neighbourhood referred to earlier, scored above the city average on every revitalisation indicator except rising income. Together with this neighbourhood there were strong signs of gentrification in the Mexican War Streets area of Central North Side, the census tract with Historic Designation in Manchester and a single census tract in East Allegheny.

The pattern of deprivation in the North Side did not then present a universal picture of disinvestment or devalorisation prior to the declaration of the programme. Even by the URA's own criteria of decline (population decline, low home ownership, increase in the African-American population, ageing population, low income, substandard housing and high crime rates) the North Side neighbourhoods did not always exhibit such symptoms. Between 1970 and 1980 owner occupancy was only declining in Fineview, house prices were increasing throughout the area and the elderly population was increasing above the average rate in only half the neighbourhoods.

The drive to home ownership and the benefits to buyers was most concerted in Manchester and Central North Side. There was no income restriction on any households in receipt of programme monies. The only restrictions on purchasers were not to have owned their own home during the previous three years or to have spent more than $100,000 on their prospective North Side home. These were waived in the case of Manchester and Central North Side. Programme requirements necessitated a 5 per cent

Table 4.2A: Selected Indicators of Revitalisation and Deprivation on North Side Census Tracts 1970-1980

N'hood	Census Tract	Owner occupation		55 years +		20-45 years old		Population Decline	
		1980 %	1970-80 % change	1980 %	1970-80 % change	1980 %	1970-80 % change	1980 %	1970-80 % change
Allegheny West	2201	11	21.0	35	-8	40	43	846	-27
California-Kirkbride	2102	47	-0.5	11	10	33	13	834	-38
	2502	43	46.0	23	-32	30	27	1047	-42
Central North Side	2202	18	19.0	34	-7	39	49	1968	-24
	2203	21	-16.0	31	2	32	8	341	-40
	2503	37	6.0	29	12	32	15	1932	-34
East Allegheny	2301	33	2.0	40	14	26	10	2385	-29
	2302	15	5.0	50	27	23	17	2123	-24
Fineview	2506	46	-1.0	25	-1	31	20	2814	-12
Manchester	2101	39	0.5	25	13	29	23	785	-13
	2103	25	0.5	28	16	30	21	1898	-29
Perry South	2501	48	9.0	26	17	32	23	1654	-36
	2603	65	6.0	23	-3	30	22	595	-17
	2604	57	-5.0	28	8	32	27	2486	-20
	2605	53	-3.0	22	-17	37	39	1998	-20
	2606	71	12.0	25	-7	3	34	591	-50

Table 4.2B: Selected Indicators of Revitalisation and Deprivation on North Side Census Tracts 1970-1980

N'hood	Census Tract	Average Median Income		New Residents (5 years or less)		4 years or More College Education		Black Population	
		1980 $	1970-80 % change	1980 %	1970-80 % change	1980 %	1970-80 % change	1980 %	1970-80 % change
Allegheny West	2201	6,221	-0.5	44	-2	11.0	1428	10	100
California Kirkbride	2102	11,550	92.0	36	-30	0.5	-100	49	39
	2502	4,519	-33.0	47	-7	0.5	-50	88	50
Central North Side	2202	7,109	47.0	98	89	9.0	255	26	114
	2203	8,282	104.0	48	-17	10.0	43	43	24
	2503	9,758	57.0	45	-34	13.0	114	75	6
East Allegheny	2301	8,589	22.0	46	29	1.0	-27	2	100
	2302	4,782	-14.0	47	1	4.0	175	7	231
Fineview	2506	9,420	-12.0	31	-8	2.0	21	40	46
Manchester	2101	9,613	71.0	43	0	9.0	1820	85	23
	2103	8,975	46.0	45	36	10.0	166	86	13
Perry South	2501	11,207	53.0	9	-79	4.0	194	30	59
	2603	11,018	6.0	46	19	2.0	200	34	30
	2604	11,297	32.0	51	11	6.0	-18	48	93
	2605	14,673	57.0	46	40	5.0	11	25	325
	2606	11,966	52.0	35	108	2.0	-10	18	163

downpayment plus closing costs which immediately prejudiced the chances of low income residents, particularly in those neighbourhoods experiencing high house price rises. The earlier designation of two historic areas in Manchester and Central North Side (Mexican War Streets) suggests that the URA was investing in areas already revitalising and therefore able to show a quick demonstration of the city's investment programme. This is a charge increasingly being laid at the door of city governments when disbursing federal grants by, amongst others, Dommel and Rich (1987), Fainstein and Fainstein (1986) and Strickland and Judd (1983). Whilst this is an attractive option, as the effects of such a strategy are quickly apparent, the more deteriorated property (less attractive to private investors) continues to decline.

The URA justified a large scale investment programme to ensure its effectiveness; however, this in turn exacerbates precisely the contradictions and polarisation already referred to. To establish whether government investment was made where it was likely to see the greatest return or to areas of greatest deprivation, public spending patterns were analysed in the light of private investment and previous revitalisation and deprivation patterns.

The bulk of government investment was made to facilitate property purchase, considered by the programme implementers as the most effective way to stabilise the area. Certain provisions were made within the bond programme, such as Equity Participation Loans (EPLs) to assist lower income purchasers. Such assistance, however, was not restricted to owner-occupants. Of the first bond issue (and by far the most significant in terms of funds raised: $20 million), 39 per cent was allocated to investors (individual loans averaging $57,064) whilst 61 per cent was allocated to owner-occupants (individual loans averaging $40,342). Of EPLs made, 56 per cent were made to investors (average loan $20,235) whilst 44 per cent were made to owner-occupiers (average loan $9,063). The URA's attitude to investor participation in the EPL scheme was ambivalent. After the second bond issue (by which time half the total programme allocation had been made) investor participation through the EPL was excluded. However, the URA was inclined to the view that investor activity promoted owner-occupation involvement. Table 4.3 shows the various degrees of investment activity versus owner-occupier revitalisation activity in the North Side neighbourhoods.

Table 4.3: Loan Activity and Investor Loan Activity Using First and Second Bond Issue Finance in North Side Neighbourhoods.

Neigh'hood	% North Side Units	Units on Which Loans Made		Loans Made	
		Number	%	Number	%
Allegheny West	6	56	7	21	5
Central North Side	22	303	41	175	40
East Allegheny	24	88	12	46	10
Fineview	11	59	8	38	9
Manchester	12	152	20	95	21
Perry South	25	97	12	66	15

Neigh'hood	Units on which Investor Loans Made		Investor Loans	
	Number	%	Number	%
Allegheny West	27	8	9	6
Central North Side	152	45	65	47
East Allegheny	47	14	19	14
Fineview	28	8	11	8
Manchester	66	19	26	19
Perry South	20	6	8	6

Source: *An Evaluation of the North Side Revitalisation Program, October 1979 - October 1983*; Urban Renewal Authority of Pittsburgh

According to the URA, the total number of loans made in Central North Side included 59 per cent on properties in the Mexican War Streets area already introduced as one of historic and architectural merit.

Property owners investing in the North Side during the URA revitalisation programme would have acted on deprivation and revitalisation information referred to earlier. Allegheny West had a greater percentage of units for which bond issue loans were allocated and a still greater percentage allocated to investors than its percentage of North Side units would account for. In 1980 it showed the greatest tendency to revitalise and performed averagely on a decline in deprivation index. Central North Side enjoyed a rate of unit improvement using bond issue finance almost twice that of the percentage of North Side units it contained. Investment activity by unit was more than double the percentage of North Side units contained by the neighbourhood.

Manchester scored higher than its share of North Side units merited in terms of general and investor loan activity but, unlike Allegheny West and Central North Side, was amongst the more deprived neighbourhoods and showed a lesser tendency to revitalise by 1980. Fineview and Perry South both received less investment than their share of units would indicate. East Allegheny displays the most glaring disparity as, whilst it contains one quarter of all North Side dwellings, total investment represents around one eighth of all North Side loans made. When census tracts are scrutinised in this neighbourhood a sharp division in experience becomes apparent. These data suggest that investment under the URA programme tended to be made in neighbourhoods (and census tracts) already showing stronger revitalisation signals.

The figures in Table 4.4 illustrate a further disparity between the share of all city capital expenditure and share of dwellings in the North Side. Positive imbalances can be seen for Allegheny West, Central North Side and Manchester in favour of investment and negatively for the remaining neighbourhoods. This also demonstrates the rehabilitation expenditure and incidence in North Side neighbourhoods and census tracts. Understandably, this follows government programme allocation (in some cases the programme will have funded the rehabilitation work), but there is also a correlation with prior revitalisation experience. Whilst Manchester shows exceptionally high expenditure on a relatively large number of properties, Central North Side and East Allegheny show selective investment (that is, higher amounts on fewer properties). California Kirkbride and Perry South both show a pattern of low investment on a few properties. When the data for census tracts are observed a marked discrepancy can be seen within East Allegheny. On the number of rehabilitations, census tract 2202 (Mexican War Streets historic area) emerges substantially ahead of its fellow Central North Side census tracts.

Table 4.4: North Side Rehabilitation Expenditure and Activity, 1981-1985

N'hood	Census Tract	Total Expenditure ($000s)	Dwelling $/Dw.	Rank	Rehab'tion %	$/Dw. Rank
Allegheny						
West	2201	1,540	2,468	8	28	4
California						
Kirkbride	2102	567	1,673	10	17	9
	2502	386	929	11	15	11
Central North						
Side	2202	2,994	2,197	9	29	3
	2203	572	2,661	7	20	8
	2503	2,731	2,968	5	25	6
East						
Allegheny	2301	5,599	4,354	3	16	10
	2302	1,105	862	12	11	14
Fineview	2506	3,647	3,091	4	31	2
Manchester	2101	2,465	5,748	2	23	7
	2103	7,457	7,744	1	34	1
Perry South	2501	1,950	2,916	6	26	5
	2603	169	826	13	14	12
	2604	693	770	14	12	13
	2605	417	552	15	8	15
	2606	115	528	16	8	15

Source: City of Pittsburgh Buildings Office

There appears to be a clear trend allying census tracts that experienced faster revitalisation and declining deprivation prior to 1980 with subsequent public and private investment. Investment since 1979 also seems to have been influenced by historic designation as census tracts containing such areas saw more rehabilitation activity.

An attempt to observe whether or not public investment leverages private investment has therefore been inconclusive. By examining the time at which public and private investment took place, only two of the six neighbourhoods for which complete data are available experienced city led investment. In Allegheny West and East Allegheny public and private investment was contemporaneous after 1981, whilst private investment led public in Manchester and California Kirkbride.

COMMUNITY REPRESENTATION IN THE NORTH SIDE

Given the disparate investment pattern in the North Side, which appears to favour areas previously showing a greater tendency to revitalise, and an investment strategy that permits higher income rehabilitators to use government funds for revitalising increasingly fashionable homes, what guides programme investment in an alleged attempt to alleviate deprivation?

The nature of community representation in Pittsburgh has been such that, while obliged to consult groups over the allocation of federally originating money, only one group per neighbourhood was consulted. Regardless of how diverse the local population or economy is in each neighbourhood, the neighbourhood planner has not sought to ensure even representation and, indeed, in most cases representation did not reflect the local socio-economic profiles. The remainder of this chapter will review the nature and activities of these neighbourhood groups in an attempt to understand better the nature of the North Side Revitalization Program delivery, to trace out the mechanisms by which social polarisation may be exacerbated rather than alleviated.

Pittsburgh has a strong neighbourhood heritage and its Rand McNally citation as "most livable city in the USA" in 1985 owed much to the feelings of intimacy residents felt towards their neighbourhood. Almost three-quarters of city residents felt that their neighbourhood was a good or excellent place to live, whilst around two-thirds felt strongly attached to their neighbourhood (Ahlbrandt and Cunningham,1980).

The neighbourhood factor was also an important marketing concept in trying to attract residents to move to Pittsburgh. To this end the Neighborhoods for Living Center was established in 1979, under the auspices of the URA and in co-operation with ACTION Housing Incorporated. ACTION Housing Incorporated is a local charitable housing foundation, founded in 1958 and in receipt of government funding. Although this centre presented a coherent picture in which the city was divided into discrete neighbourhoods, residents would not always identify with these boundaries. Moreover, single geographic units contained a range of advantage and disadvantage, revitalisation potential and public and private investment levels and, consequently, conflicting interests. From these conflicting interests emerged representation that did not always reflect the majority interest.

Each neighbourhood was assigned a planner who was responsible for notifying neighbourhood residents of planning decisions which were likely to affect them and for channeling requests for action through the appropriate city departments. Neighbourhood groups were invited to nominate a representative to attend relevant council meetings.

As well as the groups purporting to represent individual neighbourhoods, two organisations covered the North Side as a whole: the North Side Civic Development Council (NSCDC), which was essentially an economic development unit, and the North Side Leadership Conference (NSLC). This was, in fact, formed by the NSCDC after several unsuccessful attempts to unite North Side community and advocacy groups. The NSLC comprised representatives from most of the individual neighbourhoods and employed one full- and one part-time member of staff. The NSLC liaised directly with eight city agencies and nominated four representatives to sit on the NSCDC.

The North Side had, at the time of research, one community planner of eighteen months' standing. Although she had responsibility for other areas, she considered that her appointment had begun to dissolve some of the negative feelings caused by the lack of a link person. The general feeling that emanated from the City Planning Office (from directorate level downwards) was that the organisation on the North Side was both enthusiastic and sophisticated, as well as demanding. The community planner saw the NSLC as a strong and uniting force which did not create conflict between the neighbourhoods. The community planner was also aware that conflict probably did exist behind the prominence of what she perceived to be middle class agitation, but did not consider it part of her brief actively to encourage alliances that were not already formed. Rather, her role was perceived as one of shaping ideas held by groups already in existence. The individual group was seen as more important than the umbrella organisation. These individual groups are discussed in more detail.

Allegheny West

Allegheny West Civic Council (AWCC) was formed during the early 1970s to mark the distinctiveness of the area from neighbouring Manchester, which had a reputation for disadvantage. In addition to receiving subscription revenue, the AWCC received rent on a local property it owned. Allegheny West's population was predominantly white (90 per cent), had doubled its owner occupancy level from 1970 to 1980 (from a low base of 6 per cent), but had an average income of one-third of the city average. Low income was not, however, represented in the house sale prices, which were the highest in Pittsburgh (Table 4.1). Moreover, for the North Side, the neighbourhood had a relatively high percentage of households that earned more than $50,000 in 1980, close to the city average of 1.5 per cent. This suggests a high degree of polarity between low income renters and high income owner-occupiers. This trend was confirmed by a report published by the URA in 1985 that found no low income homebuyers moving into the area during the Programme period. Quite clearly 'neighbourhood' representation emanated from the latter group since all active members were home-owners.

Conflict existed both within the neighbourhood and with other North Side neighbourhood groups. Internally, the interests of the AWCC such as maintaining land in residential use and seeking effective zoning controls for this, lobbying for character street furniture and for historic designation and securing residential parking permits did not represent the interests of the wider neighbourhood population. Externally, AWCC felt that its demands were highly specific and did not benefit from a wider articulation through the North Side Leadership Conference, which it joined in 1985. The Council felt that it had only achieved a limited success in achieving the aims determined above. The main opponents in the land-use battles were the Allegheny Community College and a local developer who planned to build subsidised apartments with 25 per cent reserved for handicapped residents. The AWCC preferred to concentrate on environmental issues and gentrification. By 1987 the group's emphasis was squarely on dwelling conversions at market rates. In the Pittsburgh Neighborhood Survey, Ahlbrandt (1984) found that feelings of neighbourhood satisfaction were well below the city average, although neighbourhood attachment was greater. Whilst the AWCC were lobbying for the conversion of vacant apartments to market rate housing, the population interviewed by Ahlbrandt and Cunningham (1980) suggested that the high house prices caused the greatest concern in the area. This was considered more important than all the environmental and crime related problems prompted by the survey.

Hollow promises

The Central North Side

The Central North Side had strongly organised if partial representation since the 1960s when the Mexican War Streets area began to experience small scale renovation. This representation secured historic recognition for the area and spawned the Mexican War Streets Society. The Central North Side as a whole was, by the 1980s, represented by the Central North Side Neighborhood Council (CNSNC) but there was evidence of tension between the young people brought up in the area for whom there were slim prospects of employment (levels of unemployment consistently outstripped the city average) and householders involved in revitalisation. House prices, unlike those in Allegheny West, were not universally escalating: the average rise in house prices in the neighbourhood corresponded with the city rise. The disaffected population referred to above were not active in either of the neighbourhood societies and perceived their aims to be remote from their own needs. Of course, since they were not involved in these groups these needs failed to be expressed to the city council, although the two umbrella groups, NSCDC and NSLC, took some responsibility for this. Community feeling in the area as monitored by Ahlbrandt was low, with barely more than one half of interviewees accepting the neighbourhood as a good or excellent place to live and two-thirds (almost 20 per cent below the percentage for Allegheny West) feeling strongly attached to it. The concerns of the neighbourhoods appeared to be more with building condition (vacant structures and deterioration) than with crime related issues, house prices or non-residential environmental issues.

Economic problems were not addressed by the Ahlbrandt study and this reflects the lack of attention expressed by the neighbourhood groups to issues such as unemployment, affordable housing and employment generation. The North Side Civic Development Council placed the latter firmly on its agenda through its attempts to establish incubators for small businesses and local labour contracts in larger projects, with limited success. The Manchester Citizens Corporation was alone in lobbying for such provision, but its capability in this area became increasingly constrained towards the end of the Programme period (see below).

California Kirkbride

There had been an informal group in California Kirkbride for many years but the Charles Street-Kirkbride Area Council (CSKAC) was officially constituted in 1979 to take advantage of the UDAG. Of the active membership ninety percent were home-owners, but in contrast to the two neighbourhoods presented above, their average length of tenancy was twenty-five years. The council incompletely straddles two census tracts and 'officially' defined neighbourhoods: Perry South and California Kirkbride, and so it is difficult to establish the representativeness of its membership, although owner-occupancy rates were around half that of the active membership in both census tracts. Community satisfaction and attachment was found to be relatively low, hovering around 50 per cent. The active membership were not hostile to the interests of non-members as appeared to be the case in the two groups mentioned earlier (and East Allegheny referred to below) but felt that there was a difference in neighbourhood perception between owner occupiers and renters. The main thrust of the council's efforts had been to lobby for new housing, improve neighbourhood services and strengthen neighbourhood rapport.

This neighbourhood approach was echoed by the Fineview Citizens Council. This group was founded in 1983 under the guidance of the Perry Hilltop neighbourhood organisation. Residents had seen and been motivated by what other neighbourhoods had achieved through lobbying activities. Fineview was considered by its residents to be an old-established family neighbourhood but it was generally felt that the cohesion was being destroyed by the increasing numbers of properties converted to the rental market. This was the only neighbourhood in the North Side which experienced a drop in owner-occupancy between 1970 and 1980. Whilst renters were encouraged to participate in the neighbourhood and its organisation, lack of involvement by this group resulted in the membership being comprised of owner-occupants of long standing. Other issues that the FCC concerned itself with included the control of unruly behaviour (both by young people and by American Legion club members!), the use of vacant structures and neighbourhood welfare programmes, particularly for the elderly.

East Allegheny

In contrast, the East Allegheny Community Council (EACC) membership was dominated by new owner-occupants in recently renovated property. This contrasted with a 26 per cent owner-occupancy rate in the neighbourhood. Moreover, 55 per cent of the neighbourhood had been resident there for five years or more. The council was formed in 1979 under strong leadership guidance (the only member who had not recently moved into the area, although a home-owner). There was some committee approval for a small selective membership because "it facilitated decision making", despite its exclusivity.

Hollow promises

The council received city support for a part-time member of staff. The main focus of the council's activities was to redevelop neighbourhood housing for market rent and to this end the EACC had become involved in commercial and residential development. It had also successfully lobbied for a prestigious residential development under the Community Development Block Grant programme, although the sale prices far exceeded the borrowing capacity of the majority of local residents (median income was less than $7,000 in 1980, whilst unemployment stood at three times the city average). While city agencies have argued that the encouragement of higher income groups into a low- or moderate-income area has a stabilising effect, the lobbying efforts of an apparently unrepresentative group, which also counted amongst its achievements the zone enforcement in respect of unlicensed multi-occupancy property and the installation of street furniture with public funding in character with the prestigious Deutschland Square development, raise the question of stability for whom. These and other activities, such as commercial involvement in the conversion of a priory into a luxury hotel and the lobbying for historic designation status, created tension between the new, active residents and the majority of residents who were on low incomes and rented their homes.

The promotional literature for East Allegheny produced jointly by the EACC and the Neighborhoods for Living Center emphasised the renovation potential of the area, whilst minimising the community and family aspects concentrated on by Fineview and Charles Street-Kirkbride. Ahlbrandt found a strong attachment to the neighbourhood but a low percentage of residents (57 per cent) expressing a feeling that East Allegheny was a good or excellent place in which to live.

Manchester

Manchester Citizens Corporation (MCC) had a rather different history to other groups in the North Side. It was formed in response to the urban riots in the late 1960s, although there had previously been community activity concentrated on winning historic and architectural recognition for the area. Citizen involvement began in 1972 to coincide with the approval of a large urban renewal project. The project never materialised owing to a federal moratorium on housing funds, but the two strands of building preservation and community involvement came together in 1979 with the incorporation of the MCC. The neighbourhood was instrumental in securing the Urban Development Action Grant both through its lobbying efforts and the prevailing conditions in the area.

The MCC employed eleven members of staff at the time of investigation and ran a development corporation which was involved in renovating and constructing housing as well as providing local jobs. The MCC reported to a council of resident representatives. The organisation was complex and not without internal conflict. There was also some conflict between Manchester and neighbouring groups, largely due to the vast difference in the scale and resourcing of projects there. Alone amongst the North Side groups, the MCC aimed to maintain opportunities for housing and jobs for low and moderate households in the area. Unemployment in the area was not the highest in the North Side, but well above the city average; owner-occupancy was also low at around 30 per cent. Conversely, house prices climbed fast between 1980 and 1985, whilst median income was low (see Tables 4.2a and 4.2b). By 1987, the paid staff employed by the MCC had been reduced by half and the development emphasis had shifted to gentrification. The number of homes sold to median-to-high income earners rose while neighbourhood representatives expressed concern over the concentration of substandard property. Neighbourhood satisfaction was the lowest of all North Side neighbourhoods. From being a highly charged organisation unique in the North Side for engaging in employment and economic related issues, Manchester appeared to be following the path of Allegheny West, Central North Side and East Allegheny.

Interests in the North Side, then, do not neatly fit into neighbourhood units which dovetail into the geographic space of the area. The neighbourhood (for which physical limits may be assigned) acted as a base for a group but, often, these groups could be more accurately defined by housing and class interests than purely by locality. Although it is clear that most of these groups were not representative they were instrumental in directing government funding to projects of limited use to the majority of residents, 'neighbourhood stabilisation' apart. This raises the question of the appropriateness of organising community interests in spatial terms alone and questions the legitimacy of the community consultation process.

The operation of the communities of interest has varied from seeking to preserve neighbourhood cohesion or status quo (Fineview and Charles Street Kirkbride) to pursuing the interests of an exclusive and unrepresentative group within the neighbourhood (such as Allegheny West, Central North Side, East Allegheny and increasingly Manchester).

At the time of research there were over sixty well defined and locationally stable neighbourhood groups in the city of Pittsburgh, together with several official umbrella organisations and established routes of representation for neighbourhood groups. Although institutional sponsorship can be a positive force, it can also be counter-productive in terms of representative neighbourhood mobilisation. One formal route of expression set up in 1980 - the Home Rule Charter - was developed to provide neighbourhoods with an opportunity to form advisory boards to exercise limited powers in local government. Representatives from twenty-four predesignated districts could advise Council and the Mayor on zoning, planning, public services and other related matters. Additionally, the board could request a city departmental chief to answer questions about any relevant neighbourhood problem. Inevitably, restricting the dialogue to one neighbourhood group in each area created a problem of representativeness. Notwithstanding this, the city policy continued to approach only the designated neighbourhood group.

THE ROLE OF COMMUNITY GROUPS

The role of the community group is more than to be a channel through which individual needs and requests (however exclusive or partisan) are articulated to local government. Wilson (1988) proposed that community groups should be regarded as the interface between structure and agency and that caution should be exercised in ascribing voluntaristic impetuses to them. Both their formation and operation may be heavily constrained by the state through its managers. He later argued (1989) that public participation via community activity fostered a value-free image which obscured the involvement of state officials in facilitating the activities of institutionally recognised groups.

Yet rather than forming a point between structure and agency, perhaps the role of community groups could be better represented in terms of a continuum between civil society and the state. The point at which a group's needs and requests become institutionalised determines how far the community group is part of civil society and therefore lying outside the rubric of the state, and how far it is part of the state apparatus. Nor would this position necessarily be fixed: a group might be part of civil society at its constitution but be transformed by appropriation by the state.

Storper (1987) argues that civil society can determine the nature of capitalism itself. This may be possible through community representation and has been evident where neighbourhood groups have challenged the status quo and caused government to reappraise the practice of service delivery. Ample, if often contentious, evidence of this is given in the literature on urban social movements. There continues to be marginal evidence to suggest that 'guerillas in the bureaucracy' still exist (Needleman, 1974). However, the evidence from Pittsburgh indicates that the *community group*, instead of acting as an oppositional force, has been brought more emphatically within the institutional orbit, both through the mechanisms for consultation and as it becomes formally integrated into local policy making.

PART TWO
MISCONCEPTIONS: URBAN SOCIAL CHANGE, SALVATION AND GENTRIFICATION

The aim of this section is to examine the nexus between theory and policy in the implementation of urban programmes. We have already suggested that the notion of regeneration renders the goals of urban redevelopment unproblematic. By rallying (almost) everybody around a consensual notion of an inner city problem which needs to be resolved the actual intentions of urban policy can easily escape close scrutiny. The rhetorical thrust of urban renewal policies depends on a movement away from a depressed present without necessarily portraying too detailed a picture of the destination towards which these policies are moving.

Behind such unproblematic terms as regeneration, redevelopment, urban renaissance, revival and renewal there are many thorny issues which need to be addressed. Either explicitly or implicitly urban policy contains within it a diagnosis of the nature of decline, a prescription for regeneration and a prognosis about the future state of the city patient. It is at this point that at some level policy formulation is informed, or at least claims to be informed, not just by political expediency but also by theoretical conceptualisations of urban change. It is this point at which such social theory becomes built into policy.

In Part 2 of this volume we have tried to look at two conceptualisations of the nature of change in the city which have become institutionalised in policy formation. Both are connected to the socially prescriptive and invidious notion which has focused on the people of the city as being central to 'the problem' of urban decline. This is a notion which has found various theoretical rationalisations through time from a suggestion of a cycle of poverty which informed American urban policy in the early 1960s to an almost genetic conceptualisation of the learning (training) potential of inner city residents which was enshrined in the White Paper on the Inner Cities and Act in late 1970s Britain. Both are enshrined in the logics of officially sanctioned ansd subsidised gentrification, to improve *the social mix* of the inner city, and state sponsored training programmes of recent years.

The overall theme of Part 2 is that urban social theory is powerful but by the time it emerges in urban policy many of the central tenets that have informed policy formulation may be theoretically discredited.

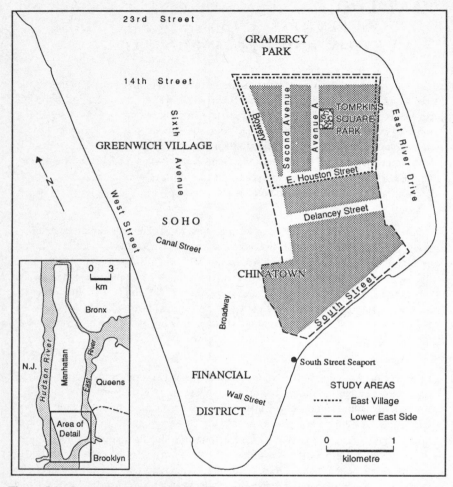

Figure 5.1: Lower Manhattan showing East Village and Lower East Side

CHAPTER 5

MAPPING THE GENTRIFICATION FRONTIER

Neil Smith

REPRESENTING GENTRIFICATION

In his definitive essay on *The Significance of the Frontier in American History*, written in 1893, Frederick Jackson Turner (1958 edn.) wrote

> "American development has exhibited not merely advance along a single line, but a return to primitive conditions on a continually advancing frontier line, and new development for that area. American social development has been continually beginning over again on the frontier. In this advance the frontier is the outer edge of the wave - the meeting point between savagery and civilization... The wilderness has been interpenetrated by lines of civilization growing ever more numerous." (1958, pp2-3)

For Turner, the expansion of the frontier and the rolling back of wilderness and savagery were an attempt to make liveable space out of an unruly and unco-operative nature. This involved not simply a process of spatial expansion and the progressive taming of the physical world. The development of the frontier certainly accomplished these things, but for Turner it was also the central experience which defined the uniqueness of the American national character. With each expansion of the outer edge by the robust pioneers, not only were new lands added to the American estate but also new blood was added to the veins of the American democratic ideal. Each new wave westward, in the conquest of nature, sent shockwaves back east in the democratisation of human nature. During the twentieth century the imagery of wilderness and frontier has been applied less to the plains, mountains and forests of the West, and more to the urban areas, especially in the East. As part of the experience of suburbanisation, the twentieth-century American city came to be seen by the white middle-class as an urban wilderness; it was, and for many still is, the habitat of crime and disease, danger and disorder, the rawness of human nature. Indeed these were the central fears expressed by a generation of postwar urban theorists who focused on urban 'blight' and 'decline', 'social malaise' in the inner city, the 'anthology' of urban life, in short, 'the unheavenly city' (Banfield, 1968). The city becomes a wilderness, or worse a jungle (Long, 1971; Sternlieb, 1971; Castells, 1976). More vividly than in the news media or social science theory, this is the recurrent theme in a whole genre of 'urban jungle' Hollywood productions, from *West Side Story* and *King Kong* to *The Warriors* and *Fort Apache*.

Anti-urbanism has been a dominant theme in American culture. Parallel to the evolution in original experiences of wilderness, the last twenty years have seen a shift from fear to romanticism and a progression of urban imagery from wilderness to frontier. Cotton Mather and the Puritans of seventeenth-century New England feared the forest as an impenetrable evil, a dangerous wilderness inhabited by 'fiery flying serpents', but with the continual taming of the forest and its transformation at the hands of human labour, the softer imagery of Turner's frontier was an obvious successor to Mather's forest of evil. There is an optimism and an expectation of expansion associated with 'frontier'; wilderness gives way to frontier when the conquest is well under way. Thus in the twentieth-century American city, the imagery of urban wilderness has been replaced by the imagery of urban frontier. This transformation can be traced to the origins of urban renewal (Abrams, 1965), but has become intensified in the last two decades, as rehabilitation by individuals and families became fashionable in the wake of urban renewal. In the language of gentrification, the appeal to frontier imagery is exact: urban pioneers, urban homesteaders and urban cowboys are the new folk heroes of the urban frontier. There are even 'urban scouts' who scout out those potentially lucrative neighbourhoods that are 'about to go'.

Just as Turner recognised the existence of Native Americans but included them as part of his savage wilderness, contemporary urban frontier imagery implicitly treats the present inner-city population as a natural element of their physical surroundings, and thus virtually invisible. The term 'urban pioneer' is as arrogant as the original notion of the pioneer in that it conveys the impression of a city that is not yet socially inhabited; like the Native Americans, the contemporary urban working class is seen as less than social, a physical threat emanating from the physical environment. Turner was explicit about this when he called the frontier "the meeting point between savagery and civilization", and although today's frontier vocabulary of gentrification is rarely as explicit, it treats the inner city population in much the same way (Stratton, 1977). One respected researcher has gone so far as to suggest that in gentrifying neighbourhoods there is a clear social difference between a "civil class" and an "uncivil class" (Clay, 1979, 37-8). The parallels go further. For Turner, the westward geographical progress of the frontier line is associated with the forging of the national spirit. An equally spiritual hope is expressed in the boosterism which presents gentrification as the leading edge of an American urban renaissance; in the most extreme scenario, the new urban 'pioneers' are expected to do for the national spirit what the old ones did: to lead us into a new world where the problems of the old world are left behind. In the words of one federal publication, gentrification's appeal to history involves the

"psychological need to re-experience successes of the past because of the disappointments of recent years - Vietnam, Watergate, the energy crisis, pollution, inflation, high interest rates, and the like" (Advisory Council on Historic Preservation, 1980, p9)

No one has yet seriously proposed that we view James Rouse (the American developer responsible for many of the highly visible downtown malls, plazas, markets and tourist arcades such as Baltimore's Harbor Place and New York's South Street Seaport) as the John Wayne of gentrification, but the proposal would be quite in keeping with much of the contemporary imagery. In the end, and this is the important conclusion, the imagery of frontier serves to rationalise and legitimise a process of conquest, whether in the nineteenth century Wild West or in the twentieth century inner city. Among the myths on which this imagery is based is the notion that gentrification is a national phenomenon, essentially American.

In fact, gentrification is a quintessentially international process. It is taking place in cities throughout North America and much of Western Europe, as well as Australia and New Zealand - that is, in cities throughout much of the advanced capitalist world. Yet nowhere is the process less understood than in the United States, where the American nationalism of the frontier motif has encouraged a provincial understanding of

Hollow promises

gentrification. The original eighteenth and nineteenth century frontier experiences were
not limited to the United States, but rather exported throughout the world. The
Australian experience of frontier, for example, was certainly different from the American,
but was also responsible (along with American cultural imports) for spawning a strong
frontier ideology. And the American frontier itself was as intensely real for potential
immigrants in Scandinavia or Ireland as it was for actual French or British immigrants in
Baltimore or Boston. Likewise, while it is nowhere as rooted as in the United States, a
frontier ideology does emerge elsewhere in connection with gentrification. The imagery
varies with geographical context. Thus in London's Notting Hill, the All Saints Road is
sometimes conceived as the 'front line' in the conflict between the local Black population
and White gentrification.

But as with every ideology, there is a real, if partial and distorted, basis for the treatment
of gentrification as a new urban frontier. In this idea of frontier we see an evocative
combination of economic, geographical and historical dimensions of development. The
frontier was simultaneously a geographical place, a line in the landscape, the leading
edge of economic development and a symbol of historical destiny. In the nineteenth
century, the expansion of the geographic frontier in the United States and elsewhere was
simultaneously an economic expansion of capital. Yet the rugged individualism that
defines the cultural substance of the frontier motif is in one important respect a myth;
Turner's frontier line was extended westward less by individual pioneers and homesteaders
than by banks, railways, the state and other speculators, and these in turn passed the land
on (at profit) to businesses and families (Swierenga, 1968; Wyckoff, 1988). In this
period, economic expansion was accomplished in part through absolute geographical
expansion. That is, expansion of the economy involved the expansion of the
geographical sway over which the economy operated.

Today, the link between economic and geographical development and supposed historical
destiny remains, giving the frontier imagery its present currency, but the form of the
link is very different. As far as its spatial basis is concerned, economic expansion takes
place today not through absolute geographical expansion but through the internal
differentiation of geographical space (Smith, 1982; 1984). Today's production of space -
geographical development - is therefore a sharply uneven process. Gentrification, urban
renewal, and the larger, more complex processes of urban restructuring are all part of the
differentiation of geographical space at the urban scale; while they had their basis in
postwar economic expansion, their larger effect today is to effect a significant
restructuring of the urban space economy. And as with the original frontier, the

mythology has it that gentrification is a process led by individual pioneers and homesteaders whose sweat equity, daring and vision are paving the way for those among us more timid. But even if we ignore urban renewal and the corporate-financed commercial, administrative and recreational redevelopment that is taking place in connection with the emerging service economy, and focus purely on residential rehabilitation, it is apparent that where the 'urban pioneers' venture, the banks, real estate companies, the state or other collective economic actors have generally gone before. In this context, it may be more appropriate to view the James Rouse Company not as the John Wayne but as the Wells Fargo of gentrification.

In the public media, gentrification has been presented as the pre-eminent symbol of the larger urban redevelopment that is taking place. Its symbolic importance far outweighs its real importance; it is a relatively small if highly visible part of a much larger process. Gentrification lends itself to such cultural abuse in the same way as the original frontier. Whatever the real economic, social and political forces that pave the way for gentrification, and no matter which banks and realtors, governments and contractors assist in orchestrating the process, gentrification can be represented as a marvellous testament to the values of a conservative do-it-yourself individualism, economic opportunity, and the dignity of work (sweat equity). From appearances at least, gentrification can be played so as to strike some of the most resonant chords on our ideological keyboard. As early as 1961, Jean Gottmann caught the reality of changing urban patterns, yet also spoke in a language amenable to the emerging ideology, when he said that the

"frontier of the American economy is nowadays urban and suburban rather than peripheral to the civilized areas". (Gottmann, 1961, p78)

With two important provisos, which have become much more obvious in the last two decades, this insight is precise. First, the urban frontier is a frontier in the economic sense, before anything else. The social, political and cultural transformations in the central city are essential to the shifts in our immediate experience and construction of everyday life, associated with gentrification, but they have also been scripted so as to camouflage the existence and operation of an economic frontier of gentrification, a frontier of profitability. Second, the urban frontier is today only one of several frontiers, given that the internal differentiation of geographical space occurs at different scales. Capital also confronts and in part constructs a global 'frontier' that encompasses the so-called urban frontier. This global connection with gentrification is acutely clear in the enthusiastic language used by supporters of the urban Enterprise Zone, an idea pioneered by the Thatcher and Reagan administrations (Anderson, 1983). To quote just one apologist, Stuart Butler (a British economist working for the American right-wing think-tank, the Heritage Foundation):

"It may be argued that at least part of the problem facing many urban areas today lies in our failure to apply the mechanism applied by Turner (the continual local development and innovation of new ideas) ... to the inner city frontier. Cities are facing fundamental changes, and yet the measures applied to deal with these changes are enacted in the main by distant governments. We have failed to appreciate that there may be opportunities in the cities themselves, and we have scrupulously avoided giving local forces any chance to seize them. Proponents of the Enterprise Zone aim to provide a climate in which the frontier process can be brought to bear within the city itself." (Butler, 1981, p3)

The circumspect observation of Gottmann and others has given way twenty years later to the unabashed adoption of the 'urban frontier' as the keystone to a political and economic programme of urban restructuring in the interests of capital.

The purpose of this chapter is to identify and map the frontier of profitability in a gentrifying neighbourhood in New York City. While this involves employing some new conceptual and methodological tools, it also functions as a larger cultural critique of ideology. New York's Lower East Side became a central battleground over gentrification following a 1988 police riot against demonstrators who were intent on retaining control of Tompkins Square Park (Smith, 1990). The park was heavily used by homeless people and widely seen, both by defenders and the city administration, as a crucial anchor as well as symbol in the progressive gentrification of the Lower East Side. In reconstructing the frontier of profitability, therefore, as it has invaded the Lower East Side, we seek not simply an economic geography but an integrated conception of the making of the landscape of gentrification.

DECODING THE FRONTIER

If the economics of urban frontier expansion are systematically obscured by the specific ideology through which the frontier is scripted, the important task would seem to involve a recovery of these constitutive economic processes. Otherwise the cultural meanings of gentrification and of struggles over gentrification would remain systematically and ideologically obscure. It is important to recognise that this is no philosophical argument for some primacy of economics; rather the culture and politics of gentrification cannot be understood without incorporating an otherwise excluded economic dimension. In short, to decode the new urban frontier it will be necessary for us to substitute the true geography for a false history. The connection with a larger spatial shift in social theory should be clear (Jameson, 1984; Soja, 1989; Harvey, 1989).

Geographically as well as historically, the gentrification frontier represents a line dividing disinvestment from reinvestment. By disinvestment is meant the relative withdrawal of capital in all its forms from the built environment; reinvestment involves the return of capital to landscapes and structures previously experiencing disinvestment. Ahead of the frontier line, properties are still experiencing disinvestment and devalorisation, through the multifarious actions of landlords, owner-occupiers, financial institutions, tenants and the state. Over a number of years, relative or absolute disinvestment and devalorisation result in the formation of a rent gap whereby the *actual* capitalised ground rent (or land value) under present use is substantially lower than the *potential* ground rent that could be appropriated at that location under a higher and better use. Behind the frontier line, some form of reinvestment has begun to supplant disinvestment. The form taken by reinvestment can vary substantially; it may involve private rehabilitation of the housing stock or public reinvestment in infrastructure, corporate or other private investment in new construction or merely speculative investment involving little or no physical alteration of the built landscape. Thus conceived, the frontier line represents the leading historical and geographical edge of urban restructuring and gentrification. Establishing the location and spread of this frontier line promises to expand our knowledge of the mechanisms of gentrification and thereby, we would hope, to enhance the ability of local neighbourhood organisations, tenant groups and residents to defend themselves against the processes and activities that have converted their communities into a new frontier. In this chapter we examine the formation and spread of the frontier line in the Lower East Side, where residential rehabilitation of the classic gentrification sort has been occurring since the 1970s. The

Lower East Side was deliberately chosen as an area of considerable social and cultural diversity and this prompts an important caveat.

Conceived in this way, the gentrification frontier is less a meeting point between development and lack of development but rather between development and purposive underdevelopment. The urban 'wilderness' is not simply discovered but actively constructed through disinvestment. Nor is it any mere conceptual fiction of a detached observer. The following depiction of the 'frontier' by a Brooklyn developer guides the economic geographer of investment.

> "The main point is that you want to be out on the frontier of gentrification. So you can't use the established financial institutions, for example, the banks. That's why you need the broker....You try to be far enough out on the 'line' that you can make a killing; not too far where you can't offload the building but far enough to still make money." (Interview with Steve Bass, December, 1986)

THE IMPORTANCE OF DISINVESTMENT

Disinvestment in urban real estate is a much neglected but crucial process for understanding urban morphology. It develops a certain momentum that gives the appearance of being self-fulfilling. Historical decline in a neighbourhood's real estate market provokes further decline since the ground rent that can be appropriated at a given site depends not only upon the level of investment on the site itself but also on the physical and economic condition of surrounding structures and wider local investment trends. It is irrational for a real estate investor to commit large amounts of capital to the maintenance of a pristine building stock amidst neighbourhood deterioration and devalorisation. The opposite process, sustained neighbourhood reinvestment, appears equally self-fulfilling for it is equally irrational for a housing entrepreneur to maintain a building in a dilapidated condition amidst widespread neighbourhood rehabilitation and recapitalisation. In any case, investment in an isolated building may indeed raise its intrinsic value but it does little to enhance the ground rent at the site and is in all probability unrecoverable insofar as the neighbourhood rent or resale levels will not sustain the necessary rise in the rent or price of the individual refurbished building. What benefits do accrue beyond the building itself are dissipated throughout a declining neighbourhood. In the second case, the neighbourhood-wide increases in ground rent that accrue from widespread recapitalisation are only partially realised by the owners of buildings who do not rehabilitate their property, although of course, short term speculative gains can be made by warehousing (keeping a building off the market while its price rises), flipping (buying a building in order simply to resell at a higher price) and other speculative practices that involve no significant reinvestment.

But whatever the economic momentum established, this does not mean that neighbourhood decline results from some irrational psychology among investors in real estate. Rather, sustained disinvestment begins as a result of largely rational decisions by owners, landlords, local and national governments and an array of financial institutions (Bradford and Rubinowitz, 1975). These represent the major groups of capital investors in the built landscape and they experience various levels of choice in their investment strategies and decisions. Clearly the state operates under a rather different set of constraints from private market actors. Level of investment, type of building(s), age of structure, geographical and market location are all contingent; much more so for financial institutions and landlords than for the home-owner, whose economic investment is simultaneously the physical commitment to a home. Whether to relinquish real estate entirely in favour of other investments - stocks and bonds, money markets, foreign currency, stock and commodity futures, precious metals - is equally an option dependent upon expected rates of profit or interest. The economic effects of state policy are also differentiated according to building and neighbourhood characteristics as well as location. However disparate these individual decisions may be, they represent a broadly rational if not always parallel or predictable set of responses to existing neighbourhood conditions.

This assumption of limited rationality in individual disinvestment and reinvestment decisions should not be construed as a spurious endorsement of the neo-classical assumption of 'economic man.' Neither do we assume such an ideal individual, nor do we attempt to generalise about aggregate patterns of urban geographical and economic development from any such ideal type of individual.

Whatever the dysfunctional social consequences provoked or exacerbated by disinvestment - deteriorating housing conditions, increased hazards to residents' health, community destruction, the ghettoisation of crime, loss of housing stock and increased homelessness - disinvestment is also economically functional within the housing market and can be conceived as an integral dimension of the uneven development of urban space.

Focusing on the relationship between housing demand and state policy, Anthony Downs makes this general point when he observes that

"a certain amount of neighbourhood deterioration is an essential part of urban development." (1982, p35)

In addition to the effects of state policies, others have highlighted the role of financial institutions in disinvestment and redlining (Harvey and Chaterjee, 1974; Boddy, 1980; Bartelt, 1979; Wolfe *et al.*, 1980) and eventually abandonment (Sternlieb and Burchell, 1973). The ultimate rationale for geographically selective disinvestment on the part of banks, savings and loans organisations and other financial institutions is to restrict the effects of devalorisation, economic decline and asset loss to clearly circumscribed neighbourhoods and thereby protect the integrity of mortgage loans in other areas. Delimiting the geography of disinvestment serves to circumscribe its economic impact.

Some attention has also focused on the functionality of disinvestment from the point of view of landlords. While Sternlieb and Burchell (1973, pxvi) have argued that landlords in declining neighbourhoods, squeezed between decreasing rent rolls and increasing costs, are as much the victims of disinvestment as its perpetrators, others have suggested a different picture. Salins argues that "most of the present and future owners of this kind of property are there by choice, and are making money". Market rationality together with state policies have "led housing entrepreneurs to make money in ways that involve the destruction of the housing stock" (Salins, 1981, pp5-6). Salins documents the process of graduated disinvestment according to which building owners become "increasingly exploitative of the property". The building is 'milked' of its rent rolls while the landlord progressively reduces and may even terminate the payment of debt service, insurance and property taxes, the performance of maintenance and repairs, and the provision of vital services such as water, heat and elevators. In all likelihood it also changes hands frequently, rarely with the benefit of traditional mortgage sources, before ending up in the hands of a 'finisher' who performs the final gutting of the building's economic value up to and including the removal of fixtures and furniture, which are scavenged for use elsewhere (Stevenson, 1980, p79). Physical and economic abandonment and arson-for-insurance are the eventual fate of many buildings. Lake (1979) corroborates this view with an intensive empirical examination of landlord tax delinquency in Pittsburgh. He points out a variety of disinvestment strategies dependent on the type of owner (landlord versus home-owner), size of holdings, the owner's perception of neighbourhood property values, etc., and identifies a 'cycle of delinquency' whereby property maintenance, property value and vacancy rates spiral downward in close relationship to each other.

At a more aggregate level, it is possible to view long term neighbourhood disinvestment as a necessary if not sufficient condition for the onset of gentrification. Sustained disinvestment by landlords and financial institutions results in the emergence of a 'rent gap' between on the one side the currently capitalised ground rent (land value) under present use and on the other the potential ground rent that could be appropriated with the conversion of the neighbourhood building stock to a higher and better use through gentrification (Smith, 1979a; 1987; Clark, 1987; Badcock, 1989). Disinvestment thereby creates the conditions for reinvestment.

No matter how trenchant or apparently self-fulfilling, neighbourhood disinvestment is reversible. There is nothing natural or inevitable about disinvestment. The fallacy in the 'self-fulfilling' thesis arises with

"the assumption that the ownership sector's expectations do not represent an economically accurate response to the dynamics ... of housing destruction" (Salins, 1981, p7).

Just as disinvestment and reinvestment are active processes carried out by more or less rational investors in response to existing conditions and changes in the housing market, the reversal of disinvestment is equally deliberate. Any individual decision by an investor or housing developer to reverse direction and to embark on a course of reinvestment rather than a disinvestment strategy may result from myriad kinds of information and perceptions. Individual perceptions about changes in the neighbourhood and in adjoining areas may contribute as much as real estate data from local real estate boards or chambers of commerce. But assuming individual investors do not control the housing market in entire neighbourhoods, successful reinvestment is contingent upon the broadly parallel actions of a range of individual investors. Whatever the individual perceptions and predilections of landlords, developers and financial lenders, the reinvestment strategy reflects a rational collective assessment of the profitable opportunities created by disinvestment and the emergence of the rent gap. The more knowledgeable, the more perceptive or simply the luckier investor may make the largest returns by responding more quickly, more accurately or even more imaginatively to the opportunities represented by the rent gap while the less knowledgeable, the less lucky and the inappropriately imaginative investor may misjudge the situation, making lower profits or even sustaining a loss.

IDENTIFYING THE FRONTIER

To identify the frontier, we are concerned with the point of reversal where disinvestment is succeeded by reinvestment. In the history of neighbourhoods, there are not always sharp reversal points or turning points. Many neighbourhoods receive a relatively steady supply of necessary funds for financing repairs, maintenance and building transfers, and therefore do not experience sustained disinvestment and physical decline. Others, having already experienced disinvestment, do not receive significant reinvestment in the existing building stock. What interests us here is a very specific aspect of the economic history of select neighbourhoods, namely the turning point where disinvestment is succeeded by reinvestment. Specifically, we want to devise an indicator that identifies this turning point in a given neighbourhood, thereby providing the sharpest indication of the onset of the broader gentrification and urban restructuring process. That is, by identifying specific turning points and generalising these across the entire neighbourhood, it is possible to construct a map of the gentrification frontier and trace its movement through time.

The most obvious indication of the economic turning point associated with gentrification would be a significant and sustained increase in mortgage financing. We already know the critical role of finance capital in the geographical division of urban space into recognisable submarkets and in place specific disinvestment (Harvey, 1974; Wolfe *et al.*, 1980; Bartelt, 1979). Where an adequate flow of mortgage money is not forthcoming, the gentrification of a neighbourhood can certainly begin but is unlikely to reach fruition. Thus, while mortgage data have been used widely by gentrification researchers (Williams, 1976; 1978; Smith, 1979b; DeGiovanni, 1983; Schaffer and Smith, 1986) and represent a very fertile data source in general, they are not especially sharp as an indicator of *initial* reinvestment associated with the turning point.

The reason for this is suggested by our Brooklyn developer. Much of the earliest gentrification activity is carried out by developers on the extreme edge of the economic frontier where traditional lenders are generally reluctant to invest. In advance of traditional sources, the actually funding mechanisms are diverse, often involve a variety of sources in some form of partnership, and are extremely difficult to trace. One common arrangement of this sort combines in partnership an architect, a developer, a building manager, a lawyer and a broker. The first three of these will work on the actual conversion of the building while the lawyer handles any problems regarding the deed transfer, loan arrangements, state subsidies and tax abatements, and any legal 'problems' resulting from the expulsion of existing tenants. All of the partners contribute financially to the project, and it is the function of the broker to secure additional private market loans on the basis of this seed money. Where building rehabilitation is organised in this manner, traditional mortgage data fail to reveal the date or dimensions of initial reinvestment.

Other researchers have used state sponsored programs, such as improvement grants in London (Hamnett, 1973) or the J-51 program in New York City (Marcuse, 1986; Wilson, 1985), as a means to date initial reinvestment. While these data have clear utility at a lower scale of analysis, they are even coarser indicators than the flow of mortgage funds, and cannot be used to detect a turning point at the neighbourhood scale. A detailed survey of building conditions and an assessment of building deterioration levels might also reveal important information regarding the onset of reinvestment, but it is important to remember that reinvestment may begin substantially in advance of a building's physical upgrading. Indeed, in a detailed survey of displacement pressures in the Lower East Side, DeGiovanni (1987, pp32, 35) found strong evidence that deterioration may actually be "an integral part of the reinvestment process" as landlords foster adverse physical conditions "to clear buildings of the current tenants" before undertaking major resale. Shifts in the physical condition of a building are better conceived as responses to economic strategies than as causes and therefore provide at best a rough proxy for reinvestment.

We propose here that tax arrears data provide a very sensitive indicator of initial reinvestment connected with gentrification. Non-payment of property taxes by landlords and building owners is one common form of disinvestment in declining neighbourhoods. Tax delinquency is in effect an investment strategy since it provides property owners with guaranteed access to capital. In so far as serious delinquency places ownership of the building in jeopardy through the threat of city foreclosure proceedings, we might expect that the extent of tax arrears in a neighbourhood is highly sensitive to reversals in the investment landscape. Where landlords and owners become convinced that substantial reinvestment is possible, they will seek to retain possession of a building whose sale price is expected to increase. Where buildings are seriously in arrears, this implies the repayment of at least some back taxes to prevent its foreclosure by the City. Redemption of tax arrears can therefore function as an initial form of reinvestment. This position is supported empirically by Lake's findings in Pittsburgh; among owners of buildings with low to moderate assessed values, there is a clear correlation between their perception of increased property values and their intention to redeem their tax delinquency status (Lake, 1979, p192; Sternlieb and Lake, 1976).

Salins judges tax arrears to be

"undoubtedly a very sensitive index of active and incipient housing destruction, especially when viewed in terms of length of delinquency, and the volume of properties at different stages of the arrears foreclosure pipeline". (1981, p17)

It follows that systematic reversals in arrears level represent an equally sensitive index of reinvestment, yet in neither context have these data been analysed at a finer level of geographic disaggregation than that of the city or (in New York City) the borough. In addition, as Lake (1979, p207) points out, "Real estate tax delinquency is but a surface manifestation of deep-rooted antagonisms" inherent in the broader processes of urban development. He has in mind the relation to changing geographical patterns of development but also urban decline and the experience of urban fiscal crisis. Tax delinquency lies on the fulcrum between growth and decline, expansion and contraction, and all that follows from this balance, and the rapid restructuring of the city at the hands of gentrification in the 1970s and 1980s adds further to the pivotal importance of arrearage trends. In this study, however, we suspend some of these broader connections and adopt a narrower perspective, focusing only on a single neighbourhood, for the purpose of devising an indicator of initial reinvestment. Peter Marcuse (1984) made the first attempt to use tax arrears data to demonstrate shifts in investment patterns in a neighbourhood threatened with gentrification. He found significant evidence of turning points in several census tracts in the Hell's Kitchen neighbourhood of New York City. The present research attempts to pursue this initial insight in the context of the Lower East Side.

NEW YORK CITY ARREARS AND FORECLOSURE PROCEDURES

Every city has its own specific procedures for determining tax delinquency and taking into public ownership buildings that surpass a certain threshold of arrearages. In New York City until 1978, foreclosure proceedings (referred to as *in rem* proceedings) could begin against buildings that were 12 or more quarters (three years) in arrears. A massive wave of residential disinvestment associated with the 1974-75 recession and the New York City fiscal crisis brought a rapid increase in delinquency rates, and in response a 1978 law, first proposed by Mayor Beame, made buildings eligible for *in rem* proceedings after only four quarters in arrears. (One and two family buildings and condominia were exempt from this change.) After four quarters in arrears, building owners have a grace period of a further quarter in which to repay taxes before the onset of *in rem* proceedings. For a further two years, an owner can still redeem the building but at the discretion of the city. In practice, the City Departments of Finance and of Housing Preservation and Development have rarely initiated proceedings against buildings that are less than 12 quarters in arrears, and although there are many complaints about the bureaucratic nature of the foreclosure procedure (Williams, 1987), the City administration is reluctant to increase its already large stock of foreclosed and often vacant buildings, and so entertains a variety of repayment schemes from building owners. Many buildings are redeemed well after the 12 quarter arrears threshold is reached without being foreclosed, others are redeemed according to individual instalment plans, and still others are transferred from one owner to another with the purchase price incorporating the redemption of outstanding tax debts. Thus in practice, the cutoff point between safe and unsafe delinquency levels is not absolute but somewhat fluid. Yet it is now clear that the city almost immediately regretted the 1978 law, and never seriously implemented the one-year foreclosure requirement (Salins, 1981, pl8). In practice, the administration has tended to adhere to the previous 12 quarters threshold.

Citywide property tax delinquency levels in New York City peaked in 1976 when over 7 per cent of the city's residential buildings were in arrears - an extraordinary figure. In the last eleven years, however, delinquency levels have steadily declined, dropping to a seventy year low of 2 per cent in 1986 (Williams, 1987). In the most immediate sense, the rapid decline in total arrears results from the easing of the recession and fiscal crisis of the 1970s and to some extent the anticipation of the tighter 1978 law. But mostly it is due to the rapid inflation of real estate prices from the late 1970s. More broadly, declining delinquency levels indicate a very significant reduction in disinvestment levels and a parallel trend toward reinvestment in previously declining real estate. Far fewer building owners were abandoning properties in the 1980s than in the 1960s and 1970s. This in turn is directly related to the larger processes of urban restructuring and to gentrification in particular. Despite these reductions in overall delinquency, disinvestment still corrodes a large section of the city's rental stock-rented dwelling units rather than owner occupied buildings. Although here too there have been significant reductions, the level of rental property delinquency remains high. In 1980, for example, 3.5 per cent of the city's residential properties were in arrears, but this figure was dominated by some 330,000 rental apartments, fully 26 per cent of the city's entire rental stock (Salins, 1981, p17). Overall disinvestment rates have declined, but from these data it would seem reasonable to argue that property tax delinquency is increasingly concentrated both geographically and economically in older neighbourhoods dominated by large tenement and other multiple unit rental housing stock. These represent the poorest neighbourhoods destroyed by massive, systematic and sustained disinvestment over a period of three to seven decades: Harlem, the Lower East Side (including the East Village section), Bedford Stuyvesant, Brownsville, East New York, the South Bronx.

THE LOWER EAST SIDE

"One must realise," writes a local art critic, "that the East Village or the Lower East Side is more than a geographical location - it is a state of mind" (Moufarrege, 1982, p73). Indeed in the early to mid 1980s, the Lower East Side was enthusiastically boosted as the newest new artistic Bohemia in New York City, drawing effusive comparison with the Left Bank or London's Soho (Figure 1). In the gentrification of the Lower East Side, art galleries, dance clubs and studios have been the shock troops of neighbourhood reinvestment, although the extraordinary complicity of the art scene with the social destruction wrought by gentrification is rarely conceded (but see Deutsche and Ryan, 1984). The area was touted as a 'neo-frontier', in a deliberate potion of urban and artistic images (Levin, 1983, p4), and surpassed the staid uptown galleries of Madison Avenue and 57th Street and even the more adventurous if thoroughly corporate art scene of neighbouring SoHo. The attraction of the East Village has been attributed in the art press to its "unique blend of poverty, punk rock, drugs and arson, Hell's Angels, winos, prostitutes and dilapidated housing that adds up to an adventurous avant-garde setting of considerable cachet". (Robinson and McCormick, 1984, p135)

The artistic influx began in the late 1970s; it was increasingly institutionalised after 1981 with the widely heralded opening of new galleries, and peaked with approximately seventy galleries in 1987. Thereafter, sharply higher rents and a financial shakeout among many galleries led to a decline in the area's art scene. In other parts of the culture industry, the Lower East Side provided the setting as well as the subject of literally dozens of 1980s novels and several movies, most notably, perhaps, Spielberg's flirtation with the gentrification genre, *Batteries Not Included.* But the romanticisation of poverty and deprivation - the area's 'unique blend' - is always limited, and the neon and pastiche sparkle of aesthetic ultra-chic only partly camouflages the harsher realities of displacement, homelessness, unemployment and deprivation in a neighbourhood converted into a new frontier at the hands of gentrification.

The housing stock of the area is dominated by four to six storey railway and dumbbell ('old law') tenements built in the late nineteenth century and now heavily deteriorated following decades of disinvestment or recently restored and roughly polished by gentrification. These are interspersed with occasional public housing complexes of ten or more storeys constructed in the immediate post-war period. Socially, even more than physically, the Lower East Side is a mosaic of yuppies and punk culture, Polish and Puerto Ricans, Ukrainian and Black working class, quiche and fern restaurants and homeless shelters, surviving ethnic churches and burned out buildings. It has been an area of intense socialist, communist and anarchist organising in the earlier part of this century, a major progenitor of New York intellectuals and at the same time an extraordinary seed bed of small entrepreneurs and businesses among recent immigrants. This exceptionally variegated history and geography would encourage us in the belief that to the extent that recognisable geographical patterns of reinvestment can be found here, they are redolent of deeper regularities in the gentrification process.

RECONSTRUCTING THE FRONTIER

Tax arrears data are collected by the Department of Finance and are available on the City's Misland database. For each census tract, a summary is available showing the extent of arrears. Taxlots in arrears are categorised according to the severity of delinquency: 3 to 5 quarters in arrears, 6 to 12 quarters, and more than 12 quarters in arrears. We can classify these as low, intermediate and serious levels of delinquency, respectively. Given the *de facto* threshold of 12 quarters before the initiation of *in rem* proceedings, low levels of arrears (3 to 5 quarters) tend not to reflect sharp and significant changes in delinquency and redemption. However arrears in the intermediate (6-12 quarters) and serious (12+ quarters) categories do reveal an interesting historical trend (Figure 5.2).

Until 1980 there is a clear inverse relationship between the number of buildings in the intermediate category and those in serious delinquency. Building owners would seem to have followed an obvious strategy: buildings are partially redeemed in 1978 and 1979 (bringing them back from the serious to the intermediate arrears category), presumably to avert the threat of foreclosure at the hands of a 1978 city-wide vesting as well as the new delinquency law. In 1980 a new wave of delinquency began as about 170 properties slipped back from intermediate to serious delinquency. After 1980, however, the inverse relationship between serious and intermediate delinquency is suspended as both categories decline significantly. Despite the national recession of 1980 to 1982, which seriously curtailed residential construction, the decline in disinvestment continues unabated. Only with the threat of a major foreclosure and vesting proceedings in 1985 is there a repeat of the inverse relationship between serious and intermediate delinquency, but this is a ripple within a larger decline in overall disinvestment. This suggests that serious reinvestment in the area began after 1980, the year of peak levels in serious delinquency. Corroborative evidence comes from sale price data. Whereas median per unit sale prices for the whole Lower East Side rose only 43.8 per cent between 1968 and 1979 (a period in which the inflation rate exceeded 100 per cent), prices between 1979 and 1984 rose 146.4 per cent (3.7 times the rate of inflation) (DeGiovanni, 1987, p27).

In order to disaggregate the arrears data geographically and to identify the gentrification frontier it is necessary first to identify a 'turning point' for each census tract. The turning point represents year of peak serious arrears for each tract. Figure 5.3 provides four illustrations of this procedure. In Figures 5.3a, 5.3b and 5.3d, the turning points are 1980, 1982 and 1976 respectively. In several cases tax arrears exhibit a bimodal distribution. In tract 34, for example (Figure 5.3c), there were fifty-four delinquent tax lots in 1976 and again in 1980. Since our concern here is the date of reversal from disinvestment to sustained reinvestment, we have taken the latest date as the turning point wherever a bimodal distribution was found.

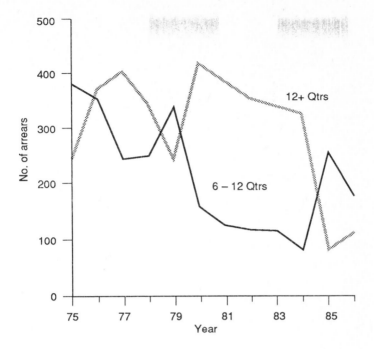

Figure 5.2: Serious (12+ quarters) and Intermediate (6–12 quarters) Tax Arrears

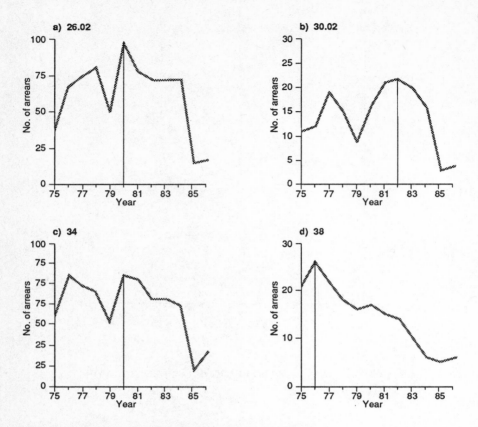

Figure 5.3: Gentrification Turning Points by Census Tract

Of the 27 tracts in the Lower East Side with private residential units, the earliest turning points were generally on the western edge of the area coming in 1975-1976; the latest lay well to the east and occurred in 1983-1985. Every tract had experienced a turning point by 1985. The resulting geographical pattern of turning points demonstrates extreme statistical autocorrelation. The turning points were mapped and, using Surfer Software, the data were generalised via a least squares method into a chorographic map of the development of gentrification. In Figure 5.4, annual contour lines join points with the same chronological turning points.

By way of interpretation, where significant space intervenes between chronological contour lines, reinvestment is diffusing rapidly; steep contour slopes indicate significant barriers to reinvestment. The frontier is most evident where there are no enclosed contours (i.e. no peaks or sink holes). Peaks, with later years at the centre of enclosed contours, represent areas of greatest resistance to reinvestment while sink holes, with earlier years at the centre, represent areas opened up to reinvestment in advance of surrounding areas. The major pattern that emerged is a reasonably well defined west to east frontier line with the earliest encroachment in the northwest and southwest of the study area. The reinvestment frontier pushes east until obstructed and slowed by localised barriers in the east and southeast.

In geographical context, the data would seem to document a gentrification frontier advancing eastward into the Lower East Side from Greenwich Village, SoHo, Chinatown and the Financial District. Greenwich Village has always been a Bohemian neighbourhood but after some decline in the 1930s and 1940s, it began in the 1950s and 1960s to experience an early gentrification. SoHo's gentrification came a few years later but was essentially complete by the late 1970s. In Chinatown, an influx of Taiwanese capital in the mid 1970s and later Hong Kong capital provided the means for a rapid northward and eastward expansion of Chinatown. Nonetheless, it is worth pointing out that the extent of pre-1975 reinvestment on the border of Chinatown to the south (Figure 5.4) may be exaggerated owing to border effects in the statistical analysis.

Barriers to the advancement of the frontier are apparent in several localised peaks, especially on east Delancey Street and on the southern edge near South Street. Delancey Street is largely commercial, a wide thoroughfare leading to the Williamsburg Bridge which connects Manhattan and Brooklyn, and its congestion, noise and impassability may well have hindered reinvestment. More generally, these peaks can be interpreted as

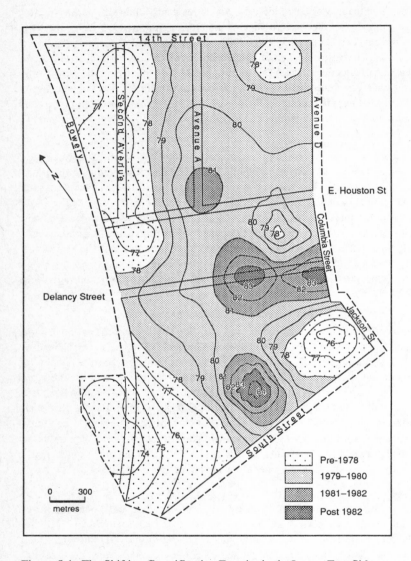

Figure 5.4: The Shifting Gentrification Frontier in the Lower East Side

demonstrating the limits of gentrification; the eastern and southern edges of the area are fringed by large public housing projects that could be expected to act as significant barriers. In addition, these nodes of resistance to reinvestment coincide with the traditional heart of the Lower East Side where disinvestment continued until as late as 1985, well into the 1980s economic recovery. This is also the poorest area, the last stronghold of a Latino population, and the focus of 'Operation Pressure Point', a gentrification-induced police crackdown on drugs that began in 1985; the year of the final turning point, as it happens.

There seem to have been two distinct periods of reinvestment in the housing stock: the first between 1977 and 1979, especially in the western and northern blocks, and in the period after 1980. The latter phase of reinvestment encompassed the southern and eastern blocks in addition to those already recapitalised in the earlier phase. While it is important to bear in mind that reinvestment in the form of tax arrears redemption does not necessarily imply the kind of productive reinvestment that betokens gentrification and urban restructuring, and might only indicate a speculative market, the reinvestment in the western/northern blocks in the late 1970s does seem to have been sufficiently sustained to prevent a major recurrence of disinvestment in the recession of 1980 to 1982. Visual evidence confirms that reinvestment in the area to the west of 1st Avenue is longer in duration, more sustained, and more broadly based, while the statistical evidence suggests that the census tracts in the east and southeast sector sustained the highest population losses (58 per cent to 74 per cent) throughout the 1970s and only began an economic upturn well into the 1980s. From 1975 to 1981, the profit frontier moved at an average speed of between 100 and 200 metres per year. It is important to add the caveat that this figure represents an averaging across a period in which the market was highly volatile: high disinvestment in 1976-1977 presaged a slow diffusion of the profit frontier, but was followed by a more rapid shift until 1980 when massive disinvestment again slowed the diffusion of the frontier until 1982. Further, these data cover only two short cycles of reinvestment and disinvestment and care is necessary in generalising the conclusions. At the very least, it seems that the concept of an economic frontier in gentrifying neighbourhoods would have to be amended to take account of the shifting pace of expansion. The diffusion of the frontier is potentially sensitive to external economic and political forces; it may be a stop and go process more than a smooth progression.

This pattern of reinvestment in the East Village coincides with casual observation about gentrification in the area. To many observers, gentrification seemed to encroach on the

East Village from its western border with the more established bohemia of Greenwich Village. The area to the north of 14th Street, including Gramercy Park but also Union Square further to the west, has been the target of early redevelopment activity, and although Stuyvesant Town (a moderate and middle income high rise complex on the north side of 14th Street further to the east) may initially have hindered the southward diffusion of higher land values, once the process began it may equally have acted as a northern anchor to the gentrification of the process. By contrast, the southern and eastern blocks experienced a deeper disinvestment and a later reinvestment. Reinvestment in the East Village began not in the area of deepest disinvestment and abandonment but on the borders (Marcuse, 1986, p166) where a killing could be made with little risk of being scalped, so to speak.

Finally, the local complexity of the pattern and its deviation from a straight line diffusion process should come as no surprise; indeed Frederick Jackson Turner, author of the nineteenth century 'end-of-the-frontier' thesis, was challenged on exactly this point, namely that while the larger frontier line may have swept through, it left behind resilient pockets of frontier existence. As with the original frontier, the gentrification line is not so much a 'wall' of equal and continuous development but a highly uneven and differentiated process.

THE POLITICS OF THE GENTRIFICATION FRONTIER

This reconstruction of the economic frontier of gentrification provides a new perspective from which the frontier ideology can be critiqued. The point is not that such a frontier is a mere invention but that it is an ideological representation of the economic basis of the frontier is omitted as a means of depicting the frontier in a more positive light. For many residents of the Lower East Side and other gentrifying areas whose neighbourhoods and communities have been converted into a frontier at the hands of the real estate market, Turner's "meeting point between savagery and civilisation" is a daily experience. The economic savagery of a gentrifying housing market is a vivid reality that scripts the politics of the frontier.

In the late 1980s, with New York's homeless population approaching 100,000, Tompkins Square, in the heart of the Lower East Side, became the temporary home for several hundred homeless people. In association with a larger gentrification strategy the

City administration and Department of Parks threatened to impose a curfew on the park. A series of increasingly aggressive anti-gentrification demonstrations ensued, culminating in a riot on 6th August 1988 by about 400 police confronting demonstrators. For one commentator, evoking the memory of Custer at Little Big Horn, the contest for Tompkins Square Park represented "one last metaphorical stand" against gentrification (Carr, 1988, p17). Over the next sixteen months the Park was occupied by up to 300 homeless people as well as squatters and housing activists, until they were forcibly evicted in December 1989 by the City.

The contest continues for 'Indian Country', as the Lower East Side has been called (Charyn, 1985, p7). If from the perspective of the pioneers it is a frontier of profitability, from the perspective of the working class 'natives' gentrification represents a frontier of struggle. It is an 'advancing wave', in Turner's terms, behind which rents are unaffordable, apartments unavailable, and the immigrant culture completely alien. In front of this advancing wave, gentrification appears to threaten the very existence of established communities; engulfment, fragmentation and displacement are the results of this 'interpenetration' by lines of gentrification, first down the main streets and then along the side streets. It is an external force, wholly uncontrolled from within, but its advance is resisted as a means to defend home and community. The parallel with Native American experience in the wild west is indeed exact.

ACKNOWLEDGEMENT

This essay builds on amended portions of two previously published papers: 'Gentrification, the Frontier, and the Restructuring of Urban Space', in N. Smith and P. Williams (eds) *Gentrification of the City* (Boston: Allen and Unwin, 1986), pp. 15-34; Neil Smith, Betsy Duncan and Laura Reid, 'From Disinvestment to Reinvestment: Tax Arrears and Turning Points in the East Village', *Housing 4* (1989), 238-52. It is presented here with permission from the publishers and co-authors. This research was assisted by National Science Foundation Grant SE897-13043. We would like to thank Fritz Nelson, who assisted with some of the data analysis, and Tanya Steinberg and Valerie Preston, who offered stimulating criticisms and commentary. Tony Lugo and Michael Siegel assisted with some of the graphics.

CHAPTER 6

WOMEN, GENDER RELATIONS AND *THE INNER CITY*

Liz Bondi

A number of writers have recently drawn parallels between contemporary changes in the character of urban areas and changes in the position of women in society. These observations relate both to the decline and disadvantage associated with inner cities and to signs of regeneration. Thus, on the one hand, urban poverty, homelessness, unemployment and other indicators of disadvantage appear to be increasingly female phenomena (Holcomb, 1986; Morrow-Jones, 1986; Millar and Glendinning, 1987). On the other hand, growing affluence among certain groups of women has been associated with the gentrification and economic revitalisation of particular inner urban localities (Markusen, 1981; Smith, 1987). These apparently contradictory trends can be resolved through claims that urban areas in general and inner cities in particular are becoming increasingly divided places, with women prominent on both sides of the divide.

The prominence of women in this context might be indicative of changes in gender relations or in the character of patriarchy that are being articulated through changes in the urban environment. In addition to their substantive importance, these references to women would seem to be symptomatic of the success of feminist geographers in getting women's issues on to the agenda. However, in this chapter it is argued that there remain serious shortcomings in current formulations of the relationship between women and the 'inner city'. In short, most studies remain wedded to theoretical positions that accord explanatory primacy to class relations and therefore subsume 'women's issues' within a class analysis rather than investigating any changes in gender identity and gender relations that might underlie the empirical evidence cited. To develop this argument attention is focused on the process of gentrification, which offers a stark example of the divisiveness of contemporary changes in inner cities. The first section outlines existing propositions concerning the role of women as members of groups involved in gentrification both as 'protagonists' and as 'victims'. The second section discusses class based analyses of gentrification, emphasising the dynamic and relational concept of class that is invoked. The third section shows how issues relating to women are subsumed within class issues, principally because the dynamic and relational nature of the gender is overlooked. This leads in the final section to a brief discussion of the relationship between capitalism and patriarchy in the 'inner city'.

WOMEN, WEALTH AND POVERTY: THE CASE OF GENTRIFICATION

Existing studies of gentrification make claims about the relationship between women and gentrification that concern both the demand for gentrified housing and the impact of gentrification on pre-existing communities. These claims cite changes in the position of women in the labour market and in the family as reasons for the prominence of women among both gentrifiers and displacees.

The position of women in the labour market

With respect to the gentrifiers, the existence of dual income households has been widely cited as a factor fuelling demand for gentrified housing. The dual income household is itself a product of the rising labour force participation of married women and, increasingly, of women with young children (Martin and Roberts, 1984; England and Farkas, 1987). Ley (1986) found a positive correlation between female participation rates and the incidence of gentrification in his ecological analysis of Canadian cities. However, more important than overall female participation rates is the number of women in well-paid career jobs since it is among these women, and the households to which they belong, that purchasing power and therefore demand for high-cost housing has increased. Markusen (1981) assumes that middle-class women are improving their access to such jobs but the evidence is mixed. The position of women as entrants to professions such as medicine and law has undoubtedly improved with the gradual dismantling of overt discriminatory practices in vocational higher education (England and

Hollow promises

Farkas, 1987). However, such changes work through all levels of a profession only slowly. Thus, women remain concentrated in lower grades, a high degree of occupational segregation persists and the wages gap shows little sign of closing (for an international survey, see Cooper and Davidson, 1984). Despite these reservations, there is some evidence of local increases in professional employment among women (albeit in the lower paid health and education sectors), and Rose (1989) demonstrates an association between such increases and the incidence of gentrification in Montreal. Moreover, there is also some North American evidence that more women than men from affluent households prefer to live in the inner city (Saegert, 1981; Wekerle, 1984). Thus, gentrification may at least partially reflect an increase in the influence of women on the locational decisions of households, stemming from improvements in their economic position (see also Bondi, 1989).

Whatever gains well-qualified women may be making in professional employment, these appear to be more than equalled by the increasing percentage of women at the opposite end of the labour market. While details vary between countries, the increase in female participation rates over the last three decades has been characterised principally by a movement into low paid service sector jobs such as cleaning, catering and clerical work, together with unskilled jobs in the manufacturing sector such as electrical assembly (Beechey, 1986; Blau and Ferber, 1985). At the same time, employment itself has become more polarised, with the workforce more sharply divided between those in secure, well-paid employment offering career and salary advancement, and those in insecure, low-paid jobs without prospects of advancement (see Pahl, 1988). This polarisation is particularly marked in urban areas and generates a social group who are economically weak and therefore vulnerable to changes in housing markets stimulated by the expanding group of affluent professionals (Williams and Smith, 1986). In many countries women form a large percentage of the poor (Glendinning and Millar, 1987; Holcomb, 1986) and therefore of those liable to become the 'victims' of gentrification.

The position of women in the family

Changes in the position of women in the labour force are closely linked to changes in the family. The affluence of households including two adults in well-paid jobs is underpinned by trends in fertility. On average, women are bearing their first child at a later age, having fewer children and returning to work sooner after each birth (Martin and Roberts, 1984; England and Farkas, 1987). These trends are particularly marked among women of higher social classes (Werner, 1985). Consequently, women are increasing their earning power both by spending a longer period in the labour force and by improving their opportunities for career advancement. Moreover, the households to which these women belong contain no or few children and therefore have more resources for expenditure on other items such as housing and associated items of consumption.

If changes in fertility contribute to the creation of potential gentrifiers, the reduced permanency of marriage is a major factor underpinning the economic vulnerability of women in other social groups. The marked increase in divorce rates has, in turn, greatly increased the number of one parent families. Responsibility for children continues to reduce earning power and the problem is compounded by the fact that the great majority of lone parents are women, most of whom still command lower wage rates than men. Within households, women have often lacked access to resources. With marital breakdown, their poverty is becoming increasingly visible (Millar and Glendinning, 1987).

Another important trend affecting women in particular is the increasing independence of old people. For some, this reflects their greater economic self-sufficiency in retirement, but for others it is more a product of changes in community and family life that reduce alternatives to living alone, and it is associated with poverty (Walker, 1987). Overall, therefore, an important consequence of the partial demise of conventional families is to leave women without the financial support of their economically more powerful menfolk. This trend reinforces the polarisation of employment referred to above and is again associated especially with inner urban areas: in both public and private rental sectors there are concentrations of one parent families and elderly people living alone in inner cities (Holcomb, 1986; Rose and Le Bourdais, 1986; Winchester and White, 1988). In areas dominated by private rental property, the risk of displacement by affluent incomers, or developers aiming to profit from them, is obvious. In areas of public sector housing, the vulnerability of tenants is reduced by state intervention but, with the curtailment of public sector housing in Britain and its limited availability in North America, entrapment in an increasingly undesirable residual sector is typical.

Social class, ethnicity and gender

This evidence suggests that the relationship between women and contemporary trends in inner city areas is deeply divided. On the one hand, there are signs that women are well represented among the gentrifiers, whether as single people or as major contributors to household income. On the other hand, there is still stronger evidence that women are over-represented among the urban poor, who, directly or indirectly, suffer negative effects as a result of gentrification.

This social class contrast is itself overlayed by ethnic divisions. In both North America and the UK, ethnic minorities are over-represented among the poor and are concentrated in inner cities. This applies especially to black Americans and Hispanics in the USA and to Afro-Caribbean and Asians in the UK. In many cases (with the principal exception of Asians) rates of female lone parenthood are also high among these groups (Brown, 1984; Holcomb, 1986). Consequently, those potentially liable to displacement through gentrification include a disproportionate number of women from ethnic minorities. The ethnic composition of displacees has not been extensively studied but Marcuse's (1986) analysis of gentrification in New York suggests that poor white neighbourhoods are more at risk than others. However, Schaffer and Smith (1986) point to signs of gentrification in Harlem, with black displacement an inevitable consequence. What is not disputed is that the gentrifiers themselves are strongly dominated by the non-minority white population.

GENTRIFICATION AS CLASS CONSTITUTION

Alongside the emergence of claims about the role of women, the literature on gentrification has been enriched by responses to critiques of the dichotomy between voluntaristic accounts stressing factors related to the demand for gentrified housing, and structuralist accounts stressing factors related to the supply of gentrified housing. Two themes are prominent in recent studies that seek to transcend this division. First, the significance of housing in the creation of new social identities has emerged as an area of study, and secondly, the role of social differentiation in gentrification has been emphasised. These two themes jointly offer an account of gentrification as a process of class constitution, within which class is interpreted in dynamic and relational terms. Each theme is examined here before developing a feminist critique that shows how gender divisions are inappropriately subsumed within such class-based analyses.

Gentrification, social identity and class: the dynamic element

Several recent studies have explored the ways in which housing in general, and gentrified housing in particular, is used to convey images connoting social position and social identity (Duncan, 1981; Jager, 1986). New residential forms indicate the carving out of new social identities. Further, it is argued that these images not only express a particular social identity, but that their creation is itself part of the process by which social groups are constituted (Saunders, 1984; Beauregard, 1986; Williams, 1986). According to Williams (1986, p66),

> "the reshaped residential environments characteristic of the gentrification process can be related clearly to the changing form and structure of social classes and their articulation with the built environment".

More specifically, gentrification is one of the processes through which a new social group, variously called the new middle class or the service class, has come into being (Smith, 1987; Thrift, 1987; Mills, 1988).

While the broad outlines of this argument are widely accepted, detailed analyses of how the urban environment is remade by, and in this remaking confers identity on, the new middle class, remain few. Exceptions are provided by Jager (1986) and Mills (1988). In a case study of the conservation of Victorian terraces in Melbourne, Jager (1986) explores how symbols associated with the class position of earlier inhabitants are reworked. He draws attention to continuities and discontinuities between an earlier leisured gentry and the professional, salaried worker typical of contemporary gentrifiers:

> "[t]hose displays of artistic consecration and possession which seek to create an aesthetic object rather than a simple material-use value indicate the class candidature of the new middle classes and define the limits to their social ascension. Failing to approximate fully to the former cultural model, that is, lacking sufficient economic capital to distance themselves fully from economic imperatives, and yet possessing sufficient cultural capital to ape that bourgeois cultural ethos, the new middle classes are forced back upon the employment of a second cultural model - that of work, investment and saving, the Victorian work ethic. The gentrifier is caught between a former gentry ethic of social

representation being an end in itself, and a more traditional petty bourgeois ethic
of economic valorization. The restoration of Victorian housing attempts the
appropriation of a very recent history and hence the authenticity of its symbols as
much as its economic profitability is in the beginning precarious. It succeeds
only to the extent that it can distance itself from the immediate past that of
working-class industrial 'slums'. This is achieved externally by esthetic-cultural
conferals, and internally by remodelling." (Jager, 1986, p83).

In other cases, gentrification involves the construction of new buildings, but
architectural features continue to seize upon and reinterpret symbols of the past. For
example, Mills (1988), in an analysis of a postmodern landscape in a gentrifying
neighbourhood of Vancouver, points out appeals to an industrial heritage alongside
attempts to evoke 'rustic nostalgia'.

The analyses of landscapes of gentrification offered by Jager (1986) and Mills (1988)
begin to fill out the broad claim that gentrification is a process of class constitution, and
represent part of a growing interest within geography in exploring cultural symbols
evident in the landscape (Gregory and Ley, 1988). There is scope for more work from
this perspective but for the purposes of the argument developed here the factor of primary
significance is that this conceptualisation of gentrification incorporates an interpretation
of class as dynamic: in the interaction between underlying structures (whether economic
or cultural) and sentient human agents, classes as empirical constructs are constantly
redefined and renegotiated. This applies equally to Marxist and Weberian formulations;
indeed in viewing gentrification as class constitution there is an attempt to transcend the
dichotomy between the production-based formulations of Marxism and the consumption-
based formulations of Weberian social theory (Williams, 1986).

Gentrification, social differentiation and class: the relational element

Gentrification also incorporates statements of individuality: embedded in the postmodern
landscape explored by Mills (1988) is a declaration of opposition to the homogeneity of
suburban living. This individuality is signalled in features produced by the do-it-yourself
labours of the gentrifiers themselves, such as the addition of brass door-knockers and the
mix-and-match interior furnishings, and in the efforts of developers to give every
apartment its own 'character'. But, as Smith (1987, p168) observes

"[t]he pursuit of difference, diversity, and distinction [which] forms the basis of the new urban ideology ... is not without contradiction. It embodies a search for diversity as long as it is highly ordered ... the perpetual search for difference and distinction ... is eternally frustrated ... (because) cultural difference itself becomes mass-produced."

The irony Smith identifies extends beyond the efforts of gentrifiers to be different from their neighbours. As Jager (1986) illustrates (see above), the articulation of a distinctive social identity necessarily involves establishing distance from other social groups. Thus, Smith (1987, p168) views gentrification as a means by which

"new middle-class individuals ... distinguish themselves from the stuffed-shirt bourgeoisie above and the working class below".

In marking themselves out from other social groups, gentrifiers rely upon direct and immediate contrasts, hence the painstaking renovation and conservation of the exterior of Victorian or Edwardian terraces. But the takeover of working-class, inner city streets, or the redevelopment of derelict inner urban sites, itself plays on the theme of polarisation: gentrification is distinctive by virtue of what it co-exists with and transforms. Its meaning resides not just in differentiation but also in contrast and colonisation. As indicated in connection with claims about women, gentrification is not only about affluence, upward mobility, renovation and revitalisation; it is equally about poverty, displacement, exclusion and marginalisation. Contrast itself depends upon invasion: the description of gentrification as urban renaissance or revitalisation implies that the neighbourhoods concerned were previously 'de-vitalized and culturally moribund' (Smith, 1982, p139). But, as Smith goes on to argue, this is a consequence not a cause of gentrification, which often destroys what were 'very vital working-class communities'.

The destruction that occurs during colonisation is part of what creates the contrast characteristic of gentrification, which is not only about social position but also about trajectory (ascendance replacing degeneration). This perspective implies that gentrification is, by definition, a process of transition. It is, therefore, liable to be self-defeating in that if an initial invasion of new territory is successful, the source of contrast may eventually be entirely expunged. Referring to gentrification in inner London, Williams (1986, p72) notes that "[t]he process of change never ceases. ... Some of the gentry have worked out their own identity through the gentrification process and, having rediscovered the essential differences between themselves and the working class, they left."

Contrast and colonisation are as much about social identity as about the physical form of the urban environment and therefore this interpretation of gentrification underpins the view of class as dynamic discussed above. In addition, the theme of social differentiation emphasises the relational character of class: the new middle class can only establish its identity in relation to other identities. Gentrification makes explicit and emphasises the relationship between social identities through geographical proximity (in the case of co-existent working-class identity), through the use of historical legacies (in the case of the identities of previous inhabitants of the same buildings or neighbourhoods), and through other landscape symbols (most notably in relation to contemporary suburban middle-class identity). In this interpretation classes are distinguished qualitatively, in contrast to a gradational view of class, which assumes that differences are of degree rather than type. Moreover, within the relational view, changes affect the whole class structure and cannot be isolated to one group. In other words, the emergence of a new middle class necessarily has repercussions beyond its own limits. Gentrification as class constitution is, therefore, about the constitution of new working-class identities as well as new middle-class identities (Rose, 1984; Beauregard, 1986; Winchester and White, 1988).

This relational view is implicit in many recent studies, and provides the theoretical background for class-based analyses of gentrification. The notion of gentrification as class constitution provides an important advance on earlier studies limited by the voluntarism of demand-side explanations or the determinism of supply-side explanations. It also avoids the narrow economism associated with approaches rooted in certain versions of both positivism and Marxism (Ley, 1980), and develops instead a framework that emphasises the interplay between 'culture' and 'economy'. However, as currently formulated, and as the next section demonstrates, these themes also serve to impede analyses that stress the importance of changes in the role of women.

WOMEN, CLASS AND GENTRIFICATION

As argued above, women's experience of, and role in, gentrification is deeply divided, and appears to be structured principally by class divisions. Perhaps as a consequence of this, recent discussions fail to consider whether gentrification might be a process of gender constitution as well as of class constitution. This section reconsiders the themes of class as dynamic and class as relational in order to show (a) how changes in the role of women are subsumed within issues of class identity and class structure, and (b) how gender could also be interpreted as dynamic and relational.

Class identity and gender identity

Within class analyses it is argued that gentrification is expressive and indeed constitutive of a new social identity, which is strongly associated with the emergence of a service class. This class is typically defined in terms of its occupational characteristics: its members enjoy well-paid jobs with security and promotion prospects, principally in management or administration, or as professionals (Thrift, 1987). Members of the service class are strongly placed in housing markets where they make a variety of choices. They are often highly mobile geographically and benefit from employer subsidies in residential relocation (Forrest and Murie, 1987). Gentrification is one possible housing choice, carrying with it a distinctive lifestyle choice through which a segment of the service class is developing a unique social identity.

Part of the lifestyle choice associated with gentrification appears to be related to changes in the position of women in both the labour market and the family (Rose, 1984; Beauregard, 1986). These changes are generally understood to operate principally via occupational position: women are gaining entry to service class (especially professional) occupations, and are increasing their scope for career progression by postponing childbearing, by having smaller families and by making extensive use of their ability to pay for childcare. This implies that women are prominent among gentrifiers because they are moving into new class positions in their own right, rather than merely as wives within households headed by men in the appropriate occupations. It can also be argued that women are prominent among the 'victims' of gentrification because changes in both urban labour markets and the family are resulting in many other women moving into very different class positions (sometimes described as forming an 'underclass') again in their own right, rather than because of the position of their menfolk.

This interpretation is problematical for two reasons. First, it ignores the issue of how the occupational position and class identity of individuals within households interact.

Secondly, despite references to women, it ignores gender in the sense of a socially constructed aspect of human identity. These difficulties are examined in turn.

Social scientists have traditionally treated social class as an attribute of households, for which the best available indicator is the occupational position of the 'head of household' (the chief earner, usually assumed to be male in households including adult men and women). This approach has been strongly criticised on the grounds that (a) it assumes that married women, under 'normal' circumstances, have no independent class position and no influence on the class position of the household; and (b) women's class position is highly unstable in that it changes on marriage, separation or if the husband's unemployment or illness results in the wife becoming 'head of household' (Walby, 1986). However, the treatment of social class as an attribute of individuals regardless of other members of the household is also problematical. Part of the problem is that existing scales for evaluating class position reflect characteristics of male employment and fail to differentiate adequately between occupations dominated by women. New scales can alleviate this problem (e.g. Murgatroyd, 1984), but the issue is more profound. There is mounting evidence to suggest that the occupational positions of husbands and wives are interacting influences on class identity (Heath and Britten, 1984; Abbott and Sapsford, 1987). Thus, social class cannot reasonably be treated as an attribute of either atomistic individuals or homogeneous households.

The technical problems that ensue in the assignment of people to gradational social classifications is not of direct relevance to this discussion. More important is an understanding of the implications for analyses of residential patterns and residential change. As Pratt and Hanson (1988) observe, the assumption that households are homogeneous units has carried over into an assumption that residential areas are generally socially homogeneous. However, their analysis demonstrates that this view is largely an artefact of the use of the occupation of the 'head of household' (presumed to be male) as an indicator of class position. When women's occupational position is taken into account social heterogeneity within and between households in supposedly homogeneous areas emerges.

In relation to gentrification, references to women's employment involve an apparently unconsidered switch from treating social class as an attribute of households to treating it as an attribute of individuals. Thus, women are inserted into existing occupational scales without any discussion of the implications for conceptualisations of class. At an empirical level, the observations prompting this shift might imply that the relationship between the occupational position and class identity of partners in gentrifying households is different from other households. There is a suggestion that gentrification is associated with a reduction in the internal role differentiation within households (Smith, 1987; Mills, 1988), and certainly greater similarity in occupational roles is likely. However, investigation of how this influences class identity is lacking.

Turning to the second issue, while the gender dimension of class identity may have been inadequately examined, the issue of gender identity remains more sorely neglected. Indeed, in the gentrification literature there is little sense that the categories 'women' and 'men' are changing; rather, the picture is one in which biologically differentiated males and females are being inserted in new ways within an evolving class structure and an evolving pattern of household organisation. 'Women' and 'men' are treated as pre-given and immutable in their gender identity, their new positions influencing only their class identity. In other words, gender as a dynamic, socially constructed form of differentiation, manifest in changing notions of masculinity and femininity, is neglected in favour of a concern with the dynamic aspect of class. At best this means that the power of feminist theory is lost, and at worst that long-discredited biological conceptualisations of differences between women and men persist by default. Even Rose (1989, p133), who argues that "changes in women's employment situation, *as mediated by other aspects of gender relations* [emphasis added], may often be constitutive of gentrification", and who offers the most strongly feminist interpretation of gentrification, remains aloof from questions of the social construction of gender identity, focusing instead on the abstract concepts of production and reproduction.

There is no intention to deny the importance of gentrification as class constitution. Instead, the aim is to open up new questions about gentrification in which the dynamic character of gender is realised. In this sense, the issue is whether gentrification is a process through which changes in gender identities are constructed and expressed. Existing feminist geography provides some leads: several studies have highlighted the relationship between suburban housing and (a) the conventional nuclear family, with its highly differentiated allocation of roles to women and men: and (b) idealisations of femininity in terms of homemaking, domesticity, emotionality, passivity and dependence, and of masculinity in terms of breadwinning, authority, rationality, active power and leadership (Davidoff, L'Esperance and Newby, 1976; Mackenzie and Rose, 1983; McDowell, 1983; Miller, 1983; Mackenzie, 1988).

There is some evidence that gentrification is associated with alternatives to the nuclear family. For example, Rose (1989) provides evidence of an association between gentrification and changes in household structure, in that one-person households, adult sharers and one-parent households headed by women in professional employment are strongly represented in neighbourhoods in Montreal undergoing gentrification. However, ideas about gender identity remain largely unexplored. If gender is treated as a dynamic concept it becomes possible to consider whether gentrification might represent redefinitions of femininity and masculinity. Certainly, it appears that among gentrifiers, ideals of femininity are being extended to include career orientation but it is far from clear whether, for example, money-making is *replacing* homemaking as a feminine ideal, or whether ideals of masculinity are undergoing changes. Further, erosion of the conventional dichotomies between the roles of women and men does not mean that the differentiation of gender identities is decreasing in strength; rather, the familiar divisions may be being replaced, as the distinction between masculinity and femininity is reworked around new themes, perhaps relating to cultural rather than economic roles (Williamson, 1987).

Historical studies suggest that the homemaking versus breadwinning idealisation originated in the differentiation of the nineteenth century middle class from other social classes (Davidoff and Hall, 1987). Thus, gender identity was itself inextricably bound up with class identity. It is likely that social groups establishing identities in the contemporary social and urban structure are also using ideas about masculinity and femininity to do so. Phillips (1987) has argued that the gender ideals of different classes were most strongly differentiated as the middle class of the mid-nineteenth century established its distinctive position. Thereafter, within a relatively stable class structure, Phillips traces a convergence between working class and middle class ideas about gender identity (especially about femininity). In so far as gentrification represents the emergence of a new form of 'middle-classness' it may entail the development of increasingly class-differentiated gender identities.

Class structure and gender structure

Despite a growing awareness that changes in the position of women in society are important in gentrification, the dominance of class analysis has obscured the issue of gender as a relational concept. This stands in contrast to the concern with class as relational apparent in the recent emphasis on gentrification as a process of urban polarisation. According to this view, urban polarisation is inherent in gentrification both in the immediate sense that upgrading and revitalisation highlight and sometimes generate downgrading and dilapidation, and in the symbolic sense that social differentiation and contrast are central to the meaning of gentrification. Thus, gentrification is bound up with the renegotiation of, and conflict over, relations between social groups (Rose, 1984; Winchester and White, 1988).

For decades, class analyses have assumed that key positions within the class structure and in class conflict are occupied by men, whether as factory bosses, stockbrokers, company directors, trade unionists, miners, dockworkers, artisans or shopkeepers. Now that women are becoming prominent in key locations within the class structure and in conflict over processes of urban social change the assumption is less tenable. However, rather than being submitted to scrutiny, the assumption is being ignored and hidden behind superficial linguistic adjustments. For example, in his discussion of social polarisation, Pahl (1988) acknowledges that poverty is principally a female phenomenon, but, like writers on gentrification, his interest is confined to the relationship between classes whose gender composition may be noted but is not considered to be intrinsic or of causal significance. Consequently, the significance of gender in the structure of power relations is ignored.

Like classes, women and men as social groups are defined relationally. That the relationship is one of power is indicated in a myriad of ways from inequalities in access to well-paid jobs, through the concentration of political power in the hands of men, to the incidence of domestic and sexual violence against women. And, like classes, change in the position of one group necessarily affects the position of others. Thus, if a group of women are strengthening their position in the job market, the relative positions of others must change. This issue has not been addressed directly in discussions of contemporary urban change, but implicit in most accounts is the assumption that only class structure is affected. As some (women) improve their economic position, others (who also happen to be women) suffer a decline. What is entirely ignored is that an increase in economic power among a sector of middle-class women erodes their historical dependence on, and therefore the relative power of, *men*. In other sectors of the population relative changes between women and men may be in the opposite direction but nevertheless this has implications for gender as well as class.

The complex and in some ways contradictory trends in the relative positions of women and men serve to highlight the distinction between the concepts of social structure and social relations. The latter, whether referring to gender or class, operates at a high level of abstraction and refers to overarching or underlying systems of power. The former operates at a lower level of abstraction and attempts to capture the broad patterns through which these power relations are organised in social practices. Consequently, changes in gender or class structure can occur without any fundamental change in gender or class relations.

While this distinction is well elaborated in class theory (see, for example, Thrift and Williams, 1987), it is often overlooked in discussions touching on gender issues. On occasion this leads to an overestimation of changes in the gender order. For example, both Smith (1987) and Mills (1988) cite with approval Markusen's (1981, p32) claim that "gentrification is in a large part a result of the breakdown of the patriarchal household". However, the potency of Markusen's claim is not appreciated: both authors assert the importance of changes in the roles of women and men but give no explanation of the implications for the deeply entrenched and pervasive system of patriarchy. In other words, they confuse positional changes that might alter the gender structure with changes in power relations. Patriarchy is a system of gender relations in which men maintain power over women (Bowlby, Foord and McDowell, 1986; Foord and Gregson, 1986). Role changes within a particular set of households are in no sense indicative of fundamental changes in power relations between women and men.

CONCLUSION: CAPITALISM AND PATRIARCHY IN *THE INNER CITY*

The treatment of gender issues in studies of contemporary urban change is confused and unsatisfactory. As the discussion presented in this chapter has shown, references to women have generally been accompanied by inadequate conceptualisations of gender. In many cases this leads to changes in the position of women being equated with changes in class position. Consequently, gender as a socially dynamic phenomenon is ignored and, by default, women and men are treated as biological constructs within a dynamic class structure. Elsewhere, gender roles are confused with gender relations, leading to misplaced claims about the imminent demise of patriarchy.

Utilising a dynamic and relational concept of gender, there is much scope for empirical investigation of the significance of gentrification in the lives of women and men. Recent analyses of gentrification as class constitution offer promising directions, which need to be expanded to consider the issue of gender constitution. This raises questions concerning the interaction between class and gender and it is therefore appropriate to conclude with a brief discussion of the theoretical framework within which this interplay might be considered in the specific context of the inner city.

Implicit in the account offered here is a position of agnosticism on the explanatory primacy of gender and class: with respect to the analysis of social change in general and contemporary urban change in particular, the primacy of class has been challenged but not replaced. This position is broadly consistent with the socialist-feminist assertion of the equally important and essentially complementary character of processes involved in the production of goods and services, and the reproduction of people. What remains disputed, however, is whether these processes are manifestations of separate capitalist and patriarchal structures or of one unitary system.

Foord and Gregson (1986) argue that capitalism and patriarchy are, respectively, specific forms of the more general objects, class relations and gender relations. This is unexceptional and serves as a useful reminder of the historically specific character of the social relations with which we are familiar. However, their decision to focus on the general, rather than the specific leads into a counterproductive search for an overarching theory of the origins of female subordination (Johnson, 1987). For the purposes of analysing contemporary urban change, the more specific concepts of capitalism and patriarchy are more appropriate points of departure.

Walby (1986) provides a lucid summary of different interpretations of the relationship between capitalism and patriarchy. She rejects the notion that capitalism and patriarchy form a single, integrated system of social relations citing "a separation ... around the rival demands for women's labour with capital and patriarchy pulling in opposite directions" (p32). Conversely, she rejects positions that treat patriarchy and capitalism as operating in entirely different spheres (as, for example, Foord and Gregson, 1986, imply). Instead, she argues that capitalism and patriarchy should be treated as analytically independent but equally ubiquitous systems. They are not separate domains in which processes of production and of reproduction operate, but they coexist, sometimes in conflict, sometimes in harness, in all aspects of human social organisation. This position is implicit in the discussion of gentrification presented here. The importance of maintaining an analytical distinction between class - the relations of capitalism - and gender - the relations of patriarchy - has been emphasised in the development of a critique of the treatment of women in studies of gentrification. At the same time, the interlocking and mutual definition of class and gender identity has been stressed.

In this interaction there is no single trajectory but, rather, there are widely divergent experiences of the contemporary inner city. For example, while Smith (1987) suggests that the contemporary women's movement has been a crucial factor responsible for translating gradual changes in the position of women in the labour force and in the family into a more rapid spatial reversal represented by gentrification, its members have also been active in community opposition to the destruction and displacement it causes. These contrasts are typical of the social polarisation that has become synonymous with the inner city. Whether these trends mark substantial changes in the social order remains to be seen, but the conflict characteristic of contemporary urban change provides unique opportunities to observe the mutual constitution of class and gender.

CHAPTER 7

'SKILLS DO NOT EQUAL JOBS'
Current misconceptions in tackling unemployment

Sara Ladbury and Clive Mira-Smith

This chapter looks at the decline of unemployment as a prominent political issue over a period of twelve months from October 1988 to October 1989.

Throughout most of 1988 the government was 'battling' with the problem of unemployment and attempting to explain it in terms of a national skills shortage. The argument put forward was that there existed a mismatch between the skills needed by employers and the skills, or lack of skills, of local people. The mismatch was to be resolved through a major new training initiative targeting the adult unemployed, the Employment Training (ET) Programme.

By October 1989, unemployment, the concept of skills shortage and the Employment Training Programme had all lost their high political profile. We will argue that the concept of skills shortage and the *solution* - the ET Programme - were simplistic responses to a far more complex problem. A gradual realisation of this complexity was one reason for their being taken off the political agenda. A second reason was a gradual awareness over the preceding twelve months of the significance of demographic changes in the UK which no longer made it necessary for the government to be seen to be focusing on unemployment.

In this chapter we will first look at the situation as it was from October to December 1988, focusing particularly on the government's response at that time to unemployment. On the basis of our own fieldwork we then analyse why that response was inadequate. In the second part of the chapter we will consider the impact demographic changes are having on the government's current approach to employment and unemployment.

THE CONCEPT OF SKILLS SHORTAGE: THE GOVERNMENT'S VIEW IN 1988

Government agencies, the Confederation of British Industry, and following this lead, the media, throughout the first half of 1988 pinpointed a shortage of skills as the major reason for high unemployment in the UK. There was a stated paradox that at a time of high unemployment there were thousands of unfilled job vacancies. A skills shortage was posited as the reason for this.

It is worth pausing to note how a skills shortage was defined at that time. A job was officially classified as hard to fill if it had remained vacant, after being advertised, for more than eight weeks. Job Centres had a list of jobs that were considered, locally and nationally, hard to fill. Men and women who had been unemployed for less than six months and who were therefore not eligible for Employment Training (ET) nonetheless became eligible if they wanted to take up training in these 'skill shortage training' areas.

The assumption in virtually all cases was that a skills shortage solely accounted for jobs being hard to fill. Thus by extension, skills shortage became the general cause for unemployment, and solutions were sought for this 'problem' alone.

The government initiated a major campaign aimed at reducing the skills shortage through training initiatives. Employment Training was one such initiative. What distinguished it from previous government training schemes was that it targeted specifically people who were unemployed. In addition there was no age barrier for adults; anyone aged between 18 and 60 who had been receiving benefit for more than six months was eligible. Its sole purpose, as its name suggests, was to get people into, or back into, work.

The whole campaign was based upon the assumption that the unemployed did not have work because they did not have the necessary skills to take up local job vacancies. The training scheme was therefore relied upon to solve two problems together - get the unemployed into work, and fill the job vacancies that 'exist in abundance'. This campaign was presented graphically in a number of advertisements, run in national newspapers and displayed on hoardings.

The visual images portrayed square blocks of wood being shaved to fit round holes - the implication being that the individual could be reshaped to fit a job opportunity. The accompanying text drove home the same message - "train the workers without jobs to do the jobs without workers". So the problem of unemployment was - at a stroke - reduced to a single manageable cause: lack of skills (see Figure 7.1).

The campaign had some considerable success and gained a level of credence not only amongst government departments, but also amongst employers, training providers, etc. The message was appealing in its simplicity and directness. The campaign was quickly taken up by employers because they were having real difficulties in recruiting staff and they accepted that skills shortages were the principal reason. This in fact 'got them off the hook' - it was neither their fault nor was the solution their sole responsibility.

The new Employment Training scheme was also geared to maximise the involvement of employers. What is more, the new ET scheme was advantageous to employers and they were not slow to recognise this. In some circumstances employers were 'headhunting' trainees and paying well over the mandatory £30 per week to training agents in order to have trainees on work placements. Job experience and job placements became main elements in the 'skilling' process.

It is important to note that opposition to ET by trades unions, voluntary groups and local councils tended to concentrate on the fact that the financial benefits to employers and trainers were considerable, whereas those to trainees were minimal. In focusing upon the pay structure of the ET programme, the fundamental assumption of the scheme - that the main cause of unemployment was a skills shortage - was never challenged.

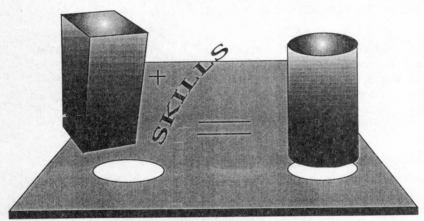

**Train the workers without jobs
to do the jobs without workers**

Figure 7.1: 'Train the workers without jobs.....' Department of Trade and Industry
Campaign

THE CONCEPT OF SKILLS SHORTAGE - THE VIEW OF THOSE OUT OF WORK

In 1988 the Department of Employment commissioned skills surveys in areas of high unemployment to ascertain the skills local people had, or did not have, and what training they required in order to fill the 'gaps' in the local labour market. In discussing the view of people out of work, we draw from one such Skills Survey carried out while we were members of a research unit based at University College London. The study was commissioned by the North Peckham Task Force (Department of Employment) to identify the skills and experience that local people had so that training initiatives could be mounted to increase the level of employment. The estate was chosen because of the existing high level of unemployment (one-third of economically active residents).

The Skills Survey was carried out on Gloucester Grove Estate in North Peckham, between April and June 1988. This work was carried out by the authors when part of the Urban Change Group at University College London. Responses were obtained from over 1,000 households, representing 87 per cent of residents. Estate residents were trained as interviewers and this accounted for the high response rate.

The survey was designed to identify the skills local people had, the training they wanted, and the barriers that prevented them from taking up training and employment opportunities. These barriers were the subject of a series of discussion groups held with local residents. While we recognised that nationally there did exist a shortage of suitably qualified and trained employees in certain sectors - Information Technology, Engineering, etc. - we wanted to find out whether lack of skills accounted for unfilled job vacancies in non-professional job activities. The government campaign on skills shortages at the time was targeting all levels of skill requirement, from professional to manual - as the advertisements said, "taxidrivers, park-keepers, taxidermists". It is particularly with these sorts of jobs in mind that we had to ask, did there exist a skills shortage?

One of the major opportunities offered by this study was to indicate why unemployed people themselves thought they were out of work. It will be recalled that as far as the government campaign was concerned, job vacancies existed solely because local people did not have the skills employers wanted and therefore they were not recruited. As far as local people on the estate were concerned, however, there were a number of reasons for their being unemployed.

In the opinion of the majority of local residents the major reasons for there being a high level of unemployment and continuing job vacancies in the area were the following:

Low levels of pay

From what respondents said, certain low paid jobs would never be attractive. Local male residents with family responsibilities categorically stated that unless they were paid at least £150 per week, it was not financially worth their while to work. This financial calculation was further corroborated by other negative aspects they perceived working would incur: minimal job satisfaction, minimal status from a job, minimal promotion prospects, decreased time with their families and friends.

The model, perhaps idealised, which was frequently given was that of apprenticeships. While initial pay and status were low, future prospects were clearly mapped out with reward being not only financial but also added responsibility, status and satisfaction.

Discrimination by employers

Both Black and White residents felt that local employers discriminated on the basis of race. Many older residents (those over 40) said their age was against them. Women wanting to come back into the workforce after having a family said they were unable to do so because of the lack of childcare facilities either in training programmes or in the workplace. The expectation of discrimination in some instances was sufficient not only to inhibit people from applying for a job, but also deterred them from going on training courses. In a meeting held after the survey between local residents and employers, the latter emphasised that they had made changes in their recruitment procedures. Residents responded that such changes were not apparent in the company's workforce and they were therefore unconvinced that anything had changed. Clearly the composition of a company's workforce was seen as the best (or the worst) indication of whether a company was likely to discriminate or not.

Status and prospects of available jobs

An additional reason for not taking up a job, a manual or low skilled job in particular, was that residents felt that such jobs did not lead anywhere. There was no way of developing skills which would enhance future job prospects. For residents with academic qualifications (particularly degrees) the status of the job was important; there was a strong disinclination to take up any job which did not recognise qualifications gained.

From our own analysis of the survey data, we would add:

Unawareness of job requirements

Very often local residents did not know exactly what particular jobs entailed. They did not apply because they did not know what skills were required of them or because they thought the necessary skills were somehow beyond them.

Lack of awareness existed principally because those out of work had lost touch - or had never been in touch - with formal employment. Likewise local employers had never been in touch with unemployed people except in interview situations across a desk. In this way myths had built up on both sides. From our work on the estate we estimated that the situation would continue until local employers met local residents out of work on their own terms - i.e. on estates, at tenants' associations, etc.

Unawareness of their own abilities and how to present these

The survey revealed that on the whole people had very little idea about 'how to market themselves', that skills gained outside the immediate context of 'work' could still be relevant.

Employment policies of companies relocating to the area

Southwark was typical of London generally in so far as jobs in traditional industries have contracted massively over the last decade, and relocation of new companies to the area has been considerable. The new companies however frequently brought their own workforces with them. The most recent available survey indicated that 98 per cent of jobs in firms relocating in the borough were filled by those already in post.

The force with which the above issues emerged from the study led us to conclude that a skills shortage was not the prime reason for high unemployment in the Peckham area. There is no reason to presume that Peckham was in any way unique. The issues which concerned residents on the Gloucester Grove Estate were those which concerned, and continue to concern, residents in all inner city areas where there is high unemployment.

The government's strategy, to introduce Employment Training, did not, nor could it, tackle the sorts of issues raised by the residents in the Gloucester Grove survey. This has accounted for the slow take-up of the programme by those out of work, the mixed reception on the part of employers, and efforts by trades unions to change aspects of the programme for the benefit of trainees. ET quite simply did not, nor does it now, address the issues that unemployed people see as important.

THE EFFECTS OF DEMOGRAPHIC CHANGE

Initial government response

The inadequacies of the ET programme were hotly debated, but only for a short time. By the beginning of 1989, another phenomenon emerged which over time drew attention away from the main debate about ET and unemployment. This phenomenon was the effect of demographic changes in the UK, or more specifically the decline in the number of school leavers entering the labour market. There was a growing awareness by government and employers alike that by 1995 there would be 1.2 million fewer 16-24 year olds in the labour force compared to 1987, a fall of more than one-fifth. Those employers who traditionally took a large proportion of their annual intake of employees straight from school were even by the beginning of 1989 experiencing difficulties in recruitment.

At first the government used the demographic changes to advertise heavily for ET. It mounted a publicity campaign to inform employers of the projected continuing decline of school leavers up to 1995. The imagery used in this campaign portrayed young people as an endangered species, showing a school leaver's head mounted on a wall plaque like an extinct species. The message to employers was - *"start thinking about a new breed of trainee, unemployed people"*. The adverts then turned into promotions for Employment Training (see Figure 7.2).

What the adverts did not do was portray older unemployed people, and women wishing to return to work, as a positive alternative to recruiting school leavers. The problem of the demographic shortage, in January 1989, was simply defined as the absence of school leavers. The solution was to train up what by implication had become a 'second grade' category of people: the unemployed who were, by implication, not skilled enough to have found jobs already. We should not be surprised that women did not enter government thinking since they did not figure in unemployment statistics and their recruitment would not bring about a fall in the official level of unemployment.

The images used in this advertising campaign were unlikely to have changed the beliefs older people had about their future employment prospects. In the Gloucester Grove survey, both men and women of 35 plus who were out of work, or who had left work to have families, felt that they had no employment prospects in the future. They thought jobs were all for the young. To convince them otherwise would have required a reversal of many years of personal experience and the effects of employment campaigns up to that time. Older people had lost confidence in themselves and in employers.

The recruitment of women

By the beginning of 1989 employers found that they had actively to look for an alternative to recruiting young people. For the first time women started to feature as the new solution to employment requirements.

THEY'LL SOON BECOME AN ENDANGERED SPECIES.

Thanks to a change in population there's soon going to be 1 million fewer school leavers.

But it needn't mean your supply of trainees will become extinct.

Just start thinking about a new breed of trainee.

Unemployed people.

Doesn't it make sense to train the workers without jobs, to do the jobs without workers?

Employment Training is the biggest training initiative Britain's ever had.

With £1.4 billion being put into it, the unemployed will get a lot out.

Up to 12 months of high quality training, for as many as 600,000 adults every year.

It's organised at a local level with local employers, so an area crying out for Taxi drivers won't get stuffed full of Taxidermists.

To find out more about training your next generation of skilled workers ring 0800 24 6000 or fill in the coupon.

Send to: Employment Training, FREEPOST (TY 895),
Brentford, Middlesex TW8 8BR. Tel. 0800 24 6000

Name (Mr/Mrs/Miss/Ms) _____

Position _____

Company name _____

Address _____

_____

Postcode _____ Tel. _____

Number of employees: _____ Number of locations: _____

Nature of Business _____

Opportunities for trainees: ☐ Office ☐ Factory ☐ Other

Company's involvement in other training schemes:
☐ Currently ☐ Previously ☐ Never IND/S

ET EMPLOYMENT TRAINING

**TRAIN THE WORKERS
WITHOUT JOBS
TO DO THE JOBS
WITHOUT WORKERS.**

Figure 7.2: Department of Trade and Industry advert for Employment Training

Several forces came together at this time to promote the recruitment of women. Firstly, employers themselves recognised the need to find an alternative labour source. Secondly, those actively working towards equal opportunities saw the opportunity to promote women's employment opportunities and be taken seriously for the first time. Thirdly, women themselves wanted to work. From the employers' point of view, there were advantages in employing women, and particularly women who had already had a family. The perceived advantages were their putative stability, level of commitment, previous skills which could be upgraded, and pay structures that the employers could get away with offering.

Those involved in equal opportunities, either as officers in individual companies, or as pressure groups working independently, responded by ensuring that all issues relating to women in the workplace were firmly placed on the political agenda. Part-time work, flexitime, job share, career breaks, all have become serious issues of debate, and more and more companies are recognising that they have to consider such options if they are to succeed in recruiting women.

The lack of childcare facilities became a national issue. Comparisons were made with other European countries' provision of childcare schemes for women returning to work. A study carried out in 1988 among the twelve EC member states found that the UK was at the bottom of the league. Only 2 per cent or less of the under-threes were in publicly funded services. Of children aged between 3 and 5 in the UK, 44 per cent had a publicly funded nursery place, less than any other member of the European Community. France offers 95 per cent of children aged between 3 and 5 a nursery place.

The number of UK employers in the private sector responding to the need for childcare facilities remains very low. A number of independent surveys have highlighted the current situation regarding childcare provision by private sector employers. A recent *Daily Telegraph* survey approached 100 major employers and found that only six provided workplace nurseries, only three offered their employees financial assistance with childcare costs. These results are substantiated by a survey carried out by the Workplace Nurseries Campaign (*Daily Telegraph*, 6 October 1989), which, based on the *Financial Times* Top 500 UK companies, found that only 20 private companies were providing work-place nurseries in Britain as of March 1989. In spite of this it is now commonly estimated that 80 per cent of new jobs over the next ten years will be taken by women.

Many of these women will be mothers, with a significant number caring for pre-school children.

If the response on the part of private employers has been minimal, the response on the part of the government has been almost non-existent. At the time of writing, the Home Office minister and chair of the Ministerial Group on Women's Issues is being accused of failing to provide resources or support for schemes he has backed verbally. Verbal support extends to guidelines for good childcare practice and for the setting up of a National Childcare Register. However the government continues to put the onus on employers to provide childcare and there is no indication that the government is willing to take on the responsibility of childcare provision itself.

The effect of demographic change as far as the government is concerned has created a dilemma. Initially, since there were fewer school leavers entering the labour market, the pressure was taken off the government as far as unemployment was concerned. However, as the emphasis has shifted to the employment of women as an alternative labour source, the government has been constrained to maintain a low profile. If it were to support the re-entry of women into the workforce, it would be under pressure to provide the necessary support facilities. Since it is clearly not prepared to do this, the new developments have been met with an almost total silence. This is in marked contrast to the high profile national campaign mounted to solve *the skills shortage* just a year previously.

PART THREE
ALTERNATIVE REALITIES

We have attempted to show how theoretically grounded notions have informed and misinformed urban policy. All policy prescriptions incorporate either explicitly or implicitly a diagnosis of the urban crisis. Although these diagnoses may at times appear to reflect more *post hoc* rationalisations of vested interest and political expediency than enlightenment wisdom, they are still rooted in a way of seeing contemporary urban life which draws its vocabulary from social science study of the inner city.

The single theme that unites the final chapters of this volume is that we do not have to see cities in this way. There are alternative ways of conceptualising city life which do not necessarily cast the losers in the urban crisis as either problems in their own right or mere victims of the machinations of macro-economic structures, which do not necessarily turn the problem of uneven development into a spatial fetish and which can base urban policy on a positive evaluation of the metropolis rather than a negative imagery of anti-urbanism.

Patrick Bond in his chapter highlights, through personal experience and theoretical analysis, the potential for an oppositional politics which attempts to confront the dominant forces of multinational capital by 'thinking globally and acting locally'.

A key theme in Mel Thompson's chapter is that an entrepreneurial way of life was the norm for many people who had long and rich experiences using entrepreneurial skills as strategies for survival in Jamaica long before they migrated to the UK. The oral history medium lends a meaning to seemingly disparate notions such as resistance and business skills which undermines easy and all too dangerous generalisations about *ethnic enterprise*.

In marked contrast to the anti-urbanism that has characterised public policy in both North America and the UK, Patricke Le Gales here illustrates not the benevolent nature of the French capitalist state but instead the possible, if limited, results of a public policy that is informed less by a fear of the evils that emanate from the city - from Dickensian horror to 'yuppie' nightmare - and marginally more by the utopian philosophies of city life.

CHAPTER 8

ALTERNATIVE POLITICS IN THE INNER CITY
The financial explosion and the campaign for community control of capital in Baltimore

Patrick Bond

Among the most powerful and damaging forces buffeting the inner city of the 1980s and 1990s is the new-found capacity of financial markets and leading financial institutions to impose upon policy-makers severe constraints not particularly related to the logic of capitalist development but rather tied to the vicissitudes of global financial speculation. As a result, more so than in earlier periods, the maldistributive consequences of the changing global economy - including job loss and deindustrialisation, destruction of community, housing displacement and homelessness, cultural gentrification, municipal fiscal crisis, etc. - have confounded even visionary urban managers. The parallel demise in the 1980s of national Keynesian welfare-state solutions to social problems has left in their place a widespread acceptance of a

> "zero-sum inter-urban entrepreneurial competition for resources, jobs, and capital, [such that] even the most resolute and avant-garde municipal socialists will find themselves, in the end, playing the capitalist game and performing as agents of discipline for the very processes they are trying to resist". (Harvey, 1989, p7)

As orthodox urban management in the USA fails to withstand the forces of hostile financial markets and address successfully the problems of the inner city, it is appropriate to focus greater attention on alternative politics. So far, it appears that the rise of finance and the relative decline of manufacturing in US cities, and the racial, ethnic and spatial divisions between the urban poor and working classes who are most affected by these tendencies, have generally left social movements and alternative political practices scattered and unable to cope. Alternative politics in the USA is, by way of definition, based in community and/or workplace and/or organisations explicitly serving the public interest; politics mostly informal, transient and unstructured, especially when in coalitional form; politics not able to wield state power, nor with immediate prospects of gaining formal power; politics vaguely able to pressure elected representatives or policy-makers on occasion but generally disconnected from more traditional tools such as the mass media and political parties. Alternative politics conceived as such perhaps offers the flexibility and imagination required to address the new urban conditions, but rarely the discipline and financial resources to do so seriously.

But on closer examination, it may be the case that the seeds of the renewal of social action can be found within the processes of its very destruction; the financial system which has fundamentally altered the urban landscape and transformed urban economic and political processes has recently begun to encounter serious resistance from subordinate classes. This chapter will explore some implications of the extraordinary dynamism of financial markets in order to make the case that even under the most difficult of objective conditions, an alternative inner city politics can be constructed, modified and maintained in a manner portentous for national and even global progressive political mobilisation and social change. The argument proceeds from a survey of evidence of the increasing role of finance in the US economy to an examination of the implications of this role for the inner city and mainstream political practices. A case study follows, from Baltimore, Maryland, once an industrial and merchant centre in the mid-Atlantic region of the US, now a major metropolitan area with a (1985) population of 2.25 million, and powered today by financial, administrative and managerial activities. Underneath what has been termed the 'glitter' of Baltimore's much-celebrated central business district renaissance lies the 'rot' of extreme social and physical decay (Szanton, 1986). Baltimore is thus as fitting a location for an alternative political culture - a culture resentful about being shut out of the city's newfound geographically concentrated prosperity - as that highly visible though fragile prosperity is fittingly emblematic of the explosive rise of finance in the economy as a whole. A concluding section reflects ways in which the campaign for community control of capital in Baltimore is profoundly relevant for national and global alternative politics.

Patrick Bond

THE FINANCIAL EXPLOSION AND THE CITY

The financial explosion in the USA

What Harry Magdoff and Paul Sweezy (1987) have called the 'financial explosion' is here taken to mean the recent relaxation of constraints on the movement and growth of financial capital. The geographical implications of this phenomenon, nationally and internationally, are only beginning to be studied (Parboni, ·1981; Daly and Logan, 1986; Corbridge, 1988; Thrift and Leyshon 1988). Little empirical work exists on the urban manifestations of the growth of finance (Meyerson, 1986; Florida, 1986a, 1986b; Thrift, Leyshon and Daniels, 1987). But there is indisputable evidence of the critical new role finance plays in the US economy, especially since 1979 when the Federal Reserve tripled the cost of credit.

The term 'finance' refers, quite simply, to external funding, i.e. not internally-generated funds like corporate profits, household wages, or government tax revenues. Corporations, for example, can raise external funding through either debt (credit) or equity (new stock, deeds, titles and other so-called 'fictitious' paper representations of capital). It is primarily the former, the credit system, with which we are concerned in the urban context.

The increase in total US debt owed to both domestic and (net) international creditors has been explosive in the 1980s when considered relative to gross national product. Outstanding debt of all types rose from a steady ratio of around 150 per cent of GNP in the 1960s and 1970s to 230 per cent at year-end 1988. The total of about $12 trillion was, at that point, divided into $11.4 trillion in domestic debt and $530 in net international debt. If the standard role of credit is in merely facilitating new investment and lubricating the payment system, the rise of the debt mountain far beyond historical levels - the buildup of what may be called 'overaccumulated financial capital' - is a reflection of speculative investment ultimately very unlikely to achieve validation in the productive economy. (Added to this category would be the post-1982 rise of the New York stock market and of various other investment arenas far beyond the underlying values they are meant to represent.) While it is important to consider other significant aspects of technological, institutional and geographical deregulation of financial markets that were set in motion at the global level as early as the 1960s (Mayer, 1985), the enormous recent increase in debt, representing a 'financial fix' to the current crisis of general capital overaccumulation

(Harvey, 1982:ch.10), offers lessons of greatest consequence for alternative inner city politics.

More precisely, economists Christopher Niggle (1986) and Robert Pollin (1986, 1987, 1989) have traced the roots of the rise of US finance, especially the enormous expansion of debt, directly to the post-1966 decline in the average rate of profit in the productive (especially manufacturing) sphere of the economy, and in the consequent need for firms to increase borrowing simply to remain competitive. One logical outcome of the decline in profits was that, beginning in 1973, non-supervisory workers were pressured to accept declining per capita real wages (Bluestone and Harrison, 1988). That phenomenon largely explains the unprecedented rise in household indebtedness, considered a necessary evil by low- and middle-income consumers attempting to maintain their standards of living (Pollin, 1987). Similarly, the rise in federal government indebtedness, Magdoff and Sweezy (1987) and Pollin (1989) argue, is a function of macroeconomic countercyclical mechanisms brought into play as normal Keynesian fiscal stabilisers lost their boost. Thus the recent explosive demand for credit in the US economy is apparently quite closely linked to deeper economic processes that began in the late 1960s. Once set in motion, the financial explosion took on a logic of its own - 'Ponzi financing', to use Minsky's (1977) term - as the economy moved progressively deeper into debt and loans were taken out by economic actors of all types simply to repay interest on past loans. By the 1980s, the demand for credit had engendered a dramatic increase in both the volume and types of financial intermediation supplied, since 'real' (i.e. corrected for inflation) interest rates in that decade were set and remained at historically high levels, drawing capital into financial markets and offering creditors ample return on their investment.

It is vital, in any analysis of rising US indebtedness, to consider the inevitable consequences: rising foreclosures and bankruptcies by corporations and consumers, some of which cannot be socialised through government bailouts. The result, throughout the 1980s, was a dramatic increase in failures of financial institutions, especially savings and loans, and increasing fragility in the financial system as a whole. This problem and the struggles it fosters over who bears the burden of the necessary devaluation of overaccumulated financial capital, have enormous implications for alternative politics.

Patrick Bond

THE IMPACT OF THE FINANCIAL EXPLOSION ON INNER CITY DEVELOPMENT AND MAINSTREAM POLITICS

What are some of the urban correlates of the explosive new role finance plays in fuelling the US economy? For the largest cities, and even for smaller ones fortunate to be blessed with a growing set of financial institutions (e.g. Wilmington, Delaware; Charlotte, North Carolina; Hartford, Connecticut), financial deregulation is changing the urban landscape in several related ways. Most obviously, the new urban economic form increasingly substitutes the infrastructure of an industrial economy with those attributes fit especially for a financial centre - e.g. new downtown office buildings, central city-oriented rail and subway systems, a proliferation of postmodern urban spectacles culturally consistent with finance, and specialised space and services for other businesses or activities related to finance. In the USA, as Davis (1985, p109) describes it

"The postmodernist phenomenon seems irreducibly specific to the reckless overbuilding of commercial space that has taken place since 1974, continuing frenetically even through the trough of the severe 1981-82 recession. As everyone knows, this great construction bubble has been inflated, not by expanding civilian industrial production, but by oil rents, third world debts, military outlays, and the global flight of capital to the safe harbour of Reagan's America. This hypertrophic expansion of the financial service sector is not a new, higher stage of capitalism - even in America speculators cannot go on endlessly building postmodernist skyscrapers for other speculators to buy - but a morbid symptom of the financial overaccumulation prolonged by the weakness of the US labour movement and productive capital's fears of a general collapse."

Thus, an especially significant urban implication of the financial explosion is the high rate of price inflation in prime downtown commercial real estate. Increases in real estate prices are related both to a) the central business district boom centred on financial services and related industries, and to b) the decline in real manufacturing profits and the general search by capital (mediated by financial institutions) for higher-earning speculative outlets such as commercial real estate. The consequences of higher land values include the collapse of small and mid-sized companies as rent costs become prohibitive, a phenomenon felt globally. On this basis, Massey (1986, p46) notes that in the case of London

"[W]hile the financial sector continues to flourish, and to consolidate British banking capital's position within the shifting international division of labour, intranationally such a structure can only have hastened the precipitate decline of smaller and manufacturing industry within London."

Much the same can be said for so many US cities whose financial institutions and developers have bid up land prices far above their historic costs.

And it is not only commercial real estate, but also the inner city housing market that becomes rife with (strategically located) speculation. Upon formerly working class neighbourhoods and warehouse districts, financial capital imposes new condominium construction and historic property restoration, much of it for the employees of the mushrooming banking, insurance, real estate and business services industries. Ironically, while gentrification picked up speed in the 1980s, there was a simultaneous deepening of 'redlining' practices (i.e. discrimination by lending institutions) against the low-income residential neighbourhoods located further from the central business district, as financial institutions' requirements for economies of scale (Marcuse, 1979) and standardised loans which could be securitised for sale on secondary markets (Florida, 1986a) conflicted with the provision of less profitable small single-family home mortgages. This has been shown, recently, by a new spate of redlining studies in places as diverse as Washington, DC (Shlay, 1985), Chicago (Shlay, 1986, 1988), Philadelphia (Goldstein, 1985), Milwaukee (Squires and Velez, 1987), Wilmington (Goldstein and Shlay, 1988), Atlanta (Dedman, 1988), and New York (Williams, 1988), and in a national study of savings and loan associations (Dedman, 1989). As will be described below, both phenomena - gentrification and redlining - have generated widespread resistance by community-based forces.

There is a wide range of other implications of financial deregulation for the relationship between the urban economy, the state, politicians and subordinate classes. Contestation of the changing urban form is engaged in by actors and coalitions as diverse as City Hall, the local and regional financial industry, other corporate players with headquarter or key branch-plant administrative functions, landed capital, large- and mid-sized local industrial capitalists, small business people, cultural entrepreneurs, and political activists. Bankers, typically the most active representatives of financial capital, generally sit at the centre of the corporate power elite both nationally (Mintz and Schwartz, 1985; Kotz, 1978) and in local settings (e.g. Ratcliff, Gallagher and Ratcliff, 1979). This is a function, in the USA at least, not so much reflective of the classic 'finance capital' merger of banking, industrial and commercial capital (Hilferding, 1981) but rather of their capacity to build a 'community of interest' (Herman, 1981) that tends to submerge real conflicts that should logically arise over the banks' geographical allocation of credit. Banks, after all, have more in common with their corporate brethren - especially retailers and the local media - as members of the local 'growth machine' (Molotch, 1976). Although there is plenty of evidence that the banks' horizons are widening beyond their headquarter city base (Logan and Molotch, 1987, p206) and that other lenders are replacing once-key banking functions related to municipal finance (Sbragia, 1986, p217), the banks' need for an ever-expanding local retail and business deposit base keeps their commitment to local growth quite strong.

The role of finance in urban development is not limited to manipulation of land markets and local business power structures. In an age of interurban entrepreneurial competition and simultaneous financial fragility, banks and other financial institutions often become intricately involved in local and national political processes, sometimes in extra-legal ways. In 1989 financial scandals toppled governments in Japan, Greece and Jordan; similarly, the clearest US evidence of the role of finance in politics during the mid- and late-1980s may have been the extensive efforts of the savings and loan (S&L) industry to influence key members of the Congress, especially leaders of the Democratic Party. Once the reform party of liberals, labour and minorities, the Democrats' first and third ranking members of the House of Representatives were forced to resign in 1989 mainly because of widespread allegations of corruption involving the taxpayer bailout of a thousand or more failing S&Ls (Bond, 1989b, 1989c).

S&Ls had traditionally served simply as suppliers of home mortgage loans, but deregulation in the early 1980s allowed the industry new powers to make direct investments in commercial ventures, even in 'junk bonds'. The S&L crisis was itself ultimately a function of processes set in motion by the global financial explosion: interest rate fluctuations; a dramatic world commodity price decline borne of the Third World debt crisis and IMF-imposed export-oriented policies; the subsequent decline of US farm land prices and extensive foreclosures; the global oil glut (again emanating in large part from debtors like Mexico, Nigeria and Venezuela desperate for hard currency); and the subsequent collapse of speculative real estate investments in Texas, Colorado and southern California. As straightforward embezzlement and ill-considered commercial loans exacerbated the structural crisis and brought the bailout cost to an estimated $335 billion, the role of finance in mainstream politics became acute. Tens of millions of dollars in campaign contributions, much of it from desperate S&Ls, swamped politicians (including urban leaders such as the mayor of Los Angeles, who in 1989 faced FBI investigations over ties to financial institutions).

The S&L crisis is no mere detour in the discussion of finance and urban development, for the vital role S&Ls had historically played in allocating credit to neighbourhood housing and hence in shaping the urban form was fundamentally altered by the financial explosion. The decline of that role in the 1980s concomitant with the rise in speculative S&L investments partly explains the exceedingly uneven development of inner city housing markets during the period. The S&L crisis also shows the degree to which by the late 1980s the Democratic Party had become, at the local level in most urban jurisdictions, a well-oiled machine heavily influenced by financiers (it was simply not worth the bankers' money to invest in Republican Party politicians in major cities since they rarely gained office). The signals such political relations send to inner city activists about their electoral prospects are unmistakable. In addition, alongside financial capital's influence-peddling, so starkly revealed by the S&L crisis, several other factors have kept grassroots activists and organisations away from electoral politics: the political decline of organised labour, the failure of the Jesse Jackson presidential campaigns to gain major concessions from the Democratic Party, and the lack of a viable third party to challenge the Democrats and Republicans.

So it is to those practising alternative (non-electoral) inner city politics - i.e. progressive representatives of the poor and working classes - that we must turn to find resistance to the financial explosion. The strength of campaigns for community (rather than financial institution) control of capital depends on their alliances, constituencies, style and aspirations, and on constraints imposed by local and global forces. To examine these with the objective of applying lessons in other urban, national or global settings, it is important to choose an appropriate case study (Baltimore, Maryland) and to properly set the context.

THE FINANCIAL EXPLOSION AND THE CAMPAIGN FOR COMMUNITY CONTROL OF CAPITAL IN BALTIMORE

Urban development and financial capital in Baltimore

Contrary to the widespread publicity which centres on the downtown Inner Harbor renaissance, the urban crisis is still pronounced in Baltimore. The city proper has 760,000 residents, 61 per cent of whom are African-American. 'Charm City' is characterised by classic inner city problems like widespread poverty (24 per cent of the city population lives below the poverty line); the loss of manufacturing establishments (55 per cent between 1960 and 1984); relatively high unemployment, especially for African-American youth; increasing numbers of households headed by women (from 35 per cent in 1970 to 53 per cent in 1983); inadequate educational resources ($3,100 per student as opposed to $4,300 in the suburbs) and a high dropout rate (next to worst among the largest fifteen US cities); housing decay; racial tension; a rising crime rate and drug epidemic; a health crisis; etc.; all making Baltimore, according to the Joint Economic Committee of the US Congress, the fifth 'neediest' city in the country (Szanton, 1986; Levine, 1987a). But all this surrounds what is considered by many to be one of the United States' most spectacular central business district renaissances (*The Economist*, 1988; Berkowitz, 1984, 1987), although even on its own terms such a claim is disputed (Levine, 1987a, 1987b; Nugent, 1984).

It is worth dissecting the financial forces behind the dual city effect. Baltimore is an old-fashioned town, one whose leading banks, distasteful about any inner city investment, had to be dragged into the downtown development effort during the reign of the legendary entrepreneurial mayor, William Donald Schaefer (1971-86). Said the mayor in 1982: "Baltimore banks are just conservative, that's all, absolutely conservative. They're loosening up a little now, but it's been a difficult process" (Englund, 1982). That conservatism may have derived from extreme industry concentration. According to the US House Banking Committee's famed 'Wright Patnam Report' (1968, p4), "In some cities banking in general, and trust banking in particular, is dominated by one or two banking institutions. This appears to be particularly the case in Baltimore ..." where the five largest banks held 97.7 per cent of all commercial bank deposits in the mid-1960s. The report (1968 p927) went on:

"There are also in Baltimore a remarkable number of interlocking relationships among the officers and directors of commercial banks, insurance companies, and mutual savings banks. Among the five largest commercial banks, four insurance companies and four savings banks, a total of 13 competing financial institutions, there are no less than 30 such interlocks."

To shake the banking industry and other financiers from oligopolistic lethargy, Schaefer organised a 'Trustee for Loans and Guarantees' system in 1976 through which two men, one a private banker and the other the city finance director, controlled the investment of some $150 million of public monies in private sector redevelopment projects (Smith, 1980; Levine, 1987a). State financing initiatives geared to catalysing inner city redevelopment and gentrification are not unusual (Smith, 1979), and in Baltimore between 1962 and 1980, $330 million of government investments were pumped into the downtown area to attract just $375 million in private capital. Indeed, throughout Baltimore from 1976 to 1983, the city's economic development agency was alone responsible for financing $540 million in projects, with funds derived from federal Urban Development Action Grants, US Small Business Administration and Economic Development Administration loan programmes, State of Maryland programmes, and industrial revenue bonds. Such strong public sector encouragement was apparently the prerequisite, but eventually, at about the time US financial markets began their explosive growth, Baltimore's banking industry joined other leading corporate forces to help develop the Inner Harbor and other major downtown projects.

In spite of their early reluctance to engage in downtown investment, today, a graphic sense of the banks' role atop the Baltimore hierarchy can be found in the writings of geographer David Harvey (1987, p6):

"[S]kylines have the habit of representing what power is all about... Consider, first, the pinnacle of downtown monumentality - the Maryland National Bank building and the insolent Citibank building that rises like an upraised finger by its side. It is interesting first to note that the two tallest buildings in the city are those of financial institutions, silently testifying to the fact that Baltimore has only one of the Fortune 500 largest manufacturing companies headquarters in its region, that it has for long been a branch-manufacturing plant city, leaving the reins of bourgeois power to the large financial institutions."

Harvey and Chatterjee began studying Maryland National and the city's other financial institutions in the early 1970s. What they discovered became a classic article in urban studies (1974): the Baltimore housing finance market was highly differentiated according to different kinds and qualities of credit suppliers. The result was a patterned mosaic of class- and race-segregated capital flows, one consistent with the maximum extraction of absolute rent from the city's poorest, 'redlined' neighbourhoods. In contrast, White working class ethnic areas fared relatively well, since their sources of financial capital for housing were

"small, community-based savings and loan institutions that operate without a strong profit orientation and which really do offer a community service". (Harvey, 1985, p72)

But for a variety of historical reasons relating to racist 'block-busting' practices, the savings and loan associations which were active in low- and even moderate-income African-American residential areas played a destructive role. Their investments, via loans to housing speculators and others abusing Federal Housing Association mortgage guarantee programmes, gave them a high rate of return but ultimately quickened processes of disinvestment (Dilts, 1971). The only housing finance available for the actual residents (not speculators) in large blocs of the inner city, especially those close to the central business district, was in the form of cash or private loan transactions.

As Neil Smith (1984) has argued, the systemic devalorisation of space (i.e. in the urban housing market, disinvestment) may be a requirement for a successful return of capital back into that space. In Baltimore's case, the see-sawing of capital away from the downtown neighbourhoods, a process which reached extremes in the mid-1970s, reversed in the late 1970s and 1980s with the Inner Harbor renaissance. Thus, many of the formerly redlined areas are now the most thoroughly gentrified. This process is continually in flux, depending on the movement of capital for its vitality and direction. A new concern in Baltimore is that the redevelopment payoff for the devalorisation of inner city neighbourhoods has reached its limits, and that the see-saw of capital back into the downtown area may already have swung too far. Again, David Harvey (1987, p9):

"The generalised over-investment in shopping malls, entertainment facilities, high-priced condos, financial services, convention centers, sports stadia (which Baltimore now intends to construct in Camden yards in the hope of luring a football team) throughout urban America spells trouble for some cities of which Baltimore may or may not be one. The failure of the Power Plant (Inner Harbor entertainment complex) conversion and the difficulty of selling off those high-priced (waterfront) condos is a warning light of excess investment in urban redevelopment of this sort."

Ironically, it is at the very moment when Baltimore's downtown development may have peaked that overcompetitive financial capital is flooding the city. The disastrous collapse of Maryland's speculative State-chartered S&Ls in 1985, along the lines laid out above, allowed New York's Chase Manhattan and Pittsburgh's Mellon Bank to enter the local market through bailouts, while Citicorp (the United States' largest bank) promised economic development benefits to gain its Maryland foothold. An interstate banking law designed to integrate Baltimore banks into the south-eastern market paved the way for more new competition, and simultaneously released Maryland institutions to search for greener fields in which to invest inner city Baltimore deposits.

The volatility of the new interstate regulatory arrangement was evidenced by a shake-out of sorts, with several smaller Maryland financial institutions becoming the junior partners in mergers with regional (i.e. above $5 billion in asset size) and super-regional (above $20 billion) banks based in the new financial centres of Charlotte, North Carolina, and Richmond and Norfolk, Virginia. A telling indication of the loss of local control was the profusion of new bank names. Venerable Maryland institutions such as Suburban Federal, Central Savings Bank, Bank of Bethesda, and others were suddenly adorned with fancy new logos designed by the growing postmodern industry of corporate name-change specialists: Sovran, Crestar, Meritor, Signet and NCNB Corp. Maryland's politicians and elites began to wonder if indeed their local banks - which, reflecting more the culture of Old Money than the gung-ho buccaneer banking mentality of an NCNB, for instance, were much more cautious about interstate expansion (Maryland National led the way with a major acquisition of a Washington, DC bank in 1986) - would be able to play catch-up, or if it was not already too late. This was, of course, a matter of no small concern, since finance, insurance and real estate sectors are among the fastest-growing sectors in the nation and the region, and to maintain Baltimore's employment growth in these sectors, it was assumed, required the administrative centralisation of banks close at hand, not in the middle of North Carolina.

In Baltimore, the confluence of all these factors - increased competition and turbulence in the financial industry concomitant with its greater power, intensification of land speculation, construction of the Inner Harbor urban spectacle, and decline of the city's traditional economy - left promises of the American dream hollow for hundreds of thousands of inner city residents. Many of Baltimore's citizens, as members of various kinds of organisations, have come to understand this, and have fought it as part of a general movement for community control of capital.

The Maryland Alliance for Responsible Investment

Local progressive activists didn't lose too much sleep worrying about whether the influx of Citibank, Chase, Mellon, NCNB and the other huge banks would harm indigenous financial sector employment and reduce the local corporate command and control functions. In their dealings with locally-based banks and S&Ls, their concerns for nearly two decades had focused on home mortgage lending patterns.

Whether the redlining of Baltimore's inner city was based on race or on class, it periodically brought activists out to protest during the 1970s. But following minor concessions to Baltimore's few militant 'Alinskyite' community groups, and even despite the passage of the federal Community Reinvestment Act of 1977 (which 'encourages' banks and S&Ls to reinvest deposits in low-income areas) (Federal Financial Institutions Examination Council, 1985), the lending discrimination inevitably reappeared in the 1980s. The nation's leading expert on geographic flows of housing finance, Anne Shlay, noted that in the early- and mid-1980s redlining was especially severe in Baltimore (1987a, 1987b). The city's banks, particularly the largest, Maryland National Bank (Shlay, 1989), showed extreme bias in lending, favouring high-income White suburbs by a large margin over low-income inner city African-American neighbourhoods. Dedman (1989) analysed mortgage lending by Baltimore's savings and loans from 1985 to 1988 as part of a national study, and found that the local ratio of successful loan applications by Whites as compared to successful loan applications by African-Americans exceeded the national average (which was more than two-to-one). Such discriminatory bias was one of the prime motivators - but not the only one - of the next round of popular resistance to financial capital.

In the mid-summer of 1986, Baltimore community leaders began an unprecedented organising effort, the Maryland Alliance for Responsible Investment (MARI). More than 150 people, representing all the major progressive constituencies in the city, attended MARI's founding convention ('Community and Capital') at the major local African-American university. The participation of activists from the civil rights, housing, community development, labour and student movements was a coalition-building feat, carried out with vigour by a talented populist organiser based at Maryland Citizen Action Coalition. Perhaps the most challenging task in such an effort, in Baltimore and elsewhere in the US, is ensuring active participation in and 'ownership' of the project by as many coalition partners as possible right from the beginning. With MARI, this was achieved early on, thanks to some very well-timed luck: a $438 million merger deal was announced between Maryland National Bank (MNB) and one of Washington, DC's largest in August 1986, which would increase MNB's asset size to $13 billion. As a result of this announcement, within three months of MARI's birth, its initial activist campaign began. It is useful to mention the political orientation of key MARI leaders who helped develop the MNB campaign and to examine that campaign in depth, exploring especially its internationalist components, before proceeding to a assessment of MARI's other projects and future prospects. The common threads that run through the politics of most of the two dozen MARI steering committee members are a commitment to multi-racialism and affirmative action, a populist anti-corporatism which has deep roots in US grassroots politics, and an internationalism that is well-developed in

some ways though not in others. While most of the leaders would label their
political predilections as progressive, some might say liberal and a few radical.
Their commitment to the politics of a broad, united front was not automatic in the
USA in the mid-1980s, but grew from disparate experiences in political organising.
The true social base of MARI is thus mixed, but perhaps of primary importance is
the group's racial justice message and focus on the aspirations of the African-
American middle class for mortgages, small business loans, and access to better
banking services in their neighbourhoods. The politics of MARI can be conceived
of as 'rainbow' in the sense that Jesse Jackson articulated in his presidential
campaigns. Indeed, the leaders of MARI represent the main constituencies that form
progressive rainbow politics at the local and national levels.

MARI versus Maryland National Bank

Using the leverage offered by the Community Reinvestment Act, MARI threatened
to intervene in MNB's merger application to the Federal Reserve on the grounds that
the bank was in violation of the anti-redlining law (the equivalent of a lawsuit can
be filed with the Federal Reserve against a bank, alleging discrimination). Knowing
that such leverage could cost the bank dearly, both in terms of the delay to its
expansion and the bad publicity that would be generated, MARI organisers polled
the community to assess its complaints about MNB and to develop demands that
could be made to its senior officers. In exchange for agreeing to MARI demands,
the bank would then not be subjected to the redlining lawsuit and other protest
actions.

Several issues arose in what became a four month campaign against MNB, and this
had the effect of encouraging a diverse and lively set of activists, organisers and
progressive leaders to join MARI and to commit time, energy and funds to its work.
The primary concern of MARI member organisations was redlining. From the
neighbourhoods of Baltimore, MNB received $390 million in deposits in 1985, but
its lending within the city was limited in volume, especially in low-income and
African-American areas. According to a MARI leaflet (1986)

"In the years 1981-1983 (the most recent years for which complete data are
available), MNB made only 124 mortgage loans in the city of Baltimore -
just 25 % of the bank's total mortgage lending in the metro area. And within
the city, lending was heavily biased: White areas received 71 per cent of the
loans, even though they represent only 34 per cent of the population;
predominantly Black neighborhoods received only 15 % of the loans, even

though they account for 46 % of the city's residents. Regardless of race, Baltimore's low- to moderate-income neighbourhoods received only 37 % of MNB's mortgages, even though they contain 65 % of the population."

And there were other criticisms of MNB business practices. MARI (1986) argued that the bank's high-priced deposit accounts were shutting low-income savers out of the retail banking market: "A November 1985 survey by Baltimore magazine compared the cost of services and accounts at ten major banks serving the Baltimore area. MNB ranked as either the most or second most expensive bank for every service fee and charge listed." MNB came under fire from the NAACP civil rights organisation because of its lack of high-ranking African-American officers and directors. MARI also complained about the bank's insufficient loyalty to the Maryland economy; in 1982, Maryland National Corporation (the bank's parent company) had moved its credit card operations to neighbouring Delaware in order to raise interest charges above the usury ceiling then in effect in Maryland. And other criticisms of the bank, especially from the AFL-CIO trade union federation, centred around MNB's role in the Maryland corporate power structure. At MARI's founding conference, the second-ranking local official of the AFL-CIO presented a populist manifesto against the power, scandals and vulnerability of financial markets, and he added some concerns of organised labour in Maryland. A corporate 'political action committee' (a special interest group which raises funds to give to politicians in exchange for favourable votes on key legislation) had recently formed in Annapolis for the sole purpose of attacking Maryland's pro-labour legislation. At the heart of the political action committee was MNB, and this prompted the AFL-CIO to begin organising a boycott of the bank. Later, the union federation instead chose the opportunity to work with MARI, join negotiations with MNB, and raise other labour demands (e.g., a commitment to using trade unionists rather than non-union companies for new bank construction projects, and a neutrality pledge if a union was to be organised at the bank).

In the course of analysing these issues, especially the lack of MNB lending in low-income areas, MARI researchers began to understand where the bank's investments were going. One area of special concern was MNB's international loan exposure, because it pointed up the vivid contrast between the bank's risk-averse inner city lending policy and its Third World lending. MARI (1986) concluded,

"MNB is heavily involved with the international debt crisis. MNB had more than $350 million in international loans as of December 1985, up from $296 million in 1984. This includes $94 million to Mexico, and $49 million to

Brazil. It is widely acknowledged that the $152 million in MNB loans to Latin America will never be paid back. The increasing load of international debt deprives Maryland of money that could be invested in jobs and community development."

MARI knew that the impact of $1 trillion in Third World external debt was felt not only by poor and working people in the Third World, but also by US producers of exports, especially in manufacturing. Because Latin American countries expanded their own exports - increasingly, from their light manufacturing industries - and curtailed their imports from US firms drastically, all in order to raise and preserve hard currency to repay the international banks, US companies and farms laid off more than one million workers in the early 1980s (Debt Crisis Network Working Group, 1986). In Baltimore, changes in the international division of labour had adversely affected the industrial and merchant sectors for many years, and the collaboration of Baltimore financial capital (led by MNB) in the destruction of local jobs was not taken lightly. By way of requesting the bank's endorsement of a then-controversial Third World debt relief proposal offered by Senator Bill Bradley (Democrat - New Jersey), MARI demanded that MNB recognise its role in the debt crisis as well as the need for debt relief (a radical concept at the time, considering the 1985 Baker Plan orientation towards new bank loans to the Third World). The Bradley Proposal, most importantly, placed the financial burden of debt relief on the banks themselves, rather than on the taxpayer.

MNB was not only exposed in Latin America, but had also made tens of millions of dollars in loans to repressive countries like South Korea ($79 million in exposure in 1984) and South Africa, whose artificially-low labour costs and exports undercut US production. This was made public at a time when Baltimore's student, religious and activist communities were focusing increased attention on the US role in supporting the South African economy. Among other loans, in 1973 MNB had participated in a highly controversial $50 million syndication to the South African Finance Ministry, which led to pickets and prompted the Baltimore Federation of Federal Credit Unions to close its account (Hauck *et al.*, 1983). In 1984 the bank still had $18 million in South African loans outstanding (JHU Coalition for a Free South Africa, 1986). The bank also maintained 'correspondent banking relationships' with the three major South African banks (Barclays, Standard and Volkskas), which enabled funds to be automatically transferred from Baltimore on behalf of international merchant clients. These relationships were initially denied by the bank, but college students from Johns Hopkins University investigating MNB learned of them and then wired money to South Africa, thus proving their existence. The students then formally joined MARI as part of their own strategy to put pressure on MNB; the bank had, at its peak, eleven of its directors serving as

Trustees of the university, most of them in leadership positions and fervently opposed to the students' demand that Hopkins sell its South Africa-related investments (Bond, 1987).

A month of vivid student demonstrations, including the construction of an anti-apartheid 'shanty' outside the bank headquarters, ultimately forced MNB to cut its South Africa ties in early November (*Washington Post*, 1986). Simultaneously with the student protest, formal negotiations between MARI and MNB had begun and were proceeding behind closed doors. In mid-November a breakthrough was reached. In exchange for the community's support of MNB's expansion into Washington, DC, MNB signed a five-year agreement that committed the bank's 'best efforts' to lending $50 million in low-income neighbourhoods at below-market interest rates; radically altered the bank's loan application practices and previously conservative standards for creditworthiness; set up an oversight committee for the agreement that included three MARI members; made available $50,000 annually in funding for community-based home loan counsellors through the bank's charitable contributions budget; increased MNB's affirmative action programmes for recruiting Black employees; created a new MNB 'lifeline' low-cost savings and checking account; contained an endorsement of the Bradley Proposal for bank-financed Third World debt relief; and sent notice to the rest of Baltimore financial capital that a new populist movement could make even the most powerful institution surrender concessions at the bargaining table (*Baltimore Sun*, 1986).

This is not to say that the MARI campaign against MNB was problem-free. There were disagreements over the role of the students, who were seen by some as a militant distraction from the more serious community development negotiating process. (The students failed, ultimately, in their efforts to win divestment of South Africa-related stocks at Johns Hopkins University.) And the decision to drop some of the labour-related demands at a crucial stage in the process may have weakened MARI's long-term attractiveness to trade unions. On the demands relating to MNB's international business, what seemed like solid victories may have been pyrrhic. MARI later learned that while MNB had cut its South Africa ties, its new Washington subsidiary hadn't. MNB's endorsement of the Bradley Proposal was not as contrary to its self-interest as originally assumed, since many regional banks with Third World exposure similar to MNB's (e.g. First Wachovia in North Carolina, First Bank of Boston, Provident in Philadelphia and Riggs in Washington) were simultaneously acting in various ways to reduce the perceived market value of Third World debt. This was done in order to harm the major New York banks, which both had much higher Third World debt exposure levels and represented the regional banks' most intense competition in an era of interstate banking expansion. Most importantly, the signing of the MARI-MNB agreement was only to be the first step in increasing community control of capital; its implementation would prove to be arduous as a result of MNB's intransigence on supplying support staff and on making prompt credit decisions. MARI meetings for the next three years were regularly devoted to finding creative ways to force the bank to comply with its undertaking, including threats of another formal intervention to the Federal Reserve.

'Thinking globally, acting locally': Expanding the campaign and MARI's alliances

Ultimately, MARI decided the only way to keep MNB and other financial institutions from considering the community group a 'paper tiger' was to remain on the attack and deepen the MARI agenda. One way to do this was through lobbying the handful of friendly legislators in the Maryland Statehouse in Annapolis and Baltimore's newly elected mayor Kurt Schmoke. MARI achieved small, highly compromised successes in 1987 and 1988 in efforts to gain a State Community Reinvestment Act, and in 1988 won a seat on the board of directors of Schmoke's underfunded and corporate-dominated Baltimore Community Development Bank.

Another step to shake up Baltimore's financial community was taken in a campaign against another bank, the (then) $30 billion North Carolina National Bank (NCNB) which was acquiring a small Baltimore bank. The campaign against NCNB, though not initially successful in arriving at an agreement, did raise consciousness, address new issues and include new constituencies. A rally attracting more than a thousand people was held at NCNB's Baltimore headquarters in May 1987, eloquently addressed by Jesse Jackson. For the first time, MARI raised the issue of bank ties to repressive regimes in Central America, having found documentation of NCNB financing of helicopter sales to Guatemala and textile factory equipment to El Salvador. The attendance of exiled Guatemalan labour leader Frank LaRue at the demonstration with Jackson prompted support from local anti-US intervention activists. The anti-apartheid groups in Baltimore joined in, since NCNB had very strong South Africa connections, as one of just three US banks ever to have an office in that country. In 1985, NCNB's chairman was quoted in Charlotte's main newspaper as saying, "South Africa's a wonderful place. I love it ... I grew up in a segregated society and that didn't kill anyone."

At the May 1987 demonstration, Jackson called on NCNB to "redline South Africa, and greenline inner city Baltimore," and endorsed more 'street heat' against the bank. The local offices of the United Auto Workers and United Steel Workers unions joined MARI against NCNB on the grounds that the bank's lead position in a $200 million loan to Ford Motor Company for a new car plant in Mexico would cost their members' jobs. The Amalgamated Clothing and Textile Workers Union objected to the decline in NCNB loans to the North Carolina textile industry at the same time El Salvador and other countries with repressive labour practices were getting NCNB textile-related loans. The American Baptist Churches had already filed shareholder resolutions against NCNB at annual meetings, calling for an examination of the human rights implications of such loans, and their national office supported the MARI campaign. Although MARI ultimately reached an agreement on the community development issues in late 1988, the international issues - especially the South Africa ties - remain on the agenda.

Thus during its first three years, MARI employed a variety of programmes, strategies and tactics. Alternative politics is characteristically experimental in nature, yet there was, in the political trajectory of MARI, a logic of purposive collective action that corresponded quite closely to the objective conditions imposed by the explosion of the Baltimore (and global) financial sector. MARI's first three-year period contained victories and defeats for the organisation, but what is most important to consider is MARI's desire to address some of the major global and local manifestations of the financial explosion. It is in the struggle for community control of capital in Baltimore, as much as in any setting in alternative inner city politics in the USA in the 1980s, that the notion of 'thinking globally, acting locally' has its concrete expression.

Like many such efforts across the USA, MARI began with a populist anti-corporate politics which energised its participants. Its internationalist consciousness set it at the cutting edge of the community reinvestment movement in the US, even if the group's awareness of international capital flows occasionally fed protectionist impulses. MARI's subsequent attempt to gain a self-consciously coopted position in the Baltimore power structure through lobbying and participation in the Community Development Bank is not a bad sign for, as Manuel Castells notes, when grassroots movements win,

"their programmes (and sometimes their leaders) are institutionalised. Institutions become reformed, but social challenges are integrated. This is a positive process of social change, though one that does not exhaust the potentials of urban (or other) movements". (1985, p60)

Castells (1985, p61) calls this "the productive fading away of social movements, which have been 'betrayed' and fulfilled at the same time".

MARI's work is by no means done, nor can the group rest on its laurels. Ahead lies the enormous task of raising consciousness about the power and fragility of financial institutions throughout Baltimore's population. In tackling this role, MARI is poised actively to search out the larger and ultimately more confrontational aspects of the financial explosion. In this latter category are the 1989 S&L crisis (anticipated to last well into the 1990s); the role of financial institutions in forcing wage cuts and plant closings on the employees of overindebted companies; the coming wave of corporate and consumer bankruptcies; the risky new activities of banks engaged in 'off balance sheet transactions' (e.g. currency and interest rate swaps, commitments and contingencies, options, etc.); the entry of banks into the stock market; the shift of manufacturing firms' capital into financial functions (e.g. General Motors into home mortgages and Ford into S&Ls); the crisis in pension funds etc.

MARI has increasing numbers of allies for such campaigns. The Baltimore Rainbow Coalition advanced a programme for a municipal insurance company, with assets to consist primarily of community development investments (along the lines suggested by Jackson in his 1988 presidential campaign). The Mid-Atlantic Coalition for Responsible Investment, a church-based corporate responsibility lobbying group, has been working closely with MARI on South Africa issues. A coalition of community reinvestment groups like MARI throughout the South-East, organised by the Charlotte-based populist Southern Finance Project, began developing strategy for an unprecedented region-wide campaign against several financial institutions in 1988. MARI also maintained close ties with its Washington, DC equivalent, the Metro Area Fair Banking Coalition. Most significantly, MARI joined a national coalition effort, the Financial Democracy Campaign (based at the Institute for Southern Studies and the Association of Community Organizations for Reform Now [ACORN]), which in 1989 signed up hundreds of progressive organisational endorsements, tackled the S&L crisis with some success, and attracted to its leadership Jackson and the populist folk hero, Texas Agricultural Commmissioner Jim Hightower (Bond, 1989a).

Though these are extremely promising alliances, MARI cannot be satisfied with this level of networking and regional/national activities, because in the near future Baltimore financial capital will be subject to much stronger international influences than ever before. The early 1990s will witness investors from Singapore, Malaysia, Hong Kong and Australia sinking in excess of $100 million into the Inner Harbor as part of a $600 million highly speculative project in the former Bethlehem Steel Corporation shipyard. Already by 1989, Bangkok Bank of Thailand had lent $30 million towards the completion of 1,590 condos and 200,000 feet of shopping and office space in what is considered an overbuilt location. The final Harborview complex will include six towers higher than 20 stories, according to the 1987 master plan (Gunts, 1988). And in another major incursion by international capital, Allied Irish Banks completed its purchase of First Maryland Bancorp, the city's second largest with $6 billion in local assets, in late 1988.

To address these capital flows and all that they represent, MARI may need international, not merely national allies. Potential allies already exist, in nascent forms. For example, responding to the recent economic turmoil caused by the international debt crisis, there have been widespread Third World populist revolts against financial capital, some well organised (Walton, 1987). And indeed there are new organisations in Latin America, the Philippines and across Europe springing from the resistance to international financial capital with which MARI may at some point develop working links (George, 1988; Potter, 1988). But even MARI's internationalist activism is, for now, mainly locally oriented and self-interested, based as it is on using banks' international ties to taint them with racism, in the case of South Africa, or to suggest they are not sufficiently patriotic, as with the NCNB loan to Ford in Mexico. It is difficult enough for MARI to think globally and act locally, and so to act globally as well - truly in the interests of the poor and working people of the world - may stretch the limits of even this innovative organisation.

But objective conditions may force the issue. As Harvey puts it,

> "The arrival of Citibank and the Bank of Bangkok suggests that the 'third worldisation' of Baltimore at the hands of international finance capital is surely at hand, unless some sort of coalition, a rainbow coalition perhaps, can be built that will turn the rot beneath the glitter into the rich seed-bed of an alternative social movement." (1987, p22)

To arrive at such a coalition and social movement, the contestation of control over local capital flows must intensify. And the alternative politics of the inner city exemplified by Baltimore's struggles against financial capital must be reproduced elsewhere. For as urban managers have learned, the overarching constraints of financial capital enforce upon the urban economy an entrepreneurialism and competition in laxity that mobile forms of financial capital find easy to take advantage of. It is therefore appropriate to conclude with some reflections on the prospects for an alternative politics of the inner city, like that of MARI, to develop simultaneously elsewhere. The issue is to what degree the Baltimore experience is (and should be) generalisable, and the exploration of this question revisits some recent debates about urban politics and social movements.

THE POTENTIAL FOR EXPANDING URBAN POLITICAL RESISTANCE TO THE FINANCIAL EXPLOSION

The National Community Resistance Movement

The combination of the financial explosion with "the resurrection of locality in an age of hyperspace," as Erik Swyngedouw (1989, pp25-6) terms the recent period,

> "resulted in the formation of a multi-nodal spatial system of control and decision-making and a compressed spatial system on the one hand and of a highly divergent mosaic of interconnected places on the other... In the age of hyperspace, in which money can flow 'at the twinkle of an eye' from one fragmented place to another as the Starship Enterprise moves at starspeed from one end of the galaxy to another, locality again becomes the place of regulating daily social and economic life in the face of a global accumulation process."

How fragmented, how particular, then, is the Baltimore experience of local resistance to the regulatory grip of financial capital? Surprisingly, MARI is not terribly unusual. Since the pathbreaking early-1970s organising of Chicago-based National People's Action won passage of several federal anti-redlining statutes, the community reinvestment movement has blossomed. It is true that macroeconomic conditions have had much to do with this, and not always in the manner expected: McCarthy finds that

> "As interest rates decline, [US neighbourhood] activism increases, and as interest rates rise, activism decreases." (1981, p119)

By most accounts, it was the increased interstate banking mergers and acquisitions beginning in 1984 that spurred the dramatic rise in community reinvestment campaigns. Local chapters of the national community group ACORN alone filed several dozen lawsuits annually against banks during the mid- and late-1980s. There are more than one hundred independent community reinvestment coalitions throughout the USA like MARI, coalitions which have as roots thousands of campaigns for better low-income housing and equitable community economic development (Bradford and Schersten, 1985). Even major trade unions - the United Mine Workers, the International Paper Workers, the Amalgamated Clothing and Textile Workers, the Service Employees International Union, the Hotel Employees and Restaurant Employees, and others - are signing on, combining their community support work with efforts to target the banks which provide crucial financial support to hostile companies. Organised labour has also begun a variety of job retention programmes which rely on the community control of capital philosophy, instead of leaving local economic development strategies solely to their metropolitan growth machines (Swinney, 1989).

Some major victories have been won in recent years, including a Chicago Community Reinvestment Alliance effort that gained $120 million in concessions from First National of Chicago, a $350 million seven-year commitment from the Crocker-Wells Fargo merger in California, and a Pittsburgh campaign which gained $135 million from Pittsburgh National Bank. All told, the community reinvestment movement has won more than $5 billion in lending concessions for low-income areas during the 1980s, according to the Washington, DC-based Centre for Community Change, which helps co-ordinate bank campaigns across the USA (Centre for Community Change, 1988). Some of the funding, especially below-market lump-sum loans, has been targeted at direct community credit institutions such as community development credit unions (loosely organised by the National Federation of Community Development Credit Unions in Brooklyn, NY) or community loan funds (organised by the Greenfield, Massachusetts-based Institute for Community Economics). Experiences with banks such as MNB which promise $50 million or more in loans but are hesitant to follow through (or if they do, enthusiastically promote gentrification) have spurred the community reinvestment movement to go further in demanding from banks formal community control, and actually gaining access to bank advisory boards to administer the loan concessions.

These groups, especially in their aggregate (and organised with trade unions and consumer activists in 1989 as the Financial Democracy Campaign), have reached a stage of consciousness and action a step beyond classic urban movements of local control and self-management, since they make demands not solely around 'collective consumption' (e.g. increased housing, transportation, education, services, etc. normally achieved through challenging the state) but in the much larger arena where capital and community meet. What is new, argues Susan Fainstein, is that

"Community activists of the 1980s have an increasingly sophisticated view of the relationship between the productive economy and the condition of their localities. They have therefore sought ways of escaping the limits imposed by the vulnerability of cities in relation to the private sector." (1987, p329)

Those limits can be overcome through a variety of mechanisms; the diverse programmes, strategies and tactics of MARI - with street campaigns, legislative battles and alternative institution-building - attest to the possibilities.

There are caveats to these campaigns, of course, that apply across the board in alternative urban politics: mainly that there tends to be a profusion of middle class leadership (Pickvance, 1985, p43); that stultifying bureaucratic procedures such as bank merger litigation represents a classic routinisation of politics (Reintges, 1989; Oberschall, 1979); and that the community-oriented nature of such politics detracts from larger struggles for social justice. Castells (1983, p329) raises (and answers) the question:

"Why the emphasis on local communities? Have people not understood that they need an international working class movement to oppose the multinational corporations, a strong, democratic parliament, reinforced by participatory democracy, to control the centralised state, and a multiple, interactive communication system to use the new technologies of the media to express (not to suppress) the cultural diversity of society? Why, instead of choosing the right ones, do people insist on aiming at the local targets? For the simple reason, that, according to available information, people appear to have no other choice."

What the MARI experience suggests, however, is that 'no other choice' is not a satisfactory response, given the international nature of the forces that are brought to bear upon the urban form during the financial explosion. Naturally, there are other internationalist efforts in progress in the USA which address the 'hyperspace' problem, ranging from trade union internationalism (International Labor Rights Working Group, 1988) to formal sister city programmes (Bulletin of Municipal Foreign Policy), to other creative community statements of solidarity (Benjamin, 1988). And in addition to MARI, groups in Philadelphia, Brooklyn, Massachusetts and Chicago are linking the redlining campaigns to international financial issues such as loans to South Africa, the Third World debt crisis, bank ties to Central America, and drug money laundering.

Ultimately, of course, financial institutions are most vulnerable on issues relating to their business practices at home. It is there they are most sensitive to adverse publicity, since the only major difference between retail banks is the effectiveness of their marketing (location of branches matters much less since the advent of automatic teller machines). Hence, colourful protests and picket lines can make a big difference. It is also in the local (and especially inner city) setting that the greatest concentration of financial industry power can be observed. Harvey (1985, p88) contends that urbanism has "been transformed from an expression of the production needs of the industrialist to an expression of the controlled power of finance capital, backed by the power of the state, over the totality of the production process", which would include, undoubtedly, the reproduction process and attendant community-based conflicts. If this is true, and the evidence of the impact of the financial explosion on the inner city in Baltimore and elsewhere is compelling, then it is important to conceive of the forces struggling for community control of capital, linked with trade unions in corporate campaigns, as perhaps, ultimately, the greatest challenge that can be offered in the current context to capital and the political power it exercises. "The questions arise", insists Goldstein (1980, p150), "of whether community economic development can: 1) successfully produce qualitative improvements in the objective economic conditions of the working class and the poor; 2) produce 'nonreformist' reforms in the road toward socialism; and 3) if it can, under what conditions?"

The end of the financial explosion? From community control of capital to political economic transformation

There are at least four reasons why an alternative politics of the inner city, and of society at large, can expect to make substantial headway on these questions by expanding globally informed attacks, like MARI's, on local financial capital. First, the consciousness-raising aspects of the activist critique of the financial explosion are vital to any further political economic transformation, especially since, as Michael Smith puts it

"In the present US political economy the cultural acceptances of free-wheeling capitalism has assumed hegemonic status. The symbolism of 'public-private partnership' has elevated mundane corporate-government interplay into a sign of public interest and civic virtue." (1988, p108)

Smith seeks means to "focus popular consciousness on the social costs of 'public-private partnership' and the profit system itself"; of these costs surely the financial explosion and the power relations which it has created represent the system's most obvious Achilles heel.

Second, any chance for an alternative, radical inner city electoral project requires that growth machines and local financial power be wrested from financial institutions. Unlike Britain (Boddy and Fudge, 1984), the USA has limited experiences with municipal socialism (Clavel, 1986, describes the uneven and mainly unsatisfying results of progressive urban management in Cleveland, Chicago, Hartford, Berkeley, Santa Monica and Burlington). In various cities, some community forces have found ways of making productive alliances with local capital (Swanstrom, 1987), and, as in the case of Chicago, some alternative urban economic development has occurred in the nooks, crannies and margins of corporate power (Swinney, 1989; Giloth and Mier, 1989). But more typical, one might presume, would be the recent Cleveland experience in which the populist regime of Mayor Dennis Kucinich was aggressively undermined and ultimately destroyed by local banks (Logan and Molotch, 1987, p233). Financial capital may offer the major ideological and material opposition to progressive urban politics, bolstered in many cases by its stranglehold over Democratic Party officials (as described above). Evidence from Baltimore suggests that to counter this, and ultimately to dissociate labour and other potentially progressive forces (e.g., small business associations and civic groups) from the growth machine, the role of local financial capital in undermining the urban employment base through its international and explicitly speculative investments can be highlighted to great effect. Third, to restructure the economy in a more democratic way, community control of capital represents a seed-bed theme that can flower and grow under conditions created by progressive political activists in local and national campaigns against financial capital. If the seeds of the next mode of production are to be found in the decay of the old, then non-profit, co-operative, democratically controlled models of economic development should be examined closely. It is in this respect that Castells makes his strongest case for urban social movements. They do, he insists,

"produce new historical meaning - in the twilight zone of pretending to build within walls of a local community a new society they know to be unattainable. And they do so by nurturing the embryos of tomorrow's social movements within the local Utopias that urban movements have constructed in order never to surrender to barbarism." (1983, p331)

These economic embryos, whether they take the form of worker-owned firms, community development credit unions, housing cooperatives, community land trusts or community development corporations, are all under constant financial strain, especially given two very severe external constraints which arose during the 1980s: the end of government subsidies, and the rise in the real interest rate. If, as one reflection of the financial explosion, the fiscal crisis of the federal government continues (and there is no reason to believe that $200 billion-plus deficits can be resolved in the near future), the co-operative seed-bed will need to be cared for through the private financial markets. One way to do so is through the community reinvestment campaigns which make available millions of dollars in new funding, especially to established community development ventures, and often at below-market rates of interest. Another is organising a national development bank (Bowles, Gordon and Weisskopf, 1983) not only to support reindustrialisation in terms of plant and equipment, but also, as Jesse Jackson is lobbying for, to support community economic development in the inner city.

What this requires, obviously, is a major government commitment to socialising financial capital, not simply nationalising failing financial institutions, as happened to the hapless Continental Illinois Bank and to hundreds of other banks and savings and loans in recent years. In a technical sense, this generally happens in the wake of a collapse, as shareholders and bank management are bailed out at taxpayers' expense. But the issue then becomes not whether the government should enter the banking business, but to what end (and on what terms) the state-owned banks' assets are invested. That is where the alternative politics of struggle against financial capital comes into play. Thus, however ironically, the best prospects for supporting co-operative economic development lie in the very fragility of the financial system which is currently imposing sometimes insurmountable burdens on poor and working people across the globe.

Fourth and most significantly, the imperative of a dramatic devaluation of overaccumulated financial capital - in other words, the end of the financial explosion - behoves activists and researchers to examine the transformative possibilities that that suggests. In the 1990s, whichever route - deflation or inflation - is taken to reduce the $12 trillion-plus debt mountain, stock and bond markets, etc. down to a value commensurate with the underlying collateral base, there will be enormous social costs. Some preliminary indications of these have already been felt in the farm belt, Rust belt and energy regions of the USA, where hundreds of thousands have lost their livelihoods, and the Third World, where millions have died from 'structural adjustment'. As the devaluation of financial assets continues and intensifies, as it necessarily must (an inverted pyramid cannot be built indefinitely), more conservative constituencies - e.g. middle class students, defaulting already at a record pace (Bond, 1989d), and homeowners with two mortgages and unmanageable credit card and auto debt (*Left Business Observer*, 1989) - will finally see it in their objective interests to join campaigns against financial capital.

Hence the greatest current possibilities for political economic transformation in the USA are probably not at the point of production, in terms of classic labour-capital conflict, but rather through populist coalitions aimed, ultimately, at democratising the economy. Though occasionally infused with racism and jingoism, US populism has a strong progressive tradition (Goodwyn, 1978) and there are some vibrant modern variants (Boyte and Riessman, 1986): the Rainbow Coalition (Navarro, 1988), Alinskyite neighbourhood activism (Boyte, 1980), resurgent anti-corporate trade unionism (Moody, 1988), Citizen Action Coalition, etc. (Boyte, Booth and Max, 1986). As Swyngedouw (1989, pp28-9) argues, "radical city politics in the absence of a global strategy which deals with the new global shifts in the patterns of global capital accumulation ... results in a vicious spiral of interterritorial competition, a competitive struggle which can only be fought around the regulation of the production/consumption nexus." The leading US populists understand that alternative politics of the inner city in the 1990s will thus surely need to think globally, and to act both globally and locally, to transform both the inner city and the political economic order as a whole. John Walton (1987, p383) posits of recent, widespread Third World riots against austerity imposed by international financial capital, "All of the protests succeeded, in the sense of shaking their societies into alert appreciation of the regressive policy effects and deepening urban poverty. In the longer run mass action has initiated a political transformation that continues to the present and suggests a realignment of the global political economy." That is an ambitious claim, and if the movement for community control of capital in the USA merely achieved such luminous heights as shaking US society into an appreciation of the damaging effects of the financial explosion, that would be a significant and worthwhile accomplishment. But if the financial explosion does come to an end, however painfully for poor, working and middle-class people across the globe, then there is more here than meets the eye. The inevitable end of the financial explosion also implies the demise of the very motor of the global economy: the financial sector that in fact has sustained consumption and investment in the shaky productive sectors.

The end of the current financial explosion is likely to be, as in the early 1930s, the beginning of a period characterised by depression, extreme interterritorial competition, the formation of enormous geopolitical economic blocs (Fortress Europe 1992, the US-Canada-Western Hemisphere bloc, the ASEAN economies), and quite possibly war and the widespread resurgence of domestic fascist movements, thus giving an added air of urgency to the current campaigns for community control of capital. Whether an alternative politics of the inner city is the right place to prepare for the end of the financial explosion and for the reconstruction of a democratic political economy is an increasingly critical question, one that only praxis will answer.

CHAPTER 9

INNER CITY MYTHS AND ETHNIC ENTERPRISE:
Black entrepreneurship in Jamaica and the UK

Mel E. Thompson

This chapter reviews the nature of entrepreneurship and the process of business development amongst working class Jamaicans prior to their emigration to the UK. Secondly, an examination of their attempts at entrepreneurial pursuits as labour migrants in Britain is undertaken, to discover the extent to which these largely pre-industrial forms of entrepreneurship have been effectively transferred from Jamaica to Britain, and finally an attempt will be made to contextualise the discussions within the contemporary debates about Black businesses in Britain generally.

Empirical data - hereinafter referred to as West Midlands Interview Data (WMID) - forms the basis of analyses in the study. WMID comprises 45 case studies of post-War labour migrants from Jamaica to the UK. The fieldwork was undertaken between 1985 and 1987. In an attempt to present the data in an authentic, largely unedited form, the speakers' contributions are presented in Jamaican creole. Unfortunately, the writer lacks the linguistic expertise to present this in the correct written form; nevertheless, the information is reasonably accessible to the reader. (For translation purposes and general information on Jamaican creole see Cassidy, F.G. and LePage, R.B., 1967; Cassidy, F.G. 1971; Roberts, P.A., 1988; Devonish, H., 1986.)

With the help of these case studies an attempt is made to look at respondents whose life histories would place them amongst the working class capitalist group. Their social and economic backgrounds are given in an attempt to locate the motivating factors behind their choices of self-employment and capital accumulation.

These case histories are not intended to be representative of Afro-Caribbean immigrants to Britain generally. Nevertheless, as both higglers and artisans were greatly represented amongst immigrant groups from Jamaica, knowledge of their backgrounds in the periphery and later integration into the UK economy may at least enable some very broad generalisations to be made about Black working class entrepreneurship and immigrant business expertise transference.

THE NATURE OF ENTREPRENEURSHIP

Any attempt to define an 'entrepreneur' - the person - or 'entrepreneurship' - the activity - within the context of working class economic activities is fraught with problems. For example, to what extent can working class proprietorship be called entrepreneurship in a traditional nineteenth century context? Does entrepreneurship necessarily involve capitalistic or profit-oriented motives? What are the criteria used for defining successful entrepreneurship? Also, importantly, to what extent can it be assumed that 'successful' entrepreneurship is transferable from one societal setting to another?

Success of individual businesses is popularly believed to be dependent on the expertise of the founder, i.e. his/her educational and experiential background. In his Foreword to Carol Kennedy's (1980) work on entrepreneurs, Sir James Goldsmith, international business magnate, wrote:

> "Entrepreneurs come in all shapes and sizes. They straddle every class and every system of education. The common theme that links them is sound judgement, ambition, determination, capacity to assess and take risks, hard work, greed, fear and luck. .... On the whole, entrepreneurs are uneducated or self educated. Any analysis of successful entrepreneurs over the past 50 years in the West, shows that formal higher education must be a great disadvantage. .... Our Western education produces specialists whereas entrepreneurs must be generalists."

Such broad generalisations as these would certainly encompass WMID respondents.

Hugh Aitkin (1967), in exploring the subject of enterprise, found that "personifying the concept" of entrepreneurship was problematic. He believed that "no person could be an entrepreneur all of the time, [but] that a great variety of persons acted as entrepreneurs some of the time' He suggested therefore that it was "better ... to adjure all talk of the entrepreneur as a real person and concentrate on entrepreneurship as a category of action"

(1967, 203-4). Despite the above, Aitkin went on to reflect that because economic theory - of which the study of entrepreneurship forms a part - has increasingly tended towards impersonalisation, there is validity in studying the individual, because, "economics is ... the study of what people do, and that sometimes what a particular individual decides to do in a particular set of circumstances can have very important consequences." Care should, however, be taken not to deduce generalisations from such individual studies. In writing of the Industrial Revolution, Flinn (in Payne, 1974, p14), wrote that the individual we now refer to as 'entrepreneur'

"organised production. He it was who brought together the capital (his own or somebody else's) and the labour force, selected the most appropriate site for operations, chose the particular technologies of production to be employed, bargained for raw materials and found outlets for the finished product."

Today, with the presence of separate commercial, financial and managerial institutions, the task is less laborious for those entrepreneurs who can afford to pay. For others, corporate institutions now exist - funded by a mixture of charitable organisations, local as well as central authorities, together with professional bodies. Thus, ignorance in these areas need no longer impede entrepreneurial pursuits.

Flinn's descriptions of the eighteenth century entrepreneur seem to fit John Benson's (1983) definition of a 'penny capitalist'. For Benson, penny capitalism is predominantly a working class phenomenon, whereas Flinn's entrepreneur was accorded no specific class status although he/she was generally believed to be lower middle class. Benson wrote that the penny capitalist should be:

"responsible for the whole process, however small: from acquiring the necessary capital, choosing a site, bargaining for raw materials, deciding the working methods, and providing the tools, to finding a market for the finished product ... prepared to assume risks in the hope of making profits .... of working class origin ... (operating) on a small scale ... his capital, his turnover and his profits should all be measured, if not in pennies, then in pounds and shillings rather than in hundreds, thousands or tens of thousands of pounds." (1983, p4)

The penny capitalist then, he summarised, "is a man or woman who went into business on a small scale in the hope of profit (but with the possibility of loss) and made him/her self responsible for every facet of the enterprise". (1983, p5)

According to Benson, some 'penny capitalism' is defensive, an attempt to buffer oneself against the worse social and economic problems. In this eventuality, the 'capitalist' has a full-time job of some sort and any work in this area is additional; a provision for a 'rainy day'. This is distinct from the working class individual who seeks economic independence through the amassing of capital. In this respect, one could argue that apart from the scale of accumulation - which is often related to variables beyond the control of the individual - penny capitalists are not very different from so-called 'real traditional capitalists'. Benson rightly points out therefore that "it is conceptually and historically impossible to distinguish clearly penny capitalists from wage-labourers below and from the petty bourgeoisie above." (1983, p5)

WORKING CLASS ENTREPRENEURSHIP - A PRAGMATIC BID FOR SELF-ADVANCEMENT?

Before closer scrutiny of WMID's entrepreneurial involvement both in Jamaica and the UK it is necessary to explore the notion of entrepreneurship and the relationship between entrepreneurial activities and capitalism, within the context of limited employment or economic alternatives, in an institutionally racist society.

Henry Rosovsky (1967) refers to the existence of entrepreneurial activities in Russian serfdom, and suggested that these enterprises formed the third part of Russian entrepreneurship. Many serfs were able to amass enormous sums of money; thus Rosovsky mentions "a serf resident of Moscow who bought his freedom for 800,000 rubles" in the 1830s, and another who would have gladly given his house and fortune of 600,000 rubles to his lord in return for his freedom.

What is relevant to note here is that some individuals - albeit a small proportion who had ownership of factors of production, skills or expertise - have been able to use their enterprise to amass capital, even under the constraining hands of serfdom or slavery.

But conspicuous results of working class initiative and enterprise, while being worthy of acknowledgement, should not be used to hide the fact that it is only the smallest minority of people who are able to circumvent the repressiveness of serfdom, slavery, autocratic state governments, or inhumane factors inherent in capitalism to gain equitable economic rewards through entrepreneurial pursuits or waged labour. Further, without safeguards, these same 'achievers' will often replicate the repression they fought to escape.

Success stories, like those mentioned above are, therefore, to be treated as 'atypical'. To do less would lead to devaluation of the struggles of thousands of enterprising people who have somehow 'failed' to make the capitalist grade. Further, the end result of pedestalising 'achievers' (the individuals), as opposed to 'achievement' (interdependent actions over which the individual does not necessarily have full control) could divert into the area of biological determinism/social Darwinism. Such futile quests are, however, not of interest here. The chapter is concerned, rather, to emphasise some of the processes involved in working class bids for economic self-determination. The case studies will invariably emphasise both the dynamism of entrepreneurial activities, i.e. 'creative responses' or processes involved in economic development, as well as specific attributes of individuals. As has been pointed out, however, this latter point is not germane to the main area of concern.

WORKING CLASS ENTREPRENEURSHIP IN JAMAICA

Colonial economic policies throughout the British Caribbean left for Zin Henry a legacy of "economic pauperisation and destitution" (Henry, 1972, pp26-8). Henry further wrote:

> "Unemployment and under-employment in large dimensions, low productivity and extremely low wages, obsolete technology, managerial inefficiency, and a vast army of unskilled and semi-literate labour force were some of the dominant features of the region's economic inheritance after some 300 years of colonialism. Apart from economic destitution and social disorganisation of the society, native manpower resources were left stifled and under-developed; for managerial, executive and administrative functions were almost entirely the sole prerogative of colonial expatriates." (Henry, 1972)

Likewise, in his comments on the economic development of Jamaica, Owen Jefferson (1977) stressed that until the 1940s there was a scarcity in the growth of secondary industries in Jamaica and this was thought to have been conditioned by official attitudes from the Crown Colony period. In the nineteenth century, the British government was reluctant to allow the expansion of urban areas in the island as this was thought to lead eventually to the growth in secondary or manufacturing industries which would detract from Britain's ability to exploit the island as an export market for manufactured goods. Jefferson wrote:

"The active promotion of secondary industry was never a feature of official policy during the period of Crown Colony Government ... the export of agricultural products and the importation of almost all the Island's requirements of manufactured goods remained basically unchanged in the period prior to the nineteen forties." (1977)

The discouragement of industrial growth in Jamaica's pre-independence period is believed to be responsible for the continuing deformity of the island's manufacturing sector.

However, colonial 'discouragement' is only part of the story as far as Jamaican industrial under-development goes. Undoubtedly, some of the answers can be found in Ferrer's observation that:

"aside from the restrictions which the authorities imposed on colonial activities competing with those of the metropolis, the structure of the export sector, as well as the concentration of wealth, were the basic obstacles to the diversification of the internal productive structure and, therefore, to the consequent elevation of the technical and cultural levels of the population, the development of social groups connected with the evolution of the internal market, and the search for new lines of exportation free from the metropolitan authority. "

The seeds of economic dynamism in Jamaica - as in most other colonies - were to be found in its export sector. It was here that potential for local capital accumulation and investment lay, and conversely, it was here too that the factors which militated against the realisation of this potential for domestic economic expansion were to be found.

The demise of colonial discouragement of economic development was accompanied by immigrating foreign entrepreneurs, often through active colonial encouragement. In the main, therefore, entrepreneurial groups have not grown out of 'local creole stock', through traditional development of 'risk-takers'. In Jamaica, as in most societies, there has always existed a pool of indigenous 'proto-entrepreneurs', usually made up of artisans, traders and merchants. Amongst these are many who, if left unhindered by external and internal factors, would make the transition from basic petty entrepreneurs (penny capitalists) to become the industrialists and manufacturers within the country. However, many of these local 'would-be entrepreneurs' were either stifled out of existence or have been forced to remain in an embryonic stage in Jamaica, through the early presence of oligopolistic groups, many of whom were relative new-comers, though their presence dates back to the 1830s.

174

In Jamaica, the work of Stanley Reid has served to highlight the presence of twenty-one families in contemporary Jamaica amongst whom most of the country's wealth and accompanying power is concentrated. Contrary to the observations of economic historians that there is often a conflict of interests between the traditional landed groups and the emergent Industrial class, this was certainly not the case in Jamaica, where there was a 'marriage' of interests rather than conflict. Indeed, this merging of interests in their turn provided a 'supportive framework for the development of the corporate economy', which is today, dominated by members of the 'twenty-one families'. Through the economic institution of the corporate firm, the members of the ruling elite are able to concentrate their power and ownership. They have been able to gain· control of public subscriptions - raised through the Jamaican Stock Exchange - while at the same time, through their monopoly of directorships, they could effectively block public involvement and participation in decision making. The twenty-one families dominate in the construction industries, the manufacturing sector, banking, distributive trade, communications, agriculture, and through comprador affiliations, they often represent foreign interests in the mining sector. In 1972, these families accounted for 125 of the 219 directorships of firms and approximately 70 per cent of chairpersons' roles in the corporate firms. Further, efforts to retain power and control of economic interests have led these families to become heavily represented in legal and financial institutions as well as directly involved in politics.

It is not simply by chance that a proportionately significant number of the respondents are involved in different enterprising activities. Many were involved in petty businesses in Jamaica and migrated in an attempt to raise more capital to expand. Further, many who had not begun the enterprises in their home country profess to having had a desire to do business there, and for some, the actual realisation of their desires took place in the country of immigration.

Table 9.1 reveals that more than a third of male respondents and almost one-quarter female respondents in the WMID said they were fully self-employed in Jamaica. In addition to this, a similar proportion of the men and approximately a quarter of the women said they were engaged in entrepreneurial activities at the same time as working for an employer. The table also shows the types of activities in which respondents were engaged as own proprietors, working on either a full or a part-time basis.

Because this is a retrospective study, the evidence proffered by respondents revealed that individually none of their activities could be deemed to have had far-reaching effects outside their immediate households or districts, although through their collective accumulation of capital they undoubtedly contributed to the economy on a macro level. This latter point is not insignificant in the Jamaican context, as in periods of the most intense economic decline, it is the higglers and other small entrepreneurs who become bastions of the economy.

Table 9.1
Engagement in entrepreneurial activities in Jamaica prior to emigration

Types of Activities	Males N = 24	Females N = 21
Baking	2	1
Butchering	1	0
Cabinet making	3	0
Carpentry	2	0
Cook (Chinese food)	1	0
Dressmaking/Embroidery Sewing/Tailoring	2	8
Farming/Agriculturalist/Cultivator	16	2
Higglering/Paper bag making	0	4
Housepainting	2	0
Kindergarten teacher	0	2
Pipefitting	1	0
Roof-shingle making	1	0
Stone Masonry	2	0

Source: West Midlands Interview Data : 1984

The complexity of motivating forces underlying the unmistakably high involvement of the respondents in small proprietorships are worth exploring. This is because of their potential for micro as well as macro implications. There is a notion that the ambition for independence, which a small business seems to confer, is somehow basic to human nature; thus, entrepreneurial pursuits are deemed to be natural human responses. An extension of this idea could be that because migrants are often amongst the most enterprising section of any society, they enter the receiving country already imbued with entrepreneurial zeal. Consequently, one could logically expect them to become involved in any activity, including small businesses, which they believe to be capable of aiding their bid for capital accumulation and - for many - a quicker return home. Of course this would be a simplistic analysis of the situation in an economically backward and resource depleted geographical area, where migration is seen by the majority of people as the only escape valve. That some are able to amass enough capital to effect emigration often has little to do with individual enterprise but sometimes more to luck, often in the form of family land legacy.

Further, it could be argued that the above entrepreneurial pursuits are in line with a tradition of peasant and artisan proprietorship common throughout the world. In these cases, they are often purely pragmatic bids for economic survival in the midst of depleted resources and economic and social under-development.

The respondents' involvement in one-person activities reflected a number of complex inter-relating factors, comprising the need for economic self-subsistence in an absence of alternative employment outlet. Additionally, there was undoubtedly a strong desire to be one's own boss or to innovate.

Importantly, when considering working class proprietorships, it is necessary to discover the extent to which these activities could be viewed as a deterrent to working class cohesion, the potential to become tools for the state to prevent workers' solidarity. But the value of the oral histories which these interviews produced is less as the basis for generalisation than in the richness and complexities of the experiences that they reveal. Only by taking individual cases in depth can such subtleties be appreciated and so most of this chapter takes just six (anonymised) extracts as exemplary.

The Higgler

Name:	J. Tallock
Age:	61
Sex:	Female
D.o.b:	3.9.1923
Parish of origin:	St Catherine
Marital status:	Separated
Age of marriage:	35
No. of children born in Jamaica:	2
No. of children born in UK:	0
Formal education:	Elementary

Family background

Mrs Tallock was one of ten children, some twins, but only the first and last (herself) was alive at the time of the interview. Apart from her eldest sister, she only remembers one brother, who she believes was 30 years old when he died.

Hollow promises

On her mother's death, Mrs Tallock went to live with her eldest sister. Her father worked away from home and only returned intermittently, until he finally left - while respondent was very young. She said she didn't know where her father was, after - 'a woman pinched him'. This trauma she believes was responsible for her mother's eventual death.

Before he left, her father worked on a sugar estate, while at the same time he had his own 'ground' where he grew bananas, cocoa, sugar cane, peas, etc. Of her mother she said:

> "Mother used to make candy and my sister used to do peppermint cake ... and do a lotta baking, but I never put my hands to it. It's only since I came here and going to the Church dem ..."

Because Mrs Tallock's mother became ill when she was very young, she had to begin work at the very early age of 11 years. At that time, she said, she was the only person in the household who worked for wages.

Personal Work Experience

In commenting on her premature entry to the labour market, Mrs Tallock replied:-

> "I'm ashamed to say it ... I was eleven. Too young ... People in Jamaica, when I was a child growing up and they have their sons and daughters leave school, they would try their best to send them on for further education.
> And whatever trade ... the father had, they would love the boy to come and be a carpenter, and the mother, if she is a dressmaker, she would love the girl to come a dressmaker. But as the years goes by, the children grow up and they have their own ... they say I don't want to be a dressmaker. I would love to sew mi own clothes, but I want a profession, different from my mother. An then, you know, some parents grieve, they seh, we try our best and you don't want to have what we have. But some parents understand ... they try to read a lot, to get to understand the generation growing up after them. So, it wasn't a custom.
> People in Jamaica used to let their children go on until some of them ... if they don't get marry ... all twenty years old, they still going on ... and they (the parents), maintainin dem and sending dem to College, and anything dey want, an where deh want to go. We used to have scholarship in Jamaica and children at 11, used to get di scholarship ... somadem go to America for certain period and come back..."

Asked about how much money she received as her first wage and about the nature of the job, she replied:

> "My first wage was five shillings for the week ... that's one shilling a day. ... I was young, but I was very quick because ... learning to read, I was very quick at

it. If you tell me anything, I don't forget it, maybe I couldn't write properly, and do figures properly, but I was quick. So when my mother took ill, and I went out to work, her friend took her down to St Thomas for a change, for we were living in Portland when my father leave St Catherine and go to work.... and dis morning we went out to a place ... it's still there ... call Stokes Hall property, to look for work, and there were big women there .. I was di only chile ... an each person get a bag-and-a-half a manure ... you know ... dat's a day's work .. you got to done dat within di day ... put it aroun di banana root."

At her mother's death she went to live with her sister and to work with a lady, doing domestic work. She did not stay long because, according to her, "they didn't treat mi very good." Consequently she went to live in Kingston in an attempt to obtain work. Of this period she reminisced:

R. After I leave my sister and went to Kingston, I started to do domestic work. Three of us live in one room... we didn't have nothing, none of us, for we were young girls.

Q. Did you know any of them before?

R. No, we just meet ... If you living with somebody, and yu fed up of di people ... 'cause you are not free, an yu can find two people... But since some people is very unfair, yu couldn't settle down until yu find three of you heading di same way ... dat is when we settle down.

Yu don't have wardrobes an all dat, yu just have yu clothes in suitcases... an we get board ... piece of board and make like a shelf. Maybe you have a job an I don't have a job ... an di other one have a job .... so if you two are working an I don't have a job yet, I do all di cooking. Maybe di domestic place yu work, yu don't have to come home an eat... but like yu have yu Sunday off .... we make big dinner, and keep di place tidy. We only had one cot... one cot share between us.

Q. When you say cot ... what do you mean?

R. Just a bed ... yu know di folding ... dose are made from canvas. If yu put it up high it comes small ... but if yu put it low, yu wide it out. .... But we all don' sleep on di one cot the same night. We share it .... one would be on di floor two in di cot ... or maybe two on di floor ... for if some of you are big, yu can't hold on it. If you have a visitor ... an your visitor is coming to visit you, we have the room tidy ... wi put up wi little table ... for you see ... you might buy di table ... I buy di chair, and di other one buy di cot ... so wi tidy the room an as soon as your visitor come ... we are off .... you see ... we may go to the theatre .... or walk about town, go to the park ... and when the visitor leave ... you know where wi are, to come an fetch us. So we didn't spy on each other, we just live an share. For no men nevva come to sleep ... we were just young girls ... visitor come an go. An if one should survive an leave and go and gawn to a little home of their home, we stay we two ... or get somebody else.

Q. What other type of work did you do in Jamaica?

R. I were in Town and I was working, and afterward I lost my job, I didn't have a job, and dis man made drinks ... and at the Racecourse he employ three of us ... I and a nex' girl and a boy. But the boy is the one dat is responsible for di money. He stand on the stan and we go around through the race-course, we make di drinks ... like ice in di glass ... and den pour di syrup in. So di money we had on us, dats all di money take back to di man for the bwoy run off wid di res'. So we had was to sen call di man, and him come an ... says he's not going to pay us because we mus know what happen.

Well I was ruthless! The other girl start crying, but I was ruthless!....So I says O.K. ... I seh to her you don' cry, come along ... and we go outside and si a policeman ... and we told it to the policeman and he says alright let's go.... and we went in and seh to di man ... you got to pay dem because deh didn't steal anything .. they could have gone as well. You know how much he gave us? Seven shilling! (instead of ten shillings). I give her a half an I took half .. an she went away crying, but I took mine and I go home and I said to di other girls .... "Well I get let down today .. di man rob us."... An I don' want to go back an do no domestic work ... I fed up a getting up early and running morning time ... and it was only cheap, it was only three shilling a week.

It's only when Bustamante come about in Jamaica before wages just gradually improve ... and di people get scared ... so if yu working with dem and you are a good worker an yu seh to dem well I'm going to bring my Union, deh quickly says "Well, how much more do you want?" You can tell dem any amount, deh pay ... cause deh was scared!

Q. Were you in the Union then?

R. No, we weren't in no Union! Nobody was in no Union, but as di Union come about, after '38, you know, the Uprising. [the employers] would seh to you "Are you a Labour Party member ?" "Yes", deh don' give you di job! ... So I'd seh (threateningly) "yu have di work ... an alright ... alright ... I'm going back to Town!!" By di time yu reach di gate dem call yu back ... yu actually black-mailing dem ... 'cause deh get scared, for dis ting deh didn't know about. An den everybody start to get brave an talk back ... for (before) yu wouldn't talk ... yu open yu mouth deh jus throw you out!

So I took my three and six and I went home, and I said to the girls, I'm going to do some higglering with my three and six. They laugh me to scorn, it was fun.

Anyhow, there was this man I knew from St Thomas, his wife run a little lodging house, but he drinks a lot, and he was drunk the day and walking through the market and the girls deh have deh tings put out an he stand on it ... mash up di tomatoe ... an they nearly kill him! I had was to go an ask how much it was I'll pay for it. Although he was drunk, he nevva forget ... and then I only had that three an six dat Sunday night an I went in di market, an he came in wid a big truck load of bananas. Everybody was buying ... everybody buying. An I said to miself, I would love to get some a dat, because it was scarce ... an dat would be a good start.

And I stand up deh and I see one a di chap an I seh to him ... "How much banana I can get for dis three-an-six?" Him seh maybe you'll get a bunch ... And he [the man she had helped] saw mi talking to di fellow, and when the fellow move off, the fellow went to him an mus be ask him if he could give me bout two for the three-an-six. "And he said who is she?" An him come up and said, "Oh I know her, give her what she want".

I seh, "No ... I got only three-an-six." He seh "Yes, you save my life." So, they give me twenty-five stem, an dat was twenty five shilling. And a lady said to mi, everybody gwine to waan buy dem whole ... don't sell dem. Daylight now ... and the higglers coming in, everybody coming in, restaurant people coming in, cook-shop people coming in ... no banana. Di others dat have, they were big higglers an they wouldn't sell dem ...

And she had some an she started to cut dem up and sell dem, an when she almost finish she said "I'll help you" She said if anybody want a whole bunch sell dem one bunch fi five shilling. While it was over-charging, but they don' have any so they'll buy it.

When it all finish I had about fifty shilling ... and I look for him, and he was going home Monday evening and I look for him an pay him, an he said, "yu sure you didn't borrow dis money?" ... And ever since ... when he come to di market, he seh to [the higglers], whatever yu have sell her, if she don't have any money give it to her, if she can't pay yu when yu going, I'll pay, and dat's where I started ... and God really bless me ... I didn't realise it at dat time, but him really bless me.

They had Banana Depot and deh used to sell di banana to di poorer people, you know, but yu can't get more than one bunch, an it was still scarce. An dat day now, I an my frien went up. We took the tram, an a hand-cart chap come after us. And when we get dere, it was about four different banana depot ... not near to each other. So di girl seh to me, "but you can't get more than one, an I can't get more than one."..... I see dis young man and I seh "Yu buying?", and him seh no him waiting fi him mother, I seh "You get in di queue an buy mi one.... the other little one seh,"I'll buy yu one Miss ..." And when I finish up from dere ... we go di other place ... mine yu, we have to give dem little money, yu know, an when I finish I get a whole hand-cart full ... about thirty stem [bunches]. We come off at Orange Street, near di Park and we start to walk from dere to Coronation Market, and crowd follow us ... Banana was very scarce.

Mrs Tallock eventually left the room which she shared with the two other girls and went to live in Trench Pen, possibly the most notorious slum area of Kingston (now called Trench Town). She acquired a room and was allowed to set up a stall at the front of the house - just inside the fence. From here she started to sell coal, wood and market goods such as fruits and vegetables.

Mrs Tallock noticed that many people on their way from work would wish to purchase some coal, but often there were no bags, so she started to make her own paper bags. To do this, she used to purchase large paper bags in which wholesale granulated sugar were imported, to make up her bags. She also found an additional source at the Condensary where dried milk was imported in multi-layered paper bags. The person at the Condensary, the middle-man who used to supply the bags, fell off a truck and died which meant that she had problems with supply. Her supplier's successor was not as keen to supply her with the dried milk bags, and after a delegation of local higglers approached her and asked whether she would be prepared to go directly to the Condensary, rather than through this supplier, she acquiesced. Mrs Tallock further stated that during shortage of supply - at various times - she approached the Cement Factory for their bags. She stressed that as long as the inside bag was removed and either discarded or cleaned and used to wrap things where food contamination was not a threat; the remaining layers of the bags were suitable to be made into smaller bags, fit for any commodity.

Of the time when she was approached by other higglers to purchase from the Condensary, Mrs Tallock said:

> "I buy must be two thousand [damaged bags were given to her]. And he said how I gwine carry it? I seh, well I don't have no transportation, but I'll take a half ... and dere was something going into Spanish Town, and I stop at di market and den get a taxi an go over.
>
> An dat's how I started there, an when I couldn't go in, I could ring him and when the milk truck is coming in, he send the bags on the milk truck, and they put dem off at Boys Town, and di hand-cart man bring dem up.
>
> Dose girls dat encourage mi to do it, afta when everybody si dem getting dese bags ... not di cement bags now ... dese are clean bags, and deh seh "Who did yu buy dat bag from?" And they might say "Miss Jane .... mi buy dem from Miss Jane." And it go on until all di customer come. So I didn't have to take it into Town. I just take it and carry it to mi house, and deh come for it."

For a while, Mrs Tallock only sold bags in the market, though she continued to sell food at her house. Later on she decided to diversify into other areas such as clothes making. At this stage, she no longer made paper bags. Instead, she continued to purchase the large ones in bulk and sold them to the group of higglers who had encouraged her to cut out the middle-man.

In addition, there was a group of young girls who used to help her to sew and do odd jobs, often unpaid. She decided, therefore, to assist by encouraging them to purchase some of the large bags from her and make up their own small bags. These small bags she then took with her to market and sold them for the girls. This was shrewd action on her part as it ensured that firstly, she was able to increase the demand for her large milk bags. Secondly, by offering to sell the made-up bags for the girls, they would continue to offer her their labour in a non-remunerative relationship; as long as they had some money coming into their hands each week, the pressure of seeking work would be reduced. Of course, for many of them it would have been almost impossible to obtain work, and if they did the wages would be very small, possibly no more than they received from the sale of their bags. Mrs Tallock said she used to sell "thousands and thousands of bags", going to the market from Friday night to Saturday until about 4.00 p.m. It was there that she got the idea to start making ready-made clothes on a large scale, for indeed, she had been selling some previously, though on a small scale. Consequently, she purchased material from 'a Syrian man', and gave the materials to a lady who had:

> "a small business ... you wouldn't call it a factory ... 'cause it was right in her house ... but a very big room ... she have a big cutting table, and she sew for most of the stores in Town .... She make shirts, she don't make nothing but shirts. I used to take shirt material up to her. Like she going to cut four, five dozen shirt, the big material is spread down on the table, and she rest the pattern

on it and cut. When she cut all the pieces, she put them into bundle and tie them, so you that coming to sew now, all the pieces are there, and you fit the shirt, put the plain top on, pass it unto the next person, an dat one might just put the collar on ... the other one put the sleeve in, the other one put the cuff in ... an it go to the last one, they put the button holes."

I asked Mrs Tallock why she decided to give someone else the shirts to be made, when she herself could sew. She replied that it was too much for her to do, so by giving the order out, she would be able to get more shirts. This was especially pertinent:

"when we used to have sugar cane in Jamaica .... crop time ... and during that season, you got to go to the market Friday ... [and] Saturday you go to the cane piece to sell. So you got a lot more things to do, and I only had just one little hand machine, I hired .... I didn't buy one of mi own yet. I had help, yes ... sometime is free labour, the girls dem just come along, and should in case they see a bit of material and they love it, they can have it, so they just come and give their help. Some been paid, but they nevva bothered about being paid. What they want is just a blouse or a skirt ... and on Saturday evenings when I come back, they used to come to meet mi down the road when I get off the bus. Everybody carry something, and then everybody expecting something. It was quite helpful. The parents would come along on a Thursday evening (to help), for every Friday morning I leave fi di country, di truck will come early and pick all the baggage up and all di passengers will assemble at Spanish Town Road."

Mrs Tallock said that during cane cutting times traders from Kingston used to go to the sugar estates where they had a ready market. This is because people came from all over the country to obtain seasonal work on the estates. They did not go home until the cane cutting season was over; this she believed lasted for between two to three months, and although the workers would write to their families and send monies home, they themselves did not return until the end of the season. Consequently they lived in 'digs' and needed to purchase necessities such as food. Mrs Tallock reported that many higglers - at these times - took food from the town to the rural estates, especially for the finale of the crop season which she called "the back money pay bill", which sometimes lasted for three days. People from other estates would congregate at two estates where all the bonuses, pay rises etc. which were owing to the workers would be paid up, because although workers received a weekly wage, they did not get any outstanding back-pay until then. This period seemed to have been a jamboree for higglers, so trucks, cars and pedestrians would turn up at the estate gates with various commodities to sell. At that time, she said, "yu free to do what yu want to do ... yu sell a lot a mixture ... raw material and such delike".

On these occasions she used to sell under-pants and other ready made clothes. Some she made herself, some she bought, while still she gave out orders to others to make up garments for her. According to Mrs Tallock:

Most traders have a tailor, sometimes [they live] in town, sometimes is out in di country ... that you would buy yu material, buy all yu trimmings; yu take dem there on a Monday, and on a Thursday on yu way to market yu collect dem (the sewn garments)

Q. Your first wage was five shillings a week. Can you remember how much you were earning just before you came here from your selling?

R. I could get about £25.00 a week.

Q. You were earning £25.00 per week ... you didn't think that was exceptional?

R. I think that was good to the time ... it was the season we were living in. At dat time, if yu doing a business an you spen £100 and yu get through the stuff quickly an yu make a £50 profit, or if yu spen a £50 an yu make a £25 profit, dat is very good business in dose days..."

I asked Mrs Tallock about the work she has done since migrating to the UK. She said she came on a Tuesday and stayed at home for the rest of that week. On the following Monday, however, she went out to look for a job, and by Tuesday, one of the ladies in the home where she lived took her to a place where she had seen a notice advertising vacancies. She was offered the job on Wednesday and commenced work on the Thursday. She related her earliest labour experience as follows:

"It was a little factory behind *The Yorkshire* pub, call Rectam. It was only 2/6d an hour. They didn't keep week in hand, and they pay you di Friday. So I went to work di Thursday morning and di Friday I had di first day's pay and they took eight shillings out of that fi insurance ... I could nevva forget, an give mi thirteen shilling an three pence. And when I went home and open the thing I was mad ... I seh, 'den how they doan ask mi if they suppose to take this money? They said, "you will learn ... they doan ask yu nothing!
I work in dat job fi seven months ... It was 2/6d an hour, an yu work fi eight hours, an they took eight shillings out of all that, di insurance."

I asked her how she felt, bearing in mind that she could earn as much as £25.00 per week in Jamaica. She said:

"You could see the grief ... I cry every night! I wanted to go home ... Once my nephew wrote to me and ask me to sen him some clothes, dat mek mi cry worse ... I didn't have di money to buy it ... an I was angry an I write him an tell him seh I doan come here to pick up money off di street of Englan ... whe yu expect mi to get ... I only just come here, not only three months yet. I was angry man ... not because I didn't want to do it, but I doan have it. "

At the time of interview in 1984, respondent had a stall in a main City market where she sold ready-made clothes. Some of these she made herself, after obtaining a loan from a finance company to purchase an industrial machine. This she uses in her rented room in a shared house, as she does not own her own property in Britain. She has, however, been able to return to Jamaica to purchase a house with an acre of land.

Mel E. Thompson

AFRO-CARIBBEAN ENTREPRENEURIAL INVOLVEMENT IN THE UK

Generally the involvement of Afro-Caribbean people in business in the UK has not attracted much research attention until recently. This increased interest must be seen in the context of the government's attempt to turn the country into a nation of small businesses as a palliative for deindustrialisation.

There is a tendency to compare the apparent 'great success' of the 'Asians' with the 'underachievement' of Afro-Caribbean people in the area of business. Education, business expertise and putative 'natural ability' are often held as the main factors responsible for 'Asian' perceived supremacy in business.

There is evidence to show differential levels of educational attainment between Afro-Caribbean and Asian men, although conventionally Afro-Caribbean women have often been shown to achieve higher educational levels than both Afro-Caribbean men and Asian men and women. Ward and Jenkins (1984), when making comparisons to explain the apparent leadership of Asians above Afro-Caribbean people in the business world, specifically referred to the 1971 Census figures which highlighted Asian supremacy in qualification and positional attainment.

Many studies have identified factors in British educational provision as being partly blameworthy for this situation (see Swann (1985) and Eggleston (1984)). Notwithstanding this, the focus on education presupposes that formal educational achievement is the basis of business enterprises and success, a view which conflicts with many observations about numerous 'successful' entrepreneurs

Other factors which are believed to contribute to relatively poor Afro-Caribbean business performance, compared to 'Asians', include the fact that they number approximately one-third of the Asian population in Britain. Thus, in terms of controlling sections of the market through specific ethnic demands the 'Asians' are at an obvious numerical advantage. While this thesis may accurately describe the contemporary situation, which can be explained partly through geographical settlement - both in terms of work and residence, language and ethnic encapsulation - to be given long-term credibility, the thesis needs to assume that retailers have a monopoly over buyers in their own ethnic groups, that monopoly control cannot be effectively penetrated by 'non-group' persons and importantly, for the long term survival of the business, that cultural demands will remain inelastic.

None of the oral history respondents used in this work expressed an intention to engage in entrepreneurial activities in the UK but two-thirds of the males who were previously engaged in business ventures became involved in entrepreneurial pursuits after immigrating (Thompson, 1989). Likewise, just under one-third of women who were previously involved in entrepreneurial activities in Jamaica became similarly involved in the UK.

The enterprises that respondents became involved in ranged from the predictable such as grocers, barbers, bakers, market stall holders to the less predictable (off-licence partner, Holiday Magic). Scrutiny of the actual areas of businesses in the UK reveals that only three - the barber shop and the two bakeries - could be termed specifically 'ethnic' enterprises. The latter would be producing hard-dough bread, buns, patties etc., specifically for the Afro-Caribbean market, but increasingly being purchased by other groups, as people become more adventurous with their food. In the same way, the barber specialised in cutting Afro-Caribbean hair - predominantly males, but boasted that he had white clientele also, including, he stressed, a doctor from the hospital close to his barber's shop.

When questioned about the outcome of their activities in the UK, four-fifths of the men involved in enterprises said their businesses had failed, while only one-fifth could boast success. Of the women one-third said their businesses failed; another third said it was difficult to determine the level of success. This was because they did sewing for private individuals and payments were irregular. In fact, it was because of this that they had felt it necessary to seek alternative forms of work intermittently. Both market stall holders felt their businesses were successful. One of these stall holders sold clothes and she attributed unqualified success to her business. The other holder sold Afro-Caribbean food, and although she said her business was successful, she pointed out that at times she found it strenuous to make a living, competing against white market holders who also sold 'ethnic' food, and who she felt often resorted to under-cutting methods which she believed contributed to the lack of progress she was making.

Unlike the male respondents, none of the women reported being involved in any working class proprietorship activities. Instead they displayed stereotypical female entrepreneurial involvements of setting up grocery shop, market stall holders and home-sewing.

Both male and female respondents exhibited greater involvement in entrepreneurial activities prior to their emigration to the UK. Further, more than half the men and almost half the women intend to become engaged in entrepreneurial activities on their return to Jamaica.

186

Extracts from five case studies have been selected to indicate two successes and three failures as judged by respondents in their entrepreneurial pursuits. Extract A differs from the others in that rather than selling commodities or offering a service, the aim was specifically to own properties - this was to be the first of others. Not all the other four extracts chosen could, technically be regarded as typifying those which would normally be included in the enclave economy sector. Secondly, although most of their clientele may have been people of their own ethnic group, the extent to which respondents set out with the intention of exploiting this market is debatable. This was not ascertained during the interviews - except for one occasion where a respondent stressed that "Black people doesn't buy from Black people in dis country". This sentiment - often expressed previously - was believed to be based on the belief that Afro-Caribbean people charged more for their goods. No serious studies have been undertaken to test check this allegation. If, however, as the evidence from most respondents seems to confirm, proprietors from this ethnic group had to use their own savings or obtain expensive finance company loans to start their own businesses, it is not surprising that they were unable to engage in many price cutting exercises as the majority would be operating at a very low profit margin.

The enclave economy is capable of generating greater business success - at least in the short term - for ethnic minority groups than the mainstream sector (a point which will be developed later); this being the case, we can assume that those respondents whose business enterprises fell within this category were afforded a slight fillip in their entrepreneurial involvement in the UK. In order to obtain a fuller understanding of the types of businesses and the eventual outcome, we now turn to the respondents themselves for explanation.

1) Extract A

Respondent:	John Preece
Age:	49
Year of arrival in UK:	1955
Education:	Elementary
Employment in Jamaica:	Carpenter
Employment in UK:	Factory labourer for six months, then carpentry.

In answer to my query about his entrepreneurial attempts in the UK, Mr Preece had this to say:

"I went into a business and lost all mi money. I lost a thousand pound. We was trying to form a company ... and the head of it was in London ... We started very well and have one shop ... property like you know ... buying property..... the bloke grab up all di money and declare bankruptcy.

> We know dem from our own district back home ... it was quite a few of us really, ... 'bout thirty, an as far as I know, nobody get back any ... £1,000 each ... my brother ... was very much in it too. ... I dare say it would be more than £1,000 because I borrow some of the money from di bank and had was to pay everlasting interest on it. So it would be more than £1,000."

Mr Preece would no doubt be classified as a member of the working class and thus, he would more readily be placed amongst Benson's penny capitalists than the petty bourgeoisie. And yet, the enterprise in which he became involved - that is, purchasing property - was certainly not a typical working class entrepreneurial pursuit. This is not the first time that respondents reported involvement in business ventures which could not be termed 'penny capitalism'.

This supports the notion that attempts to localise and predict attributes and behavioural norms for any particular group, to found grand generalisations on ethnic differentiation, may be conceptually flawed when applied to specific groups. This is particularly true of migrant labourers, who are often classified as appendages, and unwelcome ones, of the indigenous working-class. Certainly, in terms of remuneration and vulnerability to exploitation, it is difficult to differentiate them from the working class. Their heritage as rural land-owning peasant farmers, and artisans, owners of factors of production, controlling the rhythm of work, variations in the innovative ways in which they earn their living, and in several cases employing others, mean that their aspirations and actions are often not strictly working-class, despite professed loyalties. It is, therefore, not surprising, but must be seen very much as within the tradition, to find many of these respondents purchasing properties - even as members of a co-operative - in their attempts to exploit money making possibilities. These, however, are not like the 'sophisticated' forms of capitalism where a moral obligation is often absent in pursuit of amassing a disproportionately higher return of capital from the initial outlay. Working class capitalists exploiting abilities are tempered by factors such as limitations of available resources, and the fact that often their markets are made up of friends, relatives and local people to whom they are well known and feel neighbourly obligations towards.

The extent to which the outcome of respondent A's business was a reflection of the lack of pertinent educational and experiential background can only be surmised. The respondent said that the business was declared bankrupt, although whether this was due to real business management problems or fraud is not known from the information given.

2) Extract B

Respondent:	Thomas Laston
Age:	68
Year of Arrival in UK:	1960
Education:	Elementary
Employment in Jamaica:	Agricultural worker, baker
Employment in UK:	Bottle stacking, metal grinding, furnace work

Mr Laston attempted to start a bakery shortly after arriving in the country. He had gained experience in this trade through his work in Jamaica. Unfortunately, he was forced to abort this effort after one month, after falling foul of the law when he attempted to do the baking in his own home, using his domestic facilities. The neighbours reported him to the Department of the Environment who compelled him to cease this activity. Of this ill-fated attempt, the respondent said:

"I nevva inna di country so long, fi know di whole routine a di ting ... plenty frien seh I should start again ... But, as cording to how it was situate ... I [decided to] work in di factory."

I asked the respondent whether he had to borrow any money to start up that bakery, but he said he and a friend undertook the task. They didn't buy any special equipment, he said, as they were only making buns and bread, and using their own stove at home. This clearly reveals the extent to which lack of business knowledge, including operational restrictions, inhibited entrepreneurial endeavours.

Mr Laston had been in a fortunate position to have expertise in one of the areas which could have thrived as an ethnic enclave business at a time when demand was virtually guaranteed. His expertise as a baker and the absence of many Afro-Caribbean bakeries, together with the fact that this area could not readily be supplied by existing indigenous suppliers, created an almost monopolistic market. The respondent very clearly realised the potential and hoped to utilise his expertise to exploit the situation.

While, undoubtedly, many similar businesses in various less developed countries are started that way, in Britain the presence of legal environmental restriction and vigilant neighbours prevented this. Their effort, while revealing business naivety in the UK context, is no doubt similar to how respondents would have operated, had they attempted a similar exercise 'back home'. Mr Laston and his friend attempted to start the business without resorting to external sources of funding or advice. This too is typical of working class entrepreneurial attempts in Jamaica.

Hollow promises

Even with the knowledge and accessibility to sources of funding in the UK, the extent to which these would have been utilised is debatable. Nevertheless, it is a fact that the majority of those early migrant labourers did not come from a tradition of seeking funding externally, other than what could be achieved by working with a partner. Importantly, too, in 1960s Britain, information regarding possible business funding was not readily available to the working class would-be entrepreneur/capitalist.

3) Extract C

Respondent:	Delores Dare
Age:	57
Year of arrival in UK:	1954
Education:	Elementary
Employment in Jamaica:	Assistant cook in a restaurant
Employment in U.K:	Grocery shop owner

I questioned Mrs Dare about her business ventures in the UK, to which she replied that she intermittently owned two grocery shops. The first was in Bordesley Green. Later she closed that and opened another in Handsworth. The first was on the main road, and the second, in Murdoch Road, Handsworth, though not as focal as the first, was nevertheless in a reasonably busy thoroughfare.

Mrs Dare said that she rented the premises in Bordesley Green and used their own savings to start the shop rather than seeking a loan. She also purchased a house in Hay Mills. The property in Handsworth had a house attached to it, so they obtained a loan from a finance company to purchase this property, but again, used their own savings to stock the shop.

The respondent said that in Bordesley Green she catered for the general public, rather than a purely Afro-Caribbean market. She felt, however, that the Bordesley Green business did not do very well for reasons explained below:

"I suppose is because there wasn't many houses ... is mostly shops on di main road ... there wasn't many people living dere, an they don't really have to come dat way. And to be honest wid yu, Black people doesn't support Black people in dis country ... they don't."

In answer to my query about whether she had English people buying from her shop, she replied:

"Not a lot, odd one and two. I used to do mostly delivery ... because it wasn't bright ... then we have friends, so we get quite a few customers ... the one and two odd one dat came in, we had to deliver it, so then, by doing so, we get more. But den, dat's why we left and went over to Murdoch Road.

It was better ... but I took ill an I had to left ... be at home, 'cause we had a house then, we bought another house over in Hay Mills. And then I was bad, an I was away for about three months, but then when I was a bit better, I had to close it down, because it was run-down.

My husband wasn't di business type, so then ... And then, as I said, even though dere was a lot of Black people down dere, if they do come to spen any money wid yu, they really moan because they said they can get it fi one-an-six down di Indian. If yu selling it fi one-an-nine ... But they doesn't realise, even though di Indian seh one-an-six, he charging dem one-an-nine, because he weighs it on di scale an he charge dem more ... but deh doan know, yu so. I know dat's what they do to get their money, yu see. Some tings dat they sell cheap, deh mus get deh money back some way ... they have to do it some other way.

But our people doesn't support us. If deh do, deh have to moan an groan, yu know, an seh when yu go home yu gwine show-off on dem."

The respondent thinks she may try to open a paper or sweet shop later on. She would prefer to do this rather than open another grocery shop because:

"Those tings, yu doan put the price on. When yu get sweets to buy, the price of someadem is on the jar, or the bag ... dat's the retail price. Papers and tings like dat, the price is on the paper, so yu doan get no argument. But when you've got to buy things dat you have got to put the prices on, you're in trouble!

I would have made good progress in the one in Handsworth, but because I was 'bad', di ole man let it run down. ... I wasn't even better properly, I went back, but I couldn't do it on my own, because I wasn't better ... so I had was to close it down.

I left from dere and went to find myself a job, and after I got di job I was only able to open it in di mornings and in di evenings. I let di little girl open it in di morning 'cause she was going to school over dat way, and when I finish work, I used to go over, but it gets a bit too much, so I just close it."

Mrs Dare perceived herself to have fought a losing battle against the adversities of an expensive finance company loan, unhelpful spouse, competition from local 'Indian' shop-keepers, lack of customer support generally and intense haggling from Afro-Caribbean customers (a traditional custom, though respondent believed they were tinged with petty jealousy). All these, coupled with illness, she believes were responsible for the decline of her business and its eventual failure.

5) Extract D

Respondent:	Sylvester Gill
Age:	52
Year of arrival in UK:	1957
Education:	Elementary
Employment in Jamaica:	Farming and barbering
Employment in UK:	Factory worker then self-employed barber

Mr Gill opened his barber shop in 1981 so that he could become fully self-employed. What is of particular significance in this - as with other cases - is the dual/multi-disciplinary nature of his work activities. He had been cutting hair on a part-time basis previously, both in Jamaica and the UK, while holding down a full time job. In the immigration periods of the 1950s and 1960s, when most migrants' wages were very low, barbers like Mr Gill, and other artisans who were able to provide a specialised service to their ethnic communities, benefited greatly. According to him:

"I used to do it part-time when I was working at Guest Keen for sixteen years ... so I have mi two job.
When I was on early morning at Guest Keen, I finish at 2.00 an I am here at di shop by half past two ... an I go on until about 6 - 7 ... sometimes 8.00 ... and sometimes after 8.00!
When I'm on afternoons, I get sleep ... I open 9.00 o'clock until roughly half one/quarter to two, to reach work fi two o'clock, an I work until half nine. So I used to do at least twelve, thirteen, fourteen hours a day! Sixteen years! An di last of it, I tink it was killing me, an I finally decide mi mind seh, 'one time yu pass dis worl, so finish wid one job, an when I was coming out of Guest Keen I smile'."

Mr Gill said he had no regrets, and that his customers came from every nationality, English, Chinese, Indians, West Indians. He said he had slight problems but that was to be expected. He further stressed:

I feel more at ease .... I go home every night at a decent time ... between about 8.00 o'clock. Mi food [eating time] ... it's more accurate, [unlike] when yu do shifts .... Feel better health wise. I used to be that tired that when I go home and as I have something to eat an look at the television for di longest 15 to 20 minutes ... I'm off sleeping.

Mr Gill said he used his personal savings in the UK to start his business. He also referred to the fact that he had sent to Jamaica for £1,100 because, as he said, he did not believe in hire purchase, though he accepts that for large purchases like a car, it may be necessary. He believes he will expand if he has the money.

5) Extract E

Respondent:	Agnes Frazer
Age:	55
Year of Arrival in UK:	1960
Education:	Elementary
Employment in Jamaica:	Domestic work, buying and selling

Mrs Frazer only worked for a very short time in the UK because she had children and stayed at home to rear them. When her husband was made redundant, she used £60 of his redundancy money to set up a stall in Birmingham's largest market, selling Afro-Caribbean dry food. She has never borrowed any money to assist in her business.

Mrs Frazer said her business was successful. This has to be qualified, however, because 'success' appeared to have been measured more on the fact that she had managed to keep the business going, rather than allow it to fold. When asked whether she was satisfied with the progress the business was making, she replied:

"No ... but ... we'll eat in grace. If I did have a brighter sale ... if I did get more support from the West Indies community.
A White chap in di market dat sell West Indian food ... He start before us, and sometime people will tell you how he handle the West Indians dem ... (but) deh crowd him ... he will even sell ten box a yam when you doan sell one.
He used to sell ... cheaper... we complain to the market man ... they doan find out how much he sell it for. We try to compete with him, yu know, to save di sale."

I asked Mrs Frazer whether she had actively encouraged people to purchase from her and she said no, although it is more than likely she would at least have shouted out her wares to customers, while she did higglering in Jamaica (buying and selling).

It is interesting to note that once again, the respondent expressed the belief that people of her own ethnic group do not give the degree of support she expects. It is clear that they almost all tended to assume the patronage of people of their own ethnic groups to the extent that no attempts were made to actively woo either them, or people from other groups. If Afro-Caribbean proprietors had a monopoly on their food trade this may have been logical. Bearing in mind, however, the fact that the wholesalers and largest retailers both in the markets and the local shops are nearly always White, or from one of the South-East Asian groups, many comparatively more able to offer price cuts, such views are bound to lead to disappointments. Unfortunately, the rules of a capitalist market economy dictate that buyers will seek out the most competitive price and in these instances comprador affinity wanes. Further, as is mentioned later, many so called 'Indian' shop-keepers who in common sense terms are believed to be attracting the customers are themselves barely making a profit.

It would seem, then, that in order to increase sales it would have been necessary for these small business proprietors to cater for a much wider market than their own ethnic group. This, however, is easier said than done because there are several factors beyond the control of proprietors which determine where and with whom people will shop. The problem of course is compounded when racism becomes a significant factor. It is pertinent then, at this stage, to examine the extent to which 'going into business' can really be regarded as a positive tool in the fight for equity for Black people.

BLACK BUSINESS FOR BLACK INDEPENDENCE?

In his work on Black capitalism, Earl Ofari had this to say:

"Black people have the weakest commercial tradition of any people in the United States. For historical reasons, including alienation from the capitalist system and from their African communal tradition, they have been little attracted to trade shopkeeping, buying and selling, or employing labor for the purpose of exploitation ... The black masses have rarely shown an interest in black capitalism as a solution. Future programs for black liberation definitely should not include capitalism in any form." (1970, p10)

While this might be a true representation of the Black American case, it is not the historical reality for Black people of the Caribbean. Even during slavery, slaves were encouraged to keep their own vegetable gardens because of their masters' attempts to cut down on food bills. Through this practice many were able to sell a surplus and accumulate funds, even a few to purchase their freedom. Again, with Emancipation, freed slaves squatted on Crown lands and were able to market excess produce which they cultivated. In addition, there was always an artisan group such as carpenters, croupiers, etc. who were able to engage in limited entrepreneurial activities. But perhaps the most significant factor to note is that Black people, as a consequence of slavery/colonialism/immigrating entrepreneurs/imperialism in the Caribbean, were never enabled to develop the type of commercial and business traditions to equip them for advanced capitalist market competition.

For Ofari, however, probably the most crucial factor is his belief that Black capitalism is a diversion from the real struggle to devise strategies whereby all working classes "can benefit from the fruits of their labor" rather than adopt a system which historically has proved itself to be parasitic for the majority of people.

This view is in stark contrast to the beliefs of Lord Scarman, who felt that Black business development was a panacea for much of the ailment suffered by Black people in Britain, be it a sense of under-achievement, alienation or as a defence against white racism. In his report, Scarman wrote:

> "The encouragement of black people to secure a real stake in their own community, through business and the professions, is in my view of great importance if future social stability is to be secured. ... I do urge the necessity for speedy action if we are to avoid the perpetuation in this country of an economically dispossessed black population. A weakness in British society is that there are too few people of West Indian origin in the business, entrepreneurial and professional class." (1981)

Scarman's views are increasingly repeated, especially in the strong capitalist climate of Thatcher's Britain. The government has been encouraging the population at large to 'set up on their own', to combat unemployment. For Afro-Caribbean people, the pressure for them to prove their 'worth' has never been more intense, and the arena of business enterprise is the commonly chosen litmus test. It is also in this area that they are continually compared unfavourably with 'the Asians'.

Some Pan-Africanist adherents argue that only through separate development of a strong economic base will Black people begin to redress the negative power relationship between themselves and the larger predominantly racist white society. Many Black people are caught up in the paranoia of a need to display 'Black success'. However, such co-option of Thatcherite ideology, succumbing to the notion that business success is a measure of individual/group worth, implicitly results in the acceptance of the converse: a notion that inability to display overt business success is a sign of individual or group failure.

Apologetic Black people and their 'liberal/socialist minded' White 'compradors', on the other hand, provide an apologia, and they are quick to point out in defence that Black people from the Caribbean have not had a tradition of the type of individualistic capitalism practised in most advanced economies and that forms of co-operative capitalism might be more successful. Here, Afro-Caribbean people would be able to develop their own capitalist institutions without having to be controlled by, or compete with, Whites or 'Asians'.

ECONOMIC INDIVIDUALISM AND BLACK ENTREPRENEURSHIP

From the mid 1970s the British government expressed much concern about increasing urban degeneration. The 1977 White Paper policy made provision for government led regeneration programmes, but a decade later the symptoms of urban decline persisted. Amongst the reasons given for this was government's failure to anticipate the length and depth of the economic recession, failure to comprehend fully the actual nature of the task of regeneration, national government's seeming ostracism of local governments and their expertise, and a failure to mobilise and incorporate the private sector's involvement in this drive for urban regeneration. Consequently, in her 'victory speech' in the 1987 election, the Prime Minister advocated new strategies for grappling with urban decay. These were to include amongst other things, a focus on individualism as expressed through "increasing involvement of the private sector" and "more emphasis on entrepreneurial solutions" (Aldous, 1989).

Today's call for individual responsibility and self-determinism is made by the government with the knowledge that the world seems inevitably bound to undergo extensive changes in this post-industrial era. As with capitalist industrial birth, its demise will cause intense social distress through economic dislocations. Some of these are evidenced in the phenomenon of 'the divided nation' in Britain, with regional pockets of obvious material wealth juxtaposed to others in advanced stages of industrial urban decay.

Mindful of the need to address the economic and social degradation of today's inner cities, for fear of the 'rot' seeping outwards into White suburbia, 'new' urban aid programmes have been embarked on by the Conservative government (Ladbury, 1984; Keith and Rogers, Colenutt, Parkinson, this volume). It is necessary however to question the premise on which these initiatives are implemented. On the one hand they could be seen as concern for regeneration of the physical environment (within the British heritage mould). In these circumstances, capital spin-off effects for the people living in these areas are incidental, though, of course, in the neo-classical economic model, government spending on public property is bound to have a positive multiplier effect for workers through the additional employment opportunities created. Alternatively, many inner cities initiatives can be regarded as hand-holding/carrot exercises, with the intention of encouraging/prodding people towards the goals of self-determination, 'active citizenship', and individual enterprise. Neither of the above are necessarily mutually exclusive.

However, any initiative which does not seriously address structural and institutional factors which create or exacerbate social and economic problems, and perpetuate under-development of certain groups of people because of their class, ethnic origin or gender, is bound to be less effective than it could potentially be. These initiatives can exacerbate the problems of lack of employment in inner city areas, especially through the absence of safe-guarding mechanisms such as the legalisation of contract compliance and effective equal opportunity measures.

Much is discussed about the millions of pounds supposedly pumped into these areas, yet no serious attempt is made by the government to address the problem that is created when local workers are denied employment because contractors transport in their own employees, or recruit workers from outside the area. Ignorance of the dynamics involved leads to accusations about money being 'pumped' into certain areas without success. This results in faulty generalisations, which often represent 'failures' as 'something biologically lacking' in the inhabitants; in this case, the majority of Black, un/under employed inner city dwellers.

Importantly too, 'carrots', are invariably associated with 'sticks', and contrived or not, the present contraction of social welfare provision and retraction of governmental obligations performs a 'stick' role. These, together with mass unemployment, will lead to intense frustrations and hardships, and are intended to force people to devise their own plans in order to relieve personal hardships. At the same time, however, while abnegating social welfare responsibilities, the government calls for a return to the Christian virtues of the nineteenth century. This call must be viewed in context with the concern for individualism and protection of property in the midst of a growing gulf between the material wealth of the haves and have nots.

It was, after all, a nineteenth century predecessor of the government which, mindful of the potential for social unrest through the existence of rich juxtaposed to poor inter/intra regional variations, used state compulsion to force people to shoulder their own responsibilities and in consequence the 1834 New Poor Law was enacted.

It was also nineteenth century capitalism - after which Mrs Thatcher evidently hankers - that was ushered in by the 'Christian' capitalist pioneering entrepreneurs of the seventeenth and eighteenth centuries, aided by the mass of resources which Europeans were able to amass through militaristic expropriation in large parts of the rest of the world. Through the work of Max Weber we are urged to believe that their engagement in economic pursuits was goaded on by an intensity that only strong emotions like fear could instil: fear that under-achievement or failure was a sure sign of God's dissatisfaction, whereas success was a sign of divine approval. Approval could only be gained by good works within individuals' specific 'calling'.

It was opportune for the capitalists and government of the day that people accepted these doctrines. While, according to Marx, they acted as an opiate against the harshest realities of poor people's existence, they were also a protection mechanism for those who were conspicuously making large profits against a back-drop of intense economic and social hardships for the majority of people.

CONCLUSION

The above case studies and extracts have revealed the true entrepreneurial skills of Afro-Caribbean migrant labourers, conceived in terms of devising strategies to make a living for themselves. Respondents through their own words have told how, like people all over the world, they have either used the skills they had, or were forced to use initiative to devise schemes in order to be self-sufficient or 'improve themselves'. As far as exhibiting ingenuity, people like Mrs Tallock (the higgler) seemed to be second to none and like seasoned petty capitalists had certainly managed to display worthy stewardship. Many had attempted to reproduce their business enterprises in the UK with varying degrees of success.

It is relevant here to listen to Susan Nowikowski as she quotes Light (1972, p8):

"Far from expressing any 'natural aptitude' for commerce, self-employment was often the sole recourse for workers subject to extreme economic oppression."

Light regarded the early development of Chinese small businesses in the UK as "monuments to the discrimination that had created them". In concluding her work on Asian businesses too, Nowikowski was forced to stress:

"Asian business activity represents a truce with racial inequality rather than a victory over it. Despite the facade of self-determination erected by group entrepreneurs, in reality, going into business does little to change the status of group members in relation to majority society: as with members of the majority society, it simply allows a small minority to exchange the role of marginal worker for that of marginal proprietor." (1984, p209)

One aspect of the 'enclave economy' which needs to be addressed is the extent to which it can create experiential and promotional opportunities for individuals in the minority groups, through 'reciprocal obligations'. Portes and Bach stressed that:

"If employers can profit from the willing self-exploitation of fellow immigrants, they are also obliged to reserve for them those supervisory positions that open in their firms, to train them in trade skills and to support their eventual move into self-employment. It is the fact that enclave firms are compelled to rely on ethnic solidarity and that the latter 'cuts both ways', which creates opportunities for mobility unavailable in the outside." (1985, p343)

When discussing the enclave economy and its relationship to the spread of Asian businesses, Ward and Jenkins(1984) failed to indicate the role of the enclave economy in enhancing the occupational promotion of 'Asians'. For whilst it is not intended to denigrate the achievements of this group of people, one needs to be careful that the minority ethnic group's own constructs are not used to cloak a general trend of discrimination and inequality.

If the above quotation is taken as given, certain pertinent points need to be addressed. Firstly, to what extent do promotion and experience gained through these avenues provide currency in negotiations for similar positions in the wider society? Secondly, to what extent does the need for cross organisational negotiations inhibit reciprocal obligations between workers and owners in the enclave economy? For example, many 'ethnic' organisations in Britain have resorted to 'fronting' their businesses with White indigenous personnel in an attempt to attract custom from the main communities. The extent to which this is exploited in higher positions could determine the degree of promotional/experiential mobility afforded ethnic minority workers in enclave sectors. This point becomes more crucial when one considers that most of the top level business negotiations are clinched in informal gatherings or settings. Consequently, one could assume that until the principles of equality of opportunity are widely and non-judicially observed, much of the progress of one's business depends on devising strategies either to circumvent such dependency or to gain access to these gatherings. This, however, has remained an elusive quest for many professional/business magnates from indigenous working class backgrounds, and still more so for those from ethnic minority groups.

Unless these concerns can be answered positively, the enclave economy must be seen at best as "a survival strategy initiated from a location of disadvantage, and manipulating the limited resources of this position" (Nowikowski, 1984, p149). Much worse, however, it can be seen as further ghettoisation of ethnic minority groups and can be held responsible for assisting in the perpetuation of inequality of opportunities for these groups, by failing to radically confront the parameters set by mainstream capitalism. For according to Ladbury:

"The revival of the small business ethic by the government cannot therefore be explained solely in economic terms. Initial moves to implement a Small Business Policy in 1980 and 1981 suggest that the government's real concerns were not small business *per se*, but those on the economic periphery - blacks, for example, and those recently made redundant as a result of massive plant closures in the manufacturing industry. ... the main objective of the government's Small Business Policy was to win over those most likely to feel disaffected with, and directly impoverished by, Tory economic policy." (1984, p105)

The sticks applied by the Conservative government of the 1980s have the potential to be even harsher than their nineteenth century precedents over a century ago. The quality of life and indeed expectations then were vastly different from those which today's individuals have been socialised to expect as the barest necessity for humane existence. With the removal of 'protection' against low pay and other forms of capitalist exploitation, the ill effects of this are only temporarily cushioned by credit and loan facilities that have expanded with government sanction and the existence of the ever more frayed safety-net social welfare provision by the State.

Secondly, opportunities for setting up in business - whether through some kind of artisanship or service industry - presuppose the existence of an 'opportunities vacuum' capable of absorbing industries' human capital wastage, as exists amongst the mass un/under employed casualties of the world economic system. We are told that because of contraction of the industrial sector, 'service', especially in the area of technology, will be the foreign capital generator of the foreseeable future, although little consideration is paid to the long term stability of such employment opportunities.

What if the 1990s indeed proves to be the beginning of an era of international stability in the political arena, and that Britain is successful in leading the world in the business of 'service technology' and niche marketing? How, one is forced to ask, would this affect the quest for national and international Black capitalism when Black people in Britain - for various reasons - have remained unable to gain access to high levels of technological education and skills? To what extent is Black capitalism a solution to the struggle for equity and - to borrow a topical phrase - 'self-determination' within the national and international struggles for equality of opportunities and liberation? Further, what kinds of adjustments would necessarily have to be made if British Black people are to be afforded a chance to compete fairly in these areas?

Finally, it may be logical to argue that, particularly in a non-communist state, individuals of every ethnic group will be seen to operate in capitalistic ways, whether or not these are validated by terms like 'enterprising' or 'bettering oneself'. Yet any attempt by the government or other organised bodies to encourage these along ethnic lines, to promote a spurious notion of ethnic enterprise, will reinforce ethnic cleavages and help to maintain the present inequitable *status quo*. This is especially so when in Britain, none of the parliamentary parties have so far seemed keen to tackle the main problem of racism, which is largely responsible for the lack of progress of Afro-Caribbean peoples in the UK. Even to clear-thinking capitalists there is a paradox here. Hence it is *The Economist* that is seen to plead:

"The government plans a stringent fair-employment law for Northern Ireland, which will soon make it illegal not to try to employ a fair percentage of Catholics. It could use it as a model for helping British blacks. If the government were seen to attack racism more effectively, it could afford to point to ways Britain's blacks could help themselves." (*The Economist* 27/8/88)

CHAPTER 10

THOSE FRENCH INNER CITIES?
Comparative comments on the urban crisis in Britain and France

Patricke Le Gales

For an outsider an understanding of the inner city crisis immediately appears an essential concept for any understanding of contemporary urban Britain. The amount of literature about inner cities, of public policy-making, of diverse debates, makes it central, if not dominant, in urban studies. However, once the salience of *the inner city crisis* is accepted, and with some ideas about inner cities in mind, finding a clear definition of the inner city and of its crisis proves to be a difficult task.

The editors of the book have already made the point conceptually in the introduction. This chapter highlights some of the empirical contingencies about the nature of urban form and the dangers of using generalised notions of urban crisis in late capitalist societies. An alternative way of thinking about 'those inner cities', and of working on the social construction of the inner city issue, is to think in comparative terms. Yet if making comparative studies between Britain and the United States constitutes a well-established tradition in Britain, comparisons with European countries are still not so frequent.

In France, for instance, the 'inner city syndrome' does not exist as such. The urban crisis has taken different forms, one being the decline of city centres in a few cities. This

202

chapter attempts to explore the nature of the inner city crisis in France and ask why in France so little attention is paid to an issue which is so dominant in Britain.

This chapter does not pretend to provide definitive answers to this question. Exploring the history of Britain and France in order to explain the different shaping of the urban map and the current crisis would represent a considerable achievement. Instead, taking the inner city crisis as a starting point, this chapter attempts to suggest some factors which might shed some light on the differences between the British and the French contemporary urban crisis. In order to do so the chapter is divided into four parts. I begin by examining the urban crisis in France, then provide a historical context for the production of the French urban map; the third section of the chapter looks at public policy, and all three themes are then brought together in the final section, which draws on a Saint-Etienne case-study.

URBAN CRISIS IN FRANCE IN THE 1980s: SOME CONTRASTS WITH BRITAIN

It is possible briefly to contrast current urban issues in Britain and France. The decline of many British urban areas has been well-documented (e.g. the series of books edited by Hausner, 1986). As was shown in several of these studies, the cumulative effect of population departure and industrial relocation has provoked a downwards spiral in assorted urban political economies. Since the late 1960s the urban crisis has not left the political agenda.

Related to industrial decline in the late 1970s and the national economic depression, the urban crisis has taken extreme forms in various cities. Urban decay, extreme social problems, waves of urban riots, fiscal crisis; there is no lack of examples to stress the inner city crisis. On the political agenda various sorts of urban programmes have multiplied in the last ten years (Harding, 1988) and the Prime Minister herself has made the inner city a top priority.

At this superficial level French cities seem to face a better situation. On the one hand the inner city crisis does not exist as such and is limited to a small number of industrial cities. In these cases the crisis may not be so extreme as in similar northern English cities. Yet there were some cases of urban riots in the 'hot summer of 1982' in the suburbs of important French cities such as Lyon, Paris and Marseille. Larger French cities of more than 200,000 inhabitants have not faced fiscal problems. Thus far there has been nothing like the cuts which were implemented in British cities' revenue budgets in the 1980s through central government controls (Guegnant and Uhalberdorde, 1989). On the other hand, boosted by decentralisation reforms, French regional capitals, with the exception of those in the industrial North-East, have developed their national and international role. Some of them, such as Montpellier, Grenoble, Toulouse and Rennes, have become symbols of French modernisation in the 1980s. In most cities the renovation of the urban centre, including ambitious architectural and cultural programmes, was presented as a crucial element of the local economic development strategy of the city. In such places *the inner city crisis* is an alien concept.

In relation to public policy, the progressive elimination of the traditional regional policy in France, and associated decentralisation reforms, have had two sorts of consequences (Wachter, 1988). On the one hand, the State has concentrated its interventions in urban areas facing industrial decline. This was related to the State industrial policy concentrating on the modernisation of French industry. In 1984 the government launched fifteen *'Poles de Conversion'* in order to support urban areas hurt by the industrial crisis. This is an initiative which is close to an inner city policy. On the other hand, the State decided to support urban areas competitive at the European scale. In other words one may suggest that decentralisation reforms and the *'Contrats de Plan'* were in part an instrument to divert more State resources towards the already competitive cities, such as the regional capitals already cited. Finally, the *'Banlieue 1989'* programme and the *'Développement Social des Quartiers'* programme were promoted in order to cope with social and physical decay of some neighbourhoods.

There were two groups of losers in this game. Firstly, small cities and towns lost State support and did not have the political and administrative resources to compete with the main *notables* (political patrons), commonly the mayors of regional capitals, to attract public or private investment. Secondly, small industrial urban areas facing an urban crisis were forgotten. In these small urban areas, which because of their size were not designated as *Poles de Conversion*, State support was also gradually eroded and they did not have the resources to become a regional focus for investment.

So, in a sense, an urban crisis does also exist in France although it may not be as severe as in Britain. But even in the urban context *an inner city crisis* is not dominant. The French urban crisis has taken place in the suburbs of big cities; around Lyon, in Marseille, in the North-East suburbs of Paris, in Mantes-la-Jolie, in Elbeuf near Rouen, and in small urban areas which have declined and gradually almost disappeared, being too small to attract government attention (e.g. in the mining area around Bruay en Artois in northern France or in the Lorraine region).

Self-evidently, even this brief overview highlights the fact that 'the urban crisis' is a difficult issue to define. Diversity at national and local level is embodied in the histories of urbanisation, of economic development, and cultural factors. All need to be combined in an understanding of the trends specific to any city or to a country along with the more general factors common to various cities and countries. Similarly, in comparing two medium-size capitalist countries such as Britain and France it is possible to notice common trends such as the decline of traditional industrial cities, changes in the economic structure, strategies of economic and urban modernisation and the dismantling of traditional regional policies. However, such fairly rudimentary similarities are not considered in any detail in this chapter. Rather, in order to draw out some of the more interesting contrasts between the two nations, it is possible to suggest that the characteristics of the French urban crisis and the relative absence of *inner city crisis* can be traced back to the production of the French urban map and the particular nature of State policy intervention.

THE PRODUCTION OF THE FRENCH URBAN MAP: THE MINOR INFLUENCE OF INDUSTRIALISATION

Two key differences distinguish between urban structure in France and Britain. Firstly, the industrialisation of France during the nineteenth century does not explain the urban hierarchy (Duby, 1985). In fact French urban historians have described the industrialisation period as a 'parenthesis' in French urbanisation. Secondly, France remained a predominantly rural country until the second world war. The urban population represented more than half of the French population only in the 1920s. The major period of urbanisation took place in France between 1950 and 1970.

The relationship between industrialisation and urbanisation is a complex one. Whereas in Britain the development of many of the main cities was closely related to the industrial expansion of the nineteenth century, particularly in the North, in France the urban hierarchy which was dominant before the industrial revolution was mainly shaped by the administrative institutions of the *ancien régime*, dominated by regional capitals such as Bordeaux, Nantes, Rennes, Orleans, Marseille, Montpellier, Toulouse, Lyon, Grenoble and Rouen. The dominant role of Paris was already well-established. Urbanisation was specifically developed around Paris, whilst small towns flourished in the South.

The first major urbanisation cycle, which took place between 1850 and 1880, was related to the industrialisation of the country. It led to the modification of the French urban hierarchy but not to its complete change. It was characterised by the development of cities where industrialisation was taking place: in the North (Lille, Roubaix, Tourcoing), in the Lorraine region and in the Loire (Le Creusot, Saint-Etienne). This urban France from the North-East to the South-East enjoyed the most important growth over this cycle. However, this distinctive trend was paralleled by the continued growth of the Paris urban area. Despite the general urban growth of the period, Parisian primacy did not decline. Administrative and economic concentration in Paris was reinforced.

So on one level it can be argued that the French urban map was changed by nineteenth century industrialisation. Typical administrative and university cities of the *ancien régime* such as Rennes, Nîmes, Orleans, Besançon or Montpellier declined, as they were hardly touched by the industrial revolution. By contrast, Saint-Etienne became the tenth largest French city. Yet, on the other hand, it is more commonly argued that despite these changes a more remarkable feature of the period was the continuous growth of the old urban structure. Paris, Lyon, Lille and Marseille also enjoyed continuous growth as did many regional capitals.

This constitutes a marked contrast with Britain or Germany, where the industrialisation process radically reshaped the urban map. With the exception of the North and Saint-Etienne-Le Creusot, the new urban development of 1850-1880 built on a structure that was already well-established. This conservatism of the French urban structure can be traced long before and long after the nineteenth century industrialisation.

There is a second characteristic of the urbanisation process, defining the nature of state intervention in urban affairs and sometimes called the *'cycle Haussmannien'*, named after Baron Haussmann, the prefect of Paris, who managed the renovation of Paris inspired by a new vision of *the city*. This involved a conceptual and political distinction between cities and private capital. This needs to be contextualised in the light of the representation of *the city* in the work of influential philosophers and utopians such as Saint-Simon. Specifically, three main themes shaped the renovation of Paris and were subsequently applied to the majority of regional cities.

Firstly, planners decided to favour light, easy circulation and movement in preference to concentration and immobilism. Partly because of public health concerns which developed at that time, they developed an interest in the straight line, which was to benefit shopkeepers and public health as well as city aesthetics. Consciously developing a functionalist view of the city, they wanted to renovate the city centre and to create straight streets leading into the central focus of urban life.

Secondly, they echoed public concerns for the decline of city centres, in part related to public health but also expressing the fear of concentration of working-class inhabitants in city centres. The Revolutions of 1789, 1830 and 1848 had demonstrated the potential political consequences of this concentration. Consequently, in order to avoid the decline and *ghettoisation* of cities, both firms and the working classes were banished beyond the borders of the city centre.

Thirdly, Haussmann personified both the authoritarian and liberal faces of urban planning. French capitalists were interested in urban speculation. They supported the new planning, and the new bourgeois neighbourhoods which were built at that time were financed partly by the new capitalists who made a fortune during Napoleon III's reign. The city centre was also used symbolically to demonstrate the importance of the State. It followed that a whole range of important public buildings (prefecture, law courts, army caserns) were built. This was all too clear in Paris. So this Haussmannien urban planning succeeded so dramatically because it brought together strong public interventionism and successful financial mobilisation.

In short, the consequences of this urbanisation cycle for the cities were twofold. On the one hand most French cities enjoyed a complete renovation of the city centre, with new public buildings and new bourgeois neighbourhoods. However, this renovation did not reach the new industrial cities in the North or Saint-Etienne. Secondly, the strict urban planning of city centres was matched by the anarchistic development of the suburbs. In a way, city centres were seen as belonging to the public. The suburbs were thus very different. If what was seen as 'bad' - that is to say, working class people, bad health, bad housing, firms, industries - was forced outside the city centre, it developed rapidly in the suburbs. Despite some attempts to organise the suburbs, mainly inspired by the British (cf. Sellier, Garnier), the suburb was forgotten by the planners. During the early twentieth century these suburbs were the place where cheap, poor quality housing developed without public planning.

The second and most important cycle of French urbanisation took place between 1950 and 1970. As was already noted, post-war France was not as industrialised and urbanised as Britain. Until the 1950s it was still largely a rural country. Most French urbanisation has taken place since the 1950s. This period witnessed a formidable transformation: by the 1980s French levels of urbanisation were close to those of Britain or Germany. If by the 1960s many British cities were facing urban decline, most French cities were building on the economic expansion to double their population in twenty or thirty years (e.g. Grenoble, Montpellier, Orleans, Rennes). This period of massive urbanisation also saw the revenge of *ancien régime* cities against industrial cities.

The urbanisation of the period was supported by the State. With various means of intervention to control land zoning and to finance developments (most importantly through the *Caisse des Dépôts et Consignations*). Tower blocks and bars multiplied in the periphery of urban areas, accompanied by high levels of social segregation. The accelerated urbanisation put pressure on costs and implied that the massive constructions could not be too expensive. It was sometimes argued that the buildings were not supposed to last more than twenty years. By the 1970s, unsurprisingly, a particular form of *urban crisis* developed in the periphery of urban areas, a crisis of the suburbs where patterns of social segregation were most marked, reinforced by immigration and housing problems. Urban riots occurred in these sad suburbs, ghettos outside the city. By contrast, although city centres started to lose some inhabitants in the 1970s the population decline was nothing in comparison with British inner cities. Industrial firms had left the city centre a long time ago or never been there in the first place. Several city centres were nearly untouched by industrialisation.

In short, this analysis can only be superficial and requires further development. But it has highlighted the fact that the different histories of industrialisation in Britain and France have led to different types of urban crisis. Changing fortunes of industries did not affect the majority of French cities. In France, urban crisis has occurred instead in the suburbs and small towns at the periphery of urban areas.

STATE INTERVENTION: SOME LONG-TERM EFFECTS

A second range of factors might be considered in order to understand why the inner city crisis was not so deep in France: urban and regional policies. This section cannot pretend to assess the exact influence of public policies in avoiding urban crisis. However, it seems that in the long term French regional policy has had some effects. To assess its relative success in comparison to British urban policy is well beyond the scope of this chapter. This does not prevent some comparative remarks which will be re-emphasised in the case study.

French regional policy has represented a continuous effort over the last twenty-five years to decentralise and deconcentrate private and public investments. Originally, the plan was to balance, in a harmonious way, economic activities and inhabitants over the territory of the nation. French elites wanted to control Paris growth and to help peripheral regions to develop the right conditions for economic growth (Laborie, Langumier and DeRoo, 1986). The decentralisation and deconcentration movement was also seen politically as a means to secure the national unity apparently threatened by some regionalist movements, for instance in Brittany. Yet over this same period the Fordist spatial division of work accentuated the dominance of the Paris urban area. Notwithstanding this, regional policy also contributed to the economic specialisation of space (Lipietz, 1979).

The first element of the policy concerns the deconcentration of economic activities through financial incentives to locate outside Paris and a system of *agréments* similar to the Industrial Development Certificate (IDC) system in Britain. It aimed to limit new industrial and tertiary sector development in the Paris region. According to the DATAR (*Délégation à l'Aménagement du Territoire et à l'Action Régionale*), industrial deconcentrations have created about 500,000 jobs in French regions between 1955 and 1975. The rural West and the North have been the principal beneficiaries of this policy.

In the North, where cities faced the decline of their industrial base it is estimated that jobs supported by a grant accounted for one in five jobs lost in the region. It can be argued that to a certain extent voluntarist job deconcentrations in industrial cities have prevented some inner city problems.

A second aspect of the regional policy which is worth mentioning concerns *'la politique des métropoles d'equilibre'* and *'la politique des métropoles de recherche'* which was established in the late 1960s. Eight urban areas were chosen in 1963 to become regional growth centres. The idea was twofold: on the one hand the aim was to support the development of regional capitals in order to balance the growth of Paris; on the other hand this policy was a useful tool to direct important public investment to urban areas threatened by the decline of some industrial sectors. The urban areas which were chosen were as follows: Lille-Roubaix-Tourcoing, Nancy-Metz-Thionville, Strasbourg, Lyon-Saint-Etienne-Grenoble, Marseille-Aix-en-Provence-Delta du Rhône, Toulouse, Bordeaux and Nantes-Saint-Nazaire. In 1970 Rennes, Clermont-Ferrand, Dijon and Nice were added to the programme. In these urban areas the State financially supported important urban developments such as new towns, new universities, new neighbourhoods, infrastructural improvements and the renovation of city centres. Moreover, the State brought centres of research, higher education centres, banks, public services, hospitals and cultural centres to the centre of these urban areas and led a vigorous movement of investment within them.

Public investments in these urban areas were massive and reinforced by private investments and industrial deconcentrations. Assessing this policy is a difficult task. Some of these cities were already facing urban decline and some cities in the North, such as Nantes, Saint-Etienne and St-Nazaire, were even close to industrial collapse. At the very least, this policy contributed to a large scale modernisation of the designated cities, including their respective city centres. In some areas it certainly contributed to prevention of urban decay and the rapid disintegration of the urban environment. In a provocative way one may think that if significant public money had been spent in the 1960s in British industrial cities in order to renovate the physical environment and infrastructures of equivalent cities, the urban crisis of the 1980s might not have been so deep, although it certainly would not have been avoided altogether.

Furthermore, the map of the most dynamic French cities in the 1980s (Rennes, Nantes, Toulouse, Montpellier, Nîmes, Nice, Grenoble, Lyon) shows the importance of the investments of the 1960s as the base for current growth. In industrial cities such as Lille or Saint-Etienne these investments have proved essential as they emerged from the crisis. Such assertions need to be supported by more evidence; but various case studies (e.g. Montpellier, Grenoble or Toulouse) clearly stress this element (Brunet, 1989).

It must be emphasised that the committees which were planning this policy in the 1960s included powerful civil servants such as P. Delouvrier, who managed the growth of the Paris region, or J. M. Bloch Laine, chairman of the *Caisse des Dépôts et Consignations*, who were concerned by the risk of urban decline that some regional capitals might face. In contrast, at the same time in Britain urban decline was still often considered by Whitehall civil servants as a cultural problem of the population. Many authors have singled out the Inner Area Studies and the Community Development Projects of the 1970s as crucial reports providing such official *definitions* of the roots of urban decline. It is conceivable that a more interventionist regional policy - including job deconcentrations, urban renovation, cultural investments, modernisation of the infrastructure and improvement of the physical environment - might have improved the relative situation of some cities. Fifteen or twenty years later some inner city problems might not have been so acute.

This does not suggest that an interventionist public policy initiated at the appropriate time would have prevented the inner city crisis. On the contrary, various authors have shown the structural economic reasons behind inner city decline (ESRC, 1986; Robson, 1988). However things might have not been so extreme. This rapid overview also seems to suggest that public investments proved to be crucial for the economic development of some French cities about two decades later although the time scale involved prohibits premature judgement.

THE CASE OF SAINT-ETIENNE

In order to support this view, the Saint-Etienne example shows that in the case of industrial cities the problems of French and British cities are very similar. It also suggests that the support of the State has been important for the city.

Saint-Etienne is one of the few French cities which might be compared to an English industrial city. Saint-Etienne, like some cities in the North and in Lorraine, is an industrial city. As already noted its development is related to the industrial revolution of the nineteenth century. Exceptional in the French context, it renders it similar to many British cities.

As an industrial city Saint-Etienne was called the 'black city'. The Haussmann urban renovation did not affect Saint-Etienne. It was a popular city which developed in the worst conditions. Under the Second Empire Saint-Etienne was considered as one of the most dangerous cities in France, together with other industrial cities of the North. Saint-Etienne was also the worst French city for housing. The continuous waves of new workers were not matched by new housing, with 75 per cent of the flats and houses overcrowded in 1888. In the 1920s, French local estates were built on a massive scale in Saint-Etienne but despite this, housing shortage was a permanent feature of the city until the second world war.

This was not the classically planned metropolis. In spite of ambitious schemes prepared in the interwar period, Saint-Etienne did not look like a city but rather like an accumulation of firms, cheap housing and neighbourhoods which had developed without any sense of coherence. Even the bourgeois neighbourhood, built at the beginning of the twentieth century, was abandoned. In the 1930s Saint-Etienne city centre had the familiar image of the industrial city with social problems, bad housing and a poorly qualified working population. It was worse in some parts of the suburbs, where working class housing and firms were mixed. It offered a good example of inner city crisis in the 1930s, with the worst housing problems in France.

Saint-Etienne had 16,000 inhabitants at the beginning of the nineteenth century and it tripled its population every fifty years. Its local bourgeoisie was relatively weak and it did not organise the urban development of the city, although some private initiatives in education and housing were supported by local industrialists. Its working-class had a militant and anarchist tradition (Agence d'Urbanisme de la Région Stéphanoise, 1989).

After the second word war Saint-Etienne illustrated the crisis of the nineteenth century industrial cities: its urban decay was reinforced by progressively more acute economic difficulties. By contrast, its old rival in the Rhône-Alpes region, Grenoble, was enjoying a steady growth based on the links between centres of research, the university and local firms. Rare services and activities, such as research functions or a university, had never been attracted to Saint-Etienne.

In the 1960s, as part of a *'Métropole d'Equilibre'*, Saint-Etienne received some governmental support. Together with two other industrial cities, Mulhouse and Valencienne, it received some priority new investments (in the automobile sector) and a university was created. This was a major change in Saint-Etienne. For the consequences of the nature of nineteenth century industrialisation had been reflected in more than just the urban physical environment. In the long term, the economic structure also shapes the local culture and social conditions. In Saint-Etienne, as in the North of France, in textile cities like Elbeuf, the local bourgeoisie had needed only a reliable supply of labour. It had no interest in encouraging the education of the local population. It is not surprising if today nineteenth century industrial cities are marked by considerable backwardness in terms of education compared with other cities, given this blinkered vision of the elites. By contrast, as noted earlier, old regional capitals with a university such as Rennes, Grenoble and Montpellier or Aix have enjoyed steady growth since the 1950s. By 1980 Saint-Etienne had less than 6,000 students compared with 30,000 in Montpellier and 23,000 in Grenoble and Rennes.

In terms of growth, Saint-Etienne has been characterised paradoxically by both a remarkable stability and a slow decline. The ageing population did not leave the city, but then neither did the city attract new inhabitants. The poorly qualified working population did not leave the city either. As in so many cases of urban decline, the dynamic sections of the population, particularly the young, did leave.

As a declining industrial centre Saint-Etienne did not attract the sort of tertiary sector activities which were locating in Lyon and Grenoble. As well as a poorly educated labour force, the city was dominated by an industrial working class culture and a patronising local bourgeoisie with the notable absence of the *modernist* lower middle class that has led the modernisation of many French cities since the 1977 election.

Saint-Etienne industrial development was based upon three traditional industries: coal, steel, and textiles. The mines gradually disappeared during this the century and the last one was closed in 1975. The two latter sectors were still dominant by the beginning of the 1970s. Less than ten major companies dominated the local economy and these were connected to a whole range of small firms which were working for them. After 1974 the majority of these major companies were dismantled, most importantly 'Manufrance' and 'Creusot-Loire', which had 10,000 workers in Saint-Etienne in the 1970s and eventually went bankrupt. Between 1968 and 1985 the Saint-Etienne urban area lost a third of its manufacturing base. Jobs in the manufacturing sector declined from 83,000 in 1968 to 55,000 in 1982 for about 450,000 inhabitants in the urban area (230,000 in the city proper itself).

Until 1975 the growth of the building trade and small firms in the engineering sector was not sufficient to compensate for the decline of traditional industries. During the first phase of Saint-Etienne's economic crisis, the decline of the mines, a major crisis was avoided by central government regeneration policy implemented in the 1960s. Saint-Etienne benefited from the *'primes d'adaptation industrielle'*, which supported job creation and small business development in the urban area. The mining company 'Les Houilleres', state owned, was also very active, financing projects which might help the reintegration of former miners. Futhermore, several state-owned companies were encouraged to establish plants in Saint-Etienne as part of the industrial deconcentration policy. The truck firm Berliet created 1,500 jobs in the early 1970s. Overall, the area was strongly supported by State schemes and grants. Official estimates suggest that about 9,000 jobs supported by government grants were created between 1968 and 1975. In other words the growth of the building trade sector and the voluntarist regional policy just compensated for jobs lost in the manufacturing sector.

By 1975 the renovation of the city and the creation of the university were also signs of the gradual renovation of Saint-Etienne. Following its designation as part of a *Métropole d'Equilibre,* studies were undertaken in Saint-Etienne. The underdevelopment and problems of Saint-Etienne city centre consistently came out of the studies as one of the city's most important problems. The commercial sector, services, leisure activities and restaurants all appeared very much underrepresented in the local economy. Chronic deficiencies in urban planning were still seen as a major problem in the city, not least in the city centre. Within the area some neighbourhoods reflected the status of the city as a manufacturing centre (Ondaine valley, Giers valley).

In the 1960s important housing programmes were launched in order to replace the estates and houses inherited from the nineteenth century. Local authorities' efforts were directed towards the elimination of decline in the city centre and in the suburbs and to eradicate as much evidence as possible of the industrial past of the city. Many programmes were supported by the government as part of a strategy of regeneration for Saint-Etienne.

Without entering into the finer details of recent local history, these interventions demonstrated that by 1975 the city had benefited from active support from the State. Local elites were quite confident. The city had supported the closure of the mines without a serious urban crisis. New industrial jobs were slowly coming in the area. The university and the renovation of the city, along with the city centre, were all signs of the regeneration of the city. Of course tertiary sector activities were growing at a relatively slow rate when compared with other cities. However, they were so different from Saint-Etienne's traditions that their very existence was an achievement.

When the second wave of the crisis hit Saint-Etienne in the international depression that followed the 1973 oil crisis, the city went into further recession. However, the efforts of the 1960s proved to be fruitful. Without the regeneration policy pursued at that time the second industrial crisis might have provoked a crisis much deeper than the one which actually occurred. Without documenting the changes in detail I want to show how, despite the severity of the recession, Saint-Etienne never had an inner city crisis comparable to those of Liverpool and other northern English cities, or even to Coventry, a city with which it is often compared.

Most Saint-Etienne manufacturing jobs were lost after 1975 and the decline continued until 1987. Employment gains were made in the service and the public sectors. Despite the collapse of more than a third of its industrial base the unemployment rate never went above 13 per cent, even in the worst years of the crisis.

Public interventions took several forms. Firstly, various agencies were involved in the implementation of schemes or programmes designed to limit the consequences of unemployment and to prepare the retraining of the workforce. Secondly, some agencies such as the ADILE (*Association pour le Développement Industriel de la Loire*) acted as development agencies. ADILE is simultaneously a local network and the regional division of the DATAR. It acts as a development agency linking Paris, the local prefect, and local businesses, without many links with local authorities, who in Saint-Etienne have not been very active.

State intervention has also taken more direct forms. Firstly, Saint-Etienne was designated under the *'Pole de Conversion'* programme. Secondly, a *'Pole de Productique'* was established in Saint-Etienne. Under the leadership of State agencies this brought together a centre of research, a centre for the transfer of technology and various public organisations. The whole complex developed a leading role for computer applications to the productive process in France.

Under these two programmes, money was channelled to support 'new business-training programmes' and to finance premises in the form of a science park. Important resources were also specifically allocated to change the urban environment, concentrating on the derelict land that had been vacated by the old manufacturing industries and was known as the *friches industrielles*. Under the *'friches industrielles'* programme a vigorous schedule of elimination of derelict infrastructure and traces of the industrial past from the city centre was pursued. According to State representatives, between 1983 and 1986 Saint-Etienne received about £5 million per year. This money can be considered as extra money as it does not include normal programmes of central state support for local government services.

From the urban perspective the results have been quite spectacular. In less than ten years Saint-Etienne has lost its old image. The city centre has been entirely renovated, the old neighbourhoods have been restored and the premises abandoned by firms have been converted into offices, middle class housing or commercial premises. The physical transformation of the city has been seen as one of the most remarkable achievements of governmental programmes and has been stressed by many observers. The suburbs are now receiving particular attention. Various projects are now gradually being implemented. At this very basic level the effort to transform and regenerate the city centre and its housing and services may be seen as quite successful. It may also be noticed that this rapid success was fundamentally facilitated by the first wave of regeneration which started over twenty years ago.

A more detailed analysis would require a focus on the transformation of the local economy. In brief, since 1987 the economy has been buoyant, even if unemployment has not been substantially reduced. Along the new growth sector the role of the university research departments and the agencies brought together in the *'Pole de Productique'* is significant.

In terms of the social aspects of the inner city crisis, Saint-Etienne benefited from all the programmes implemented by the central government over the years under the rubric of *'le traitement social du chômage'*. It is not conceivable within the space of this chapter to compare the effects of governmental programmes on the inner city crisis. The British and French social security systems, local authorities, job centres and unemployment benefits are too different in such a brief assessment. There is no doubt however that beyond the urban and regional policy all these elements are important determinants of the inner city crisis. The connections between decline of the manufacturing sector and the inner city crisis in Britain have often been highlighted as a key element in the British inner city crisis (Robson, 1988). However, it is beyond doubt that the British and the French economic bases were and are quite different. In general the manufacturing crisis of the late 1980s and early 1980s took different forms in France, even if from place to place it could be quite similar to the British experience.

So it follows that examining the whole range of factors which have contributed to Saint-Etienne's crises and making wholesale comparisons with any British city is a demanding task which is not attempted here.

Yet in comparison to a city such as Coventry, for instance, some preliminary observations can be stressed. In many ways Coventry's decline and crisis in the 1970s was much deeper than in Saint-Etienne. Coventry lost half of its industrial jobs and the rate of unemployment went far beyond 20 per cent in the early 1980s (Coventry City Council Policy Guide, 1989) and the social problems concentrated in some of its local estates are typical inner city problems, seen for instance in the Foleshill area. Comparison must necessarily take into account the particular economic and social history of the city, yet at a superficial level it is noticeable that no renovation of Coventry centre was started prior to the 1970s. Although Coventry was designated as an Urban Programme Area, the money it received through this programme (about £4.5 million per year since 1984) did not match the money it lost through cuts in the block grant received by the city council, £23 million in real terms between 1981-82 and 1985-86 (Coventry City Council Policy Guide, 1989). Beyond these figures, the policies pursued by the Conservative government were not calculated to favour industrial cities.

Overall, in comparison with Coventry, Saint-Etienne has benefited since the 1960s from continuous support from the government in order to deal with economic restructuring and facilitate urban regeneration. Coventry and many other British cities have not.

Further comparison would require analysis at the international, national and local levels. The contrasts presented are far too superficial to pretend to make definitive generalisations but they are suggestive. However, it remains the case that the inner city crisis refers to a whole range of economic, historic and social conditions which go far beyond public policies.

The inner city crisis in France has not taken the same forms as it has in England. Firstly, it is limited to industrial cities which means it involves a small number of French cities. Secondly, for various economic and possibly public policy reasons, the crisis has not been so extreme. In a provocative way it is possible to argue that *the inner city crisis* simply does not exist in France. After all, the inner city crisis is not a given concept but refers to a social creation at the end of a social and economic process. Part of this process refers to the transformation of capitalism and the role of cities in the accumulation of capital. Only part of this process stems from the national and local, social and economic conditions and history. In other words, one may notice on the one hand that nineteenth century industrial cities have followed the same pattern of decline in France and Britain and face very similar problems. On the other hand important contrasts exist both within each country and between countries which are due to different national and local social and economic conditions. The relationship between the state and the city in the two countries exemplifies this contrast. It is perhaps in this political context that comparison with the French experience may be a useful tool to avoid a dangerous 'reification' of the concept of inner city.

REFERENCES

Abbott, P. and Sapsford, R. 1987 *Women and Social Class*, London: Tavistock

Abrams, C. 1965 *The City is the Frontier*, New York: Harper

Adcock, B. 1984 'Regenerating Merseyside Docklands: The Merseyside Development Corporation 1981-1984', *Town Planning Review*, 55, 265-89

Advisory Council on Historic Preservation 1980 *Report to the President and the Congress of the United States*, Washington, D.C.: Government Printing Office

Agence d'Urbanisme de la Région Stéphanoise 1989 *La Région Stéphanoise - 'Saint-Etienne et son Agglomération', Notes et Etudes Documentaires* N.4030-4031-4032, Paris: La Documentation Française

Ahlbrandt, R. S. 1984 *Neighborhoods, People and Community*, New York: Plenum

Ahlbrandt, R. S. and Cunningham, J. V. 1980 *Pittsburgh's Residents Assess Their Neighborhoods*, Pittsburgh: University of Pittsburgh

Aitken, H. (ed) 1967 *Explorations in Enterprise*, Cambridge, Massachusetts: Harvard University Press

Aldous, T. 1989 *Inner City Urban Regeneration and Good Design, Appendix A*, London: HMSO

Anderson, J. 1983 'Geography as Ideology and the Politics of Crisis: The Enterprise Zones Experiment'. In Anderson, J., Duncan, S. and Hudson, R. (eds), *Redundant Spaces in Cities and Regions?*, London: Academic Press

Badcock, B. 1989 'An Australian View of the Rent Gap Hypothesis', *Annals of the Association of American Geographers*, 79, 125-145

Baltimore Sun 1986 'Maryland National to Commit $50 Million to Loan Fund', 24 November

Banfield, E. C. 1968 *The Unheavenly City: The Nature and Future of Our Urban Crisis,* Boston: Little, Brown

Barnekov, T., Boyle, R. and Rich, D. 1989 *Privatism and Urban Policy in Britain and the United States,* Oxford: Oxford University Press

Bartelt, D. 1979 *Redlining in Philadelphia: An Analysis of Home Mortgages in the Philadelphia Area,* Mimeo, Institute for the Study of Civic Values, Temple University, Philadelphia

Beauregard, R. A. 1986 'The Chaos and Complexity of Gentrification'. In Smith, N. and Williams, P. (eds), *Gentrification of the City,* Boston: Allen and Unwin

Beechey, V. 1986 'Women's Employment in Contemporary Britain'. In Beechey, V. and Whitelegg, E. (eds), *Women in Britain Today,* Milton Keynes: Open University Press

Benjamin, M. 1988 'Global Exchange: 1001 Ways to Make the World a Better Place', *Food Monitor,* Winter

Benson, J. 1983 *The Penny Capitalist: A Study of Nineteenth Century Working-Class Entrepreneurs,* Dublin: Gill and Macmillan

Berkowitz, B. 1984 'Economic Development Really Works: Baltimore, MD'. In Bingham, R. and Blair, J. (eds), *Urban Economic Development,* Beverly Hills, CA: Sage

Berkowitz, B. 1987 'Rejoinder to "Downtown Redevelopment as an Urban Growth Strategy"', *Journal of Urban Affairs,* 9 (2)

Blau, F. and Ferber, M. 1985 'Women in the Labor Market: The Last Twenty Years'. In Larwood, L., Stromberg, A. H. and Gutek, B. A. (eds), *Women and Work,* Beverly Hills, CA: Sage

Bluestone, B. and Harrison, B. 1988 *The Great U-Turn,* New York: Basic Books

Boddy, M. 1980 *The Building Societies,* Basingstoke: Macmillan

Boddy, M. and Fudge, C. (eds) 1984 *Local Socialism? Labour Councils and New Left Alternatives,* London: Macmillan

Bond, P. 1987 'From Divestment to Reinvestment', *Dollars and Sense,* June

Bond, P. 1989a 'S&L Bailout: We Pay the Bill', *The Guardian,* 24 May

Bond, P. 1989b 'Wright Impaled on Sharpened Ethics Sword; Who's Next?', *The Guardian*, 1 June

Bond, P. 1989c 'House Resignations Only Scrape Surface of Congressional Corruption', *The Guardian*, 15 June

Bond, P. 1989d 'The Student Loan Crisis: Proposed Solutions Blame the Victims', *DC Scar News*, Summer

Bondi, L. 1989 'Gentrification, Work and Gender Identity'. In Kobayashi, A. (ed), *Women, Work and Place*, Montreal: McGill Queens (forthcoming)

Bowlby, S. R., Foord, J. and McDowell, L. 1986 'The Place of Gender Relations in Locality Studies', *Area*, 18, 327-31

Bowles, S., Gordon, D. and Weisskopf, T. 1983 *Beyond the Wasteland*, New York: Anchor

Boyle, R. (ed) 1985 'Leveraging Urban Development: a Comparison of Urban Policy Directions and Programme Impact in the United States and Britain', *Policy and Politics*, 13

Boyte, H.C. 1980 *The Backyard Revolution*, Philadelphia: Temple University Press

Boyte, H.C. and Riessman, F. 1986 *The New Populism: Politics of Empowerment*, Philadelphia: Temple University Press

Boyte, H.C., Booth, H., and Max, S. 1986 *Citizen Action and the New American Populism*, Philadelphia: Temple University Press

Bradford, C. and Schersten, P. 1985 'A Tool for Community Capital: Home Mortgage Disclosure Act 1985 National Survey', unpublished manuscript, Chicago: National Training and Information Center

Bradford, C. P. and Rubinowitz, L. S. 1975 'The Urban-Suburban Investment-Disinvestment Process', *Annals of the Academy of Political and Social Science*, 442, 77-86

Brown, C. 1984 *Black and White in Britain: The Third PSI Survey*, London: Heinemann

Brunet, R. and Brunet, A. 1989 *Montpellier Europole*, Montpellier: RECLUS

Brunet, R. and Sallois, J. 1989 *France: Les Dynamiques du Territoire*, Montpellier: RECLUS-DATAR

221

Bulletin of Municipal Foreign Policy, various issues

Butler, S. M. 1981 *Enterprise Zones: Greenlining the Inner City,* London: Heinemann

Butler, S. M. 1984 'Free Zones in the Inner City'. In Bingham, R. and Blair, J. (eds), *Urban Economic Development,* Beverly Hills, CA: Sage

Byrne, D. 1989 *Beyond the Inner City,* Milton Keynes: Open University Press

Carr, C. 1988 'Night Clubbing. Reports from the Tompkins Square Police Riot', *Village Voice,* 16 August

Cassidy, F. G. 1971 *Jamaica Talk: Three Hundred Years of the English Language in Jamaica,* London: Macmillan

Cassidy, F. G. and LePage, R. B. 1967 *Dictionary of Jamaican English,* Cambridge: Cambridge University Press

Castells, M. 1976 'The Wild City', *Kapitalistate,* 4-5, 2-30

Castells, M. 1983 *The City and the Grassroots,* London: Edward Arnold

Castells, M. 1985 'Commentary on C.G. Pickvance's 'The Rise and Fall of Urban Movements ...', in *Environment and Planning D: Society and Space,* 3, 55-61

Center for Community Change 1988 *The CRA Reporter,* Washington, D.C.: Center for Community Change. Various issues

Charyn, J. 1985 *War Cries Over Avenue C.,* New York: Donald I. Fine, Inc.

Church, A. 1988 'Urban Regeneration in London Docklands: A Five Year Policy Review', *Environment and Planning C: Government and Policy,* 6

City of Pittsburgh 1984 *Progress in the Neighborhoods, A Report on Capital Investment 1970-1984*

City of Pittsburgh 1983 'Six Year Development Program', *1983 Capital Budget and Community Development Draft for Discussion*

Clark, E. 1987 *The Rent Gap and Urban Change: Case Studies in Malmo, 1860-1985,* Lund: Lund University Press

Clavel, P. 1986 *Progressive Cities,* New Brunswick, NJ: Rutgers University Press

Clay, P. 1979 *Neighborhood Renewal: Trends and Strategies*, Lexington, MA: Lexington Books

Cooper, C. L. and Davidson, M. J. (eds) 1984 *Working Women in Management*, London: Heinemann

Corbridge, S. 1988 'The Debt Crisis and the Crisis of Global Regulation', *Geoforum*, 19, 109-30

Cunningham, J. V. 1980 *A Brief History of Neighborhood Organization in Pittsburgh*, Pittsburgh: University of Pittsburgh

Daly, M. and Logan, M. 1986 'The International Financial System and National Economic Development Patterns'. In Drakakis-Smith, D. (ed), *Urbanization in the Developing World*, London: Routledge

Davidoff, L. and Hall, J. 1987 *Family Fortunes*, London: Hutchinson

Davidoff, L., L'Esperance, J. and Newby, H. 1976 'Landscape with Figures: Home and Community in English Society'. In Mitchell, J. and Oakley, A. (eds), *The Rights and Wrongs of Women*, Harmondsworth: Penguin

Davis, M. 1985 'Urban Renaissance and the Spirit of Postmodernism', *New Left Review*, 151, 106-113

De Banville, E. and Verihac, J. 1973 *Saint-Etienne, le Capital Redistribué*, Saint-Etienne: CRESAL Université de Saint-Etienne

Debt Crisis Network Working Group 1986 *From Debt to Development'*, Washington, D.C.: Institute for Policy Studies

Dedman, B. 1988 'The Color of Money', *The Atlanta Journal and the Atlanta Constitution*, 1-4 May

Dedman, B. 1989 'Blacks Turned Down for Home Loans from S&Ls Twice as Often as Whites', *The Atlanta Journal and Constitution*, 29 January

DeGiovanni, F. 1983 'Patterns of Change in Housing Market Activity in Revitalizing Neighborhoods', *Journal of the American Planning Association*, 49, 22-39

DeGiovanni, F. 1987 *Displacement Pressures in the Lower East Side*, Community Service Society of New York, Working Paper

Deutsche, R. and Ryan, C. G. 1984 'The Fine Art of Gentrification', *October*, 31, 91-111

Devonish, H. 1986 *Language and Liberation: Creole Language Politics in the Caribbean*, London: Karia Press

Dilts, J. D. 1971 'Some Savings Firms Finance Speculators', *Baltimore Sun*, 20 September

Docklands Consultative Committee 1990 *The Docklands Experiment; A Critical Review of Eight Years of the London Docklands Development Corporation*', London: DCC

Dommel, P. R. and Rich, M. J. 1987 'The Rich Get Richer; the Attenuation of Targeting Effects of the Community Development Block Grant', *Urban Affairs Quarterly*, 22

Downs, A. 1982 'The Necessity of Neighborhood Deterioration', *New York Affairs*, 7, 35-8

Dreier, P. 1984 'The Tenants' Movement in the United States', *International Journal of Urban and Regional Research*, 8

Duby, G. (ed) 1985 *Histoire de la France Urbaine*, Paris: Seuil, 5 volumes (more specifically volume 4: 'La Ville de l'Age Industriel' and volume 5: 'La Ville Aujourd'hui')

Duncan, J. 1981 (ed) *Housing and Identity*, London: Croom Helm

Economist, The 1988 'Oh, Say Can You See?, 27 August, 14

Edelman, M. 1971 *Politics as Symbolic Action: Mass Arousal and Quiescence*, Chicago: Markham

Edelman, M. 1985 'Political Language and Political Reality', *P.S.*, XVIII, 10-19

Eggleston, J. 1984 *The Educational and Vocational Experiences of 15-18 Year Old Young People of Minority Ethnic Groups*, A Report Submitted to the Department of Education and Science, University of Keele: Department of Education

England, P. and Farkas, G. 1987 *Households, Employment and Gender*, New York: De Gruyter

Englund, W. 1982 'The City's Trustees Get a Narrow Okay', *Baltimore Sun*, 5 December

Fainstein, N. and Fainstein, S. (eds) 1986 *Restructuring the City*, New York: Longman. 2nd edition

Fainstein, S. 1987 'Local Mobilization and Economic Discontent'. In Smith, M. P. and Feagin, J. R. (eds), *The Capitalist City*, Oxford: Basil Blackwell.

Federal Financial Institutions Examination Council 1985 *A Citizens Guide to CRA*, Washington, DC

Florida, R. 1986a 'The Political Economy of Financial Deregulation and the Reorganization of Housing Finance in the United States', *International Journal of Urban and Regional Research*, 10, 207-31

Florida, R. (ed) 1986b, *Housing and the New Financial Markets*, New Brunswick, NJ: Rutgers University Press

Foord, J. and Gregson, N. 1986 'Patriarchy: Towards a Reconceptualisation', *Antipode*, 18, 186-211

Forrest, R. and Murie, A. 1987 'The Affluent Homeowner: Labour-market Position and the Shaping of Housing Histories'. In Thrift, N. and Williams, P. (eds), *Class and Space: The Making of Urban Society*, London: Routledge and Kegan Paul

Freycon, J.P. and Ville, J.P. 1983 *L'agglomération Stéphanoise*, for the LEDA programme EEC Saint-Etienne Sitelle

Friedland, R. 1982 *Power and Crisis in the City*, London: Macmillan

Gamble, A. 1988 *The Free Economy and the Strong State*, London: Macmillan

Gates, L.B. and Brophy, P. C. 1985 *Economic Integration: A Strategy in Neighborhood Revitalization*, Urban Renewal Authority of Pittsburgh

George, S. 1988 *A Fate Worse Than Debt*, Harmondsworth: Penguin

Giloth, R. P. and Mier, R. 1989 'Spatial Change and Social Justice'. In Beaureguard, R. A. (ed), *Economic Restructuring and Political Response*, v.34, *Urban Affairs Annual Reviews*, Newbury Park, CA: Sage.

Glendinning, C. and Millar, J. (eds) 1987 *Women and Poverty in Britain*, Brighton: Wheatsheaf

Goldberg, D. 1990 'Polluting the Body Politic: Racist Discourse and Urban Location'. In Cross, M. and Keith, M. (eds), *Racism, the City and the State*, London: Unwin Hyman

Goldstein, H. 1980 'The Limits of Community Economic Development'. In Clavel, P., Forester, J. and Goldsmith, W. W. (eds), *Urban and Regional Planning in an Age of Austerity*, New York: Pergamon Press.

Goldstein, I. 1985 'The Impact of Racial Composition on the Distribution of Conventional Mortgages in the Philadelphia SMSA', *A Case Study Working Paper*, Philadelphia: Institute for Public Policy Studies, Temple University Press.

Goldstein, I. and Shlay, A. 1988 *Getting the Credit We Deserve: An Analysis of Residential Lending in New Castle County, Delaware 1984-86*, Philadelphia Institute for Public Policy Studies, Temple University Press

Goodwyn, L. 1978 *The Populist Moment: A Short History of the Agrarian Revolt in America*, New York: Oxford University Press

Gottmann, J. 1961 *Megalopolis: The Urbanized Northeastern Seaboard of the United States*, New York: Twentieth Century Fund

Gregory, D. and Ley, D. 1988 'Culture's Geographies', *Environment and Planning D: Society and Space*, 6, 115-16

Guegnant, A. and Uhalberdorde, J-M. 1989 *Crise et Réformes des Finances Locales*, Paris: PUF-GRAL

Gunts, E. 1988 'Investors Found for Harborview', *The Baltimore Sun*, 21 September

Guskind, R. 1989 'Zeal for Zones', *National Journal*, 6 March, 1358-62

Hall, P. 1982 'Enterprise Zones: A Justification', *International Journal of Urban and Regional Research*, 16, 416-21

Hamnett, C. 1973 'Improvement Grants as an Indicator of Gentrification in Inner London', *Area*, 5, 252-61

Harding, A. 1988 'Spatially Specific Urban Programmes in Britain since 1979: The Conservative Strategy and the Problem of Policy Control', *West European Politics*, 11 (1)

Harvey, D. 1974 'Class Monopoly Rent Finance Capital and the Urban Revolution', *Regional Studies*, 8, 239-55

Harvey, D. 1982 *The Limits to Capital*, Oxford: Basil Blackwell

Harvey, D. 1985 *The Urbanization of Capital*, Oxford: Basil Blackwell

Harvey, D. 1987 'The View from Baltimore's Federal Hill', Mimeo, School of Geography, Oxford University

Harvey, D. 1989a 'From Managerialism to Entrepreneurialism: The Transformation of Urban Governance in Late Capitalism', *Geographiska Annaler Series B*, 71, 3-17

Harvey, D. 1989b *The Condition of Postmodernity: An Enquiry into the Origins of Cultural Change*, Oxford: Basil Blackwell

Harvey, D. and Chaterjee, L. 1974 'Absolute Rent and the Structuring of Space by Financial Institutions', *Antipode*, 6, 22-36

Hauck, D., Voorhees, M. and Goldberg, C. 1983 *Two Decades of Debate*, Washington, D.C.: Investor Responsibility Research Center

Hausner, V. (ed) 1986 *Critical Issues in Urban Economic Development, Vol. 1*, Oxford: Clarendon Press

Hausner, V. (ed) 1987a *Critical Issues in Urban Economic Development, Vol 2*, Oxford: Clarendon Press

Hausner, V. 1987b *Economic Change in British Cities*, Oxford: Clarendon Press

Hausner, V. 1987c *Urban Economic Change: Five City Studies*, Oxford: Clarendon Press

Heath, A. and Britten, N. 1984 'Women's Jobs Do Make a Difference', *Sociology*, 18, 475-90

Henry, Z. 1972 *Labour Relations and Industrial Conflicts in the Caribbean Countries*, Port of Spain: Colombus

Herman, E. 1981 *Corporate Control, Corporate Power*, New York: Cambridge University Press

Hilferding, R. 1981 *Finance Capital*, London: Routledge and Kegan Paul

Hill, R. C. 1984 'Urban Political Economy'. In Smith, M. P. (ed), *Cities in Transformation*, Beverly Hills, CA: Sage.

Holcomb, B. 1986 'Geography and Urban Women', *Urban Geography*, 7, 448-56

House of Commons Employment Committee 1988 *The Employment Effects of the Urban Development Corporations*, Volumes 1 and 2, London: HMSO

House of Lords Select Committee 1981 *Report on London Docklands Development Corporation, Area and Constitution Order 1980,* London: HMSO

Hudson, R. and Sadler, D. 1986 'Contesting Works Closures in Western Europe's Old Industrial Regions: Defending Place or Betraying Class?'. In Scott, A. J. and Storper, M. (eds), *Production, Work, Territory; The Geographical Anatomy of Industrial Capitalism,* London: Allen and Unwin

International Labor Rights Working Group 1988 *Trade's Hidden Costs,* Washington, DC: Institute for Policy Studies

Jager, M. 1986 'Class Definition and the Aesthetics of Gentrification: Victoriana in Melbourne'. In Smith, N. and Williams, P. (eds), *Gentrification of the City,* Boston: Allen and Unwin

Jameson, F. 1984 'Postmodernism, or the Cultural Logic of Late Capitalism', *New Left Review,* 146, 53-92.

Jefferson, O. 1977 'The Post War Economic Development of Jamaica', University of the West Indies, Jamaica: Institute of Social and Economic Research

JHU Coalition for a Free South Africa 1986 *MN Makes Apartheid Grow,* Leaflet distributed at Maryland National Bank branches

Johnson, L. 1987 '(Un)realist Perspectives: Patriarchy and Feminist Challenges in Geography', *Antipode,* 19, 210-15

Kasarda, J. 1985 'Urban Change and Minority Opportunities'. In Peterson, P. E. (ed), *The New Urban Reality,* Washington, D.C.: Brookings Institution

Kennedy, C. 1980 *The Entrepreneurs,* Newbury: Scope Books

Kotz, D. 1978 *Bank Control Over Large Corporations in the U.S.,* Berkeley: University of California Press

Krieger, J. 1986 *Reagan, Thatcher and the Politics of Decline,* Cambridge: Polity Press

Laborie, J-P., Langumier, J-F., and Deroo, P. 1986 *La Politique Française d'Aménagement du Territoire de 1950 à 1985,* Paris: La Documentation Française

Ladbury, S. 1984 'Choice, Chance or No Alternative? Turkish Cypriots in Business in London'. In Ward, R. and Jenkins, R. (eds), *Ethnic Communities in Business: Strategies for Economic Survival,* Cambridge: Cambridge University Press

Lake, R. W. 1979 *Real Estate Tax Delinquency: Private Disinvestment and Public Response*, Piscataway, NJ: Center for Urban Policy Research, Rutgers University

Lash, S. and Urry, J. 1987 *The End of Organized Capitalism*, Oxford: Polity Press

Left Business Observer 1989 various issues.

Levin, K. 1983 'The Neo-Frontier'. In Goldstein, R. and Massa, R. (eds), Heroes and Villains in the Arts, *Village Voice*, 4 January

Levine, M. 1987a, 'Downtown Development as an Urban Growth Strategy: A Critical Appraisal of the Baltimore Renaissance', *Journal of Urban Affairs*, 9

Levine, M. 1987b, 'Going Upscale Downtown,' *Baltimore Sun*, 6 September

Levine, M. 1989 'The End of National Urban Policy'. Paper presented to the 7th Urban Change and Conflict Conference, School of Advanced Urban Studies, University of Bristol, Bristol, 17-20 September

Ley, D. 1980 'Liberal Ideology and the Post-Industrial City', *Annals of the Association of American Geographers*, 70, 238-58

Ley, D. 1986 'Alternative Explanations for Inner City Gentrification: A Canadian Assessment', *Annals of the Association of American Geographers*, 76, 521-35

Lipietz, A. 1979 *Capital et son Espace*, Paris: Maspero

Liverpool City Council Planning Department 1987 *Merseyside Development Corporation: The Liverpool Experience*

Local Government Planning and Land Act 1980, C65 *Part XVI, Schedules 26-31*

Logan, J. and Molotch, H. 1987 *Urban Fortunes: The Political Economy of Place*, Berkeley: University of California Press

Long, P. 1971 'The City as Reservation', *Public Interest*, 25, 22-38.

Lubove, R. 1969 *Twentieth Century Pittsburgh: Government, Business and Environmental Change*, New York: John Wiley

MacGregor, S. and Pimlott, B. (eds) 1990 *Tackling the Inner Cities*, Oxford: Clarendon Press

MacKenzie, S. and Rose, D. 1983 'Industrial Change, the Domestic Economy and Home Life'. In Anderson, J., Duncan, S. and Hudson, R. (eds), *Redundant Spaces in Cities and Regions?*, London: Academic Press

Mackenzie, S. 1988 'Building Women, Building Cities: Toward Gender Sensitive Theory in the Environmental Disciplines'. In Andrew, C. and Milroy, B. M. (eds), *Life Spaces,* Vancouver: University of British Columbia Press

Magdoff, H. and Sweezy, P. 1987 *Stagnation and the Financial Explosion*, New York: Monthly Review Press

Marcuse, P. 1979 'The Deceptive Consensus on Redlining: Definitions Do Matter', *Journal of the American Planning Association*, October

Marcuse, P. 1984 *Abandonment, Gentrification and Displacement in New York City*, Report to the Community Services Society

Marcuse, P. 1986 'Abandonment, Gentrification, and Displacement: The Linkages in New York'. In Smith, N. and Williams, P. (eds), *Gentrification of the City,* Boston: Allen and Unwin

Markusen, A. 1981 'City Spatial Structure, Women's Household Work, and National Urban Policy'. In Stimpson, C. R., Dixler, E., Nelson, M. J. and Yatrakis, K. B. (eds), *Women and the American City*, Chicago: University of Chicago Press

Martin, J. and Roberts, C. 1984 *Women and Employment: A Lifetime Perspective,* London: HMSO

Maryland Alliance for Responsible Investment 1986 *Is Maryland National Bank Helping us Grow?*, leaflet given to member organizations

Massey, D. 1986 'The Legacy Lingers On: The Impact of Britain's International Role on its Internal Geography'. In Martin, R., and Rowthorn, B. (eds), *The Geography of De-Industrialization*, London: Macmillan.

Massey, D. and Meegan, R. 1989 'Spatial Divisions of Labour in Britain'. In Gregory, D. and Walford, R. (eds), *Horizons in Human Geography*, London: Macmillan

Mayer, M. 1985 *The Money Bazaars*, New York: Weybright and Talley

McCarthy, J. J. 1981 'Research on Neighbourhood Activism: Review, Critique and Alternatives', *The South African Geographical Journal*, 63, 107-31

McDowell, L. 1983 'Towards an Understanding of the Gender Division of Urban Space', *Environment and Planning D: Society and Space*, 1, 59-72

Merseyside Development Corporation 1981 *Initial Development Strategy*

Merseyside Development Corporation 1989a *Annual Report and Financial Statements 1988/89*

Merseyside Development Corporation 1989b Draft *New Brighton Area Strategy*

Merseyside Development Corporation 1989c *Vauxhall Area Draft Strategy*

Meyerson, A. 1986 'Deregulation and the Restructuring of the Housing Finance System'. In Bratt, R. G., Hartman, C. and Meyerson, A. (eds), *Critical Perspectives on Housing*, Philadelphia: Temple University Press

Miliband, R. and Saville, J. 1979 'The Free Economy and the Strong State'. In *Socialist Register*, London: Merlin

Millar, J. and Glendinning, C. 1987 'Invisible Women, Invisible Poverty'. In Glendinning, C. and Millar, J. (eds), *Women and Poverty in Britain*, Brighton: Wheatsheaf

Miller, R. 1983 'The Hoover in the Garden: Middle-Class Women and Suburbanisation 1850-1920', *Environment and Planning D: Society and Space*, 1, 73-87

Mills, C. 1988 'Life on the Upslope: The Postmodern Landscape of Gentrification', *Environment and Planning D: Society and Space*, 6, 169-89

Minsky, H. 1977 'A Theory of Systematic Fragility'. In Altman, E. D. and Sametz, A. W. (eds), *Financial Crises*, New York: John Wiley

Mintz, B. and Schwartz, M. 1985 *The Power Structure of American Business*, Chicago: University of Chicago Press

Molotch, H. 1976 'The City as a Growth Machine: Toward a Political Economic of Place', *American Journal of Sociology*, 82, 309-30

Moody, K. 1988 *An Injury to All*, London: Verso

Morrow-Jones, H. 1986 'The Geography of Housing: Elderly and Female Households', *Urban Geography*, 7, 263-269

Moufarege, N. 1982 'Another Wave, Still More Savagely Than the First: Lower East Side, 1983', *Arts*, 57-73

Murgatroyd, L. 1984 'Women, Men and the Social Grading of Occupations', *British Journal of Sociology*, 35, 473-97

Murray, R. 1989 'Fordism and Post-Fordism'. In Hall, S. and Jacques, M. (eds), *New Times: The Changing Face of Politics in the 1990s*, London: Lawrence and Wishart

National Audit Office 1988 *Department of the Environment: Urban Development Corporations*, London: HMSO

Navarro, V. 1988 'Social Movements and Class Politics in the U.S.'. In Miliband, R., Panitch, L. J. and Saville, J. (eds), *Socialist Register 1988: Problems of Renewal: East & West*, London: Merlin

Needleman, M. L. 1974 *Guerillas in the Bureaucracy: The Community Planning Experiment in the United States*, New York: John Wiley

Nicholson, G. 1989 'A Model of How Not to Regenerate an Urban Area', *Town and Country Planning*, 58, 52-5

Niggle, C. 1986 'Financial Innovation and the Distinction between Financial and Industrial Capital', *Journal of Economic Issues*, 20

North Side Leadership Conference and North Side Civic Development Council 1986 *North Side Action Plan*

Nowikowski, S. 1984 'Snakes and Ladders: Asian Business in Britain'. In Ward, R. and Jenkins, R. (eds), *Ethnic Communities in Business*, Cambridge: Cambridge University Press

Nugent, T. 1984 'Inner Harbor Booms, City Goes Bust', *Inside Baltimore, v.1, No. 2*, December

Oberschall, A. 1979 'Protracted Conflict'. In Zald, M. N. and McCarthy, J. (eds), *The Dynamics of Social Movements*, Boston: Winthrop Publishers

Ofari, E. 1970 *The Myth of Black Capitalism*, London: Monthly Review Press

Pahl, R. E. 1988 'Some Remarks on Informal Work, Social Polarization and the Social Structure', *International Journal of Urban and Regional Research*, 12, 247-67

Parboni, R. 1981 *The Dollar and Its Rivals*, London: Verso

Parkinson, M. (ed) 1987 *Reshaping Local Government*, Oxford: Policy Journals, Hermitage

Parkinson, M. 1985 *Liverpool on the Brink*, London: Hermitage

Parkinson, M. 1988 'Urban Regeneration and Development Corporations: Liverpool Style', *Local Economy*, 3

Parkinson, M. and Evans, R. 1990 'Urban Development Corporations'. In Campbell, M. (ed), *Local Economic Policy*, London: Cassell

Parkinson, M., Foley, B. and Judd, D. (eds) 1988 *Regenerating the Cities: The UK Crisis and the US Experience*, Manchester: Manchester University Press

Payne, P. L. 1974 *British Entrepreneurship in the Nineteenth Century*, London: Macmillan

Peat Marwick McLintock 1987 'Review of LDDC Education, Training and Employment Initiatives', Unpublished Report

Peterson, P. E. (ed) 1985 *The New Urban Reality*, Washington, D.C.: Brookings Institution

Phillips, A. 1987 *Divided Loyalties: Dilemmas of Sex and Class,* London: Virago

Pickvance, C. 1985 'The Rise and Fall of Urban Movements and the Role of Comparative Analysis', *Environment and Planning D: Society and Space*, 3, 31-53

Pollin, R. 1986 'Alternative Perspectives on the Rise of Corporate Debt Dependency: The U.S. Postwar Experience', *Review of Radical Political Economics,* 18 (1) and 18 (2)

Pollin, R. 1987 'Structural Change and Increasing Fragility in the U.S. Financial System'. In Union for Radical Political Economics, *The Imperiled Economy*, New York: Union for Radical Political Economics

Pollin, R. 1989 'Keynes is Dead!', *The Guardian,* 2 August

Portes, A. and Bach, R. 1985 *Latin Journey: Cuban and Mexican Immigrants in the United States,* Berkeley, London: University of California Press

Potter, G. 1988 *Dialogue on Debt*, Washington, D.C.: Center of Concern

Pratt, G. and Hanson, S. 1988 'Gender, Class and Space', *Environment and Planning D: Society and Space,* 6, 15-35

Rand McNally, 1985 *Annual Survey*

Ratcliff, R., Gallagher, M. B. and Ratcliff, K. S. 1979 'The Civic Involvement of Bankers: An Analysis of the Influence of Economic Power and Social Prominence in the Command of Civic Policy Positions', *Social Problems*

Reintges, C. 1990 'Urban Movements in South African Black Townships: A Case Study', *International Journal of Urban and Regional Research*, 14, 109-34

Rex, J. 1988 'Old and New Themes in Urban Redevelopment'. In Rex, J., *The Ghetto and the Underclass; Essays on Race and Social Policy*, Aldershot: Gower

Roberts, P. A. 1988 *West Indians and Their Language*, Cambridge: Cambridge University Press

Robinson, W. and McCormick, C. 1984 'Slouching toward Avenue D', *Art in America*, 72, 135

Robson, B. 1988 *Those Inner Cities: Reconciling the Economic and Social Aims of Urban Policy*, Oxford: Clarendon Press

Rose, D. 1984 'Rethinking Gentrification: Beyond the Uneven Development of Marxist Urban Theory', *Environment and Planning D: Society and Space*, 1, 47-74

Rose, D. 1989 'A Feminist Perspective of Employment Restructuring and Gentrification: The Case of Montreal'. In Wolch, J. and Dear, M. (eds), *The Power of Geography*, Boston: Unwin Hyman

Rose, D. and Le Bourdais, C. 1986 'The Changing Conditions of Female Single Parenthood in Montreal's Inner City and Suburban Neighbourhoods', *Urban Resources*, 3, 45-52

Rosovsky, H. 1967 'The Serf Entrepreneur'. In Aitken, H. (ed), *Explorations in Enterprise*, Cambridge, Massachusetts: Harvard University Press

Saegert, S. 1981 'Masculine Cities and Feminine Suburbs: Polarized Ideas and Contradictory Realities'. In Stimpson, C. R., Dixler, E., Nelson, M. J. and Yatrakis, K. B. (eds), *Women and the American City*, Chicago: University of Chicago Press

Salins, P. 1981 'The creeping tide of disinvestment'. *New York Affairs*, 6, 5-19

Sassen, S. 1989 'New Trends in the Socio-Spatial Organization of the New York City Economy'. In Beauregard, R. A. (ed), *Economic Restructuring and Political Response*, Newbury Park, CA: Sage

Sassen-Koob, S. 1984 'The New Labor Demand in Global Cities'. In Smith, M.P. (ed), *Cities in Transformation*, Beverly Hills, CA: Sage

Saunders, P. 1981 *Social Theory and the Urban Question*, London: Hutchinson

Saunders, P. 1984 'Beyond housing classes: the sociological significance of private property rights in means of consumption', *International Journal of Urban and Regional Research*, 8, 202-25

Savas, E. S. 1983 'A Positive Urban Policy for the Future', *Urban Affairs Quarterly*, 18, 447-53

Sbragia, A. 1986 'Finance Capital and the City'. In Gottdiener, M. (ed), *Cities in Stress: A New Look at the Urban Crisis*, Beverly Hills, CA: Sage

Scarman Report 1982 *The Brixton Disorders 10-12 April 1981, Report of an Inquiry*, Harmondsworth: Penguin

Schaffer, R. and Smith, N. 1986 'The Gentrification of Harlem?', *Annals of the Association of American Geographers*, 76, 347-65

Shlay, A. 1985 *Where the Money Flows: Lending Patterns in the Washington, DC-Maryland-Virginia SMSA*, Chicago: The Woodstock Institute

Shlay, A. 1986 *A Tale of Three Cities: The Distribution of Housing Credit from Financial Institutions in the Chicago SMSA from 1980-1983*, Chicago: The Woodstock Institute

Shlay, A. 1987a *Maintaining the Divided City: Residential Lending Patterns in the Baltimore SMSA*, Baltimore: The Maryland Alliance for Responsible Investment

Shlay, A. 1987b *The Underwriting of Community: Evaluating Federally Regulated Depository Financial Institutions' Residential Lending Performance within the Baltimore SMSA from 1981-84*, Baltimore: The Maryland Alliance for Responsible Investment

Shlay, A. 1988 'Not in that Neighborhood: The Effects of Housing and Population on the Distribution of Mortgage Finance within the Chicago SMSA from 1980-1983', *Social Science Research*, 17

Shlay, A. 1989 'Financing Community: Methods for Assessing Residential Credit Disparities, Market Barriers and Institutional Performance in the Metropolis', forthcoming in *Journal of Urban Affairs*

Sills, A., Taylor, G. and Golding, P. 1988 *The Politics of the Urban Crisis*, London: Hutchinson

Smith, C. F. 1980 'As Shadow Government Grows Stronger, its Accountability to the Public Lessens', *The Baltimore Sun*, 20 April

Smith, M. P. 1988, 'The Uses of Linked Development Policies in U.S. Cities'. In Parkinson, M., Foley, B. and Judd, D. (eds), *Regenerating the Cities: The U.K. Crisis and the U.S. Experience*, Manchester: Manchester University Press

Smith, N. 1979a 'Toward a Theory of Gentrification: a Back to the City Movement by Capital not People' *Journal of the American Planning Association*, 45, 538-48

Smith, N. 1979b 'Gentrification and Capital: Theory, Practice and Ideology in Society Hill', *Antipode*, 11, 24-35

Smith, N. 1982 'Gentrification and Uneven Development', *Economic Geography*, 58, 139-55

Smith, N. 1984 *Uneven Development: Nature, Capital and the Production of Space*, Oxford: Basil Blackwell

Smith, N. 1987 'Gentrification and the Rent Gap', *Annals of the Association of American Geographers*, 77, 462-5

Smith, N. 1987 'Of Yuppies and Housing: Gentrification, Social Restructuring, and the Urban Dream', *Environment and Planning D: Society and Space*, 5, 151-72

Smith, N. 1990 'New City, New Frontier'. In Sorkin, M. (ed), *Variations on a Theme (Park)*, New York: Hill and Wary (forthcoming)

Soja, E. 1989 *Postmodern Geographies: The Reassertion of Space in Critical Social Theory*, London: Verso

Solomos, J. 1988 *Black Youth, Racism and the State*, Cambridge: Cambridge University Press

South East Community Organization (SECO) 1980a Pamphlet on *Housing Speculation in Baltimore*

South East Community Organizations (SECO) 1980b *Speculation leaflet*

Squires, G. and Velez, W. 1987 'Neighborhood Racial Composition and Mortgage Lending: City and Suburban Differences', *Journal of Urban Affairs*, 9

Sternlieb, G. 1971 'The City as Sandbox', *Public Interest*, 25, 14-21.

Sternlieb, G. and Burchell, R. W. 1973 *Residential Abandonment: The Tenement Landlord Revisited*, Piscataway, NJ: Center for Urban Policy Research, Rutgers University

Sternlieb, G. and Lake, R. W. 1976 'The Dynamics of Real Estate Tax Delinquency', *National Tax Journal*, 29, 262-71

Stevenson, G. 1980 'The Abandonment of Roosevelt Gardens'. In Jensen, R. (ed), *Devastation/Reconstruction: The South Bronx*, New York: The Bronx Museum of the Arts

Storper, M. 1987 'Significance of Private Property Rights and Means of Consumption', *International Journal of Urban and Regional Research*, 8, 202-27

Stratton, J. 1977 *Pioneering in the Urban Wilderness*, New York: Urizen Books.

Strickland, D. and Judd, D. 1983 'National Urban Policy and the Shifting Priorities of Inner City Revitalisation', *Urban Analysis*, 7

Swann Report 1985 *Education for All - Great Britain, Committee of Inquiry into the Education of Children from Ethnic Minority Groups*, London: DES, HMSO

Swanstrom, T. 1987 'Urban Populism, Uneven Development, and the Space for Reform'. In Cummuns, S. (ed), *Corporate Elites and Urban Development*, New York: State University of New York Press

Swiereger, R. 1968 *Pioneers and Profits: Land Speculation on the Iowa Frontier*. Ames, Iowa: Iowa University Press

Swinney, D. 1989 'Capital Strategies and Labor', *Newsletter of the Union for Radical Political Economics*, Summer

Swyngedouw, E. 1989 'The Heart of the Place: The Resurrection of Locality in an Age of Hyperspace', *Geographiska Annaler Series B*, 71, 31-42

Szanton, P. 1986 *Baltimore 2000*, Baltimore: Goldseker Foundation

Thrift, N. 1987 'The Geography of Late Twentieth-Century Class Formation'. In Thrift, N. and Williams, P. (eds), *Class and Space: The Making of Urban Society*, London: Routledge and Kegan Paul

Thrift, N. and Leyshon, A. 1988 'The Gambling Propensity', *Geoforum*, 19, 55-69

Thrift, N. and Williams, P. 1987 'The Geography of Class Formation'. In Thrift, N. and Williams, P. (eds), *Class and Space: The Making of Urban Society*, London: Routledge and Kegan Paul

Thrift, N., Leyshon, A. and Daniels, P. 1987 'Sexy Greedy. The New International Financial System, The City of London and the South East of England', Mimeo, Bristol: Centre for the Study of Britain and the World Economy, University of Bristol

Toker, F. 1986 *Pittsburgh: An Urban Portrait*, Pittsburgh: Penn State Press

Trippier, D. 1989 *New Life for Inner Cities*, London: Conservative Political Centre

Turner, F. J. (1958 edn.) *The Frontier in American History*, New York: Holt, Rinehart and Winston

Urban Renewal Authority of Pittsburgh 1983 *An Evaluation of the North Side Revitalization Program October 1979 - October 1983*

US Department of Housing and Development 1982 *The President's 1982 National Urban Policy Report*, Washington, D.C.: HUD

US Department of Housing and Development 1984 *The President's 1984 National Urban Policy Report*, Washington, D.C.: HUD

US House Banking and Currency Committee 1968 *Commercial Banks and their Trust Activities: Emerging Influence on the American Economy*, Washington, D.C., 8 July

Wachter, S. 1988 *Etat, Décentralisation et Territoire*, Paris: L'Harmattan

Walby, S. 1986 *Patriarchy at Work*, Cambridge: Polity Press

Walker, A. 1987 'The Poor Relation: Poverty among Old Women'. In Glendinning, C. and Millar, J. (eds), *Women and Poverty in Britain*, Brighton: Wheatsheaf

Walton, J. 1987 'Urban Protest and the Global Political Economy'. In Smith, M. P. and Feagin, J. R. (eds), *The Capitalist City*, Oxford: Basil Blackwell

Ward, R. and Jenkins, R. (eds) 1984 *Ethnic Communities in Business*, London: Cambridge University Press

Washington Post 'Apartheid Foes at Hopkins Hail Bank's Decision', 11 November

Wekerle, G. R. 1984 'A Woman's Place is in the City', *Antipode*, 16, 11-19

Werner, B. 1985 'Fertility Trends in Social Classes: 1970-83', *Population Trends*, 41, 5-13

Williams, P. 1976 'The Role of Institutions in the Inner London Housing Market: The Case of Islington', *Transactions of the Institute of British Geographers*, NS1, 72-82

Williams, P. 1978 'Building Societies and the Inner City', *Transactions of the Institute of British Geographers*, NS3, 23-34

Williams, P. 1986 'Class Constitution through Spatial Reconstruction? A Re-evaluation of Gentrification in Australia, Britain and the United States'. In Smith, N. and Williams, P. (eds), *Gentrification of the City,* Boston: Allen and Unwin

Williams, P. 1988 *Race and Mortgage Lending in New York City: A Study on Redlining,* Brooklyn: Center for Law and Social Justice, Medgar Evers College

Williams, P. and Smith, N. 1986 'From Renaissance to Restructuring: The Dynamics of Contemporary Urban Development'. In Smith, N. and Williams, P. (eds) *Gentrification of the City,* Boston: Allen and Unwin

Williams, W. 1987 'Rise in Values Spurs Rescue of Buildings', *New York Times,* 4 April

Williamson, J. 1987 *Consuming Passions,* London: Marion Boyars

Wilson, D. 1985 *Institutions and Urban Revitalization: The Case of the J-51 Subsidy Program in New York City*, PhD dissertation, Department of Geography, Rutgers University

Wilson, D. 1988 'Urban Ecology, Managerialism and Neighbourhood Revitalisation: The Manhattan Experience', *South Eastern Geographer,* 28(2)

Wilson, D. 1989 'Local State Dynamics and Gentrification in Indianapolis', *Indiana Urban Geography,* 10, 19-40

Wilson, W. J. 1987 *The Truly Disadvantaged: The Inner City, the Underclass and Public Policy*, Chicago: University of Chicago Press

Winchester, H. P. M. and White, P. E. 1988 'The Location of Marginalised Groups in the Inner City', *Environment and Planning D: Society and Space,* 6, 37-54

Wolfe, J. M., Drover, G. and Skelton, I. 1980 'Inner City Real Estate Activity in Montreal', *The Canadian Geographer,* 24, 349-67

Wolman, H. 1986 'The Reagan Urban Policy and its Impacts', *Urban Affairs Quarterly,* 21, 311-35

Wong, K. K. and Peterson, P. E. 1986 'Urban Response to Federal Program Flexibility', *Urban Affairs Quarterly,* 21, 293-309

Wyckoff, W. 1988 *The Developer's Frontier; The Making of the Western New York Landscape*, New Haven: Yale University Press

INDEX

Thatcher, M., 2, 10, 17, 90, 195, 197, 204; government and urban policy, 42; Thatcherism, 14-19, 20, 196
Thompson, M., 27, 186
Thrift, N., 119, 124, 143
Toledo, Ohio, 9
Toxteth, 51
Trades union movement, 15, 129
Trickle-down, 32-34
Trippier, D., 4, 16, 19, 23, 27 38
Turner, F. J., 85, 88, 108, 109
UDAG, 149
UDC, 2, 8, 10, 11, 16, 18, 19, 24, 26, 36, 37, 38, 40, 42, 43, 44, 45, 46, 57; and accountability, 50-52; and official criticism of, 37, 43; and leverage, 40-41; and government policy, 31, 40, 43, 57; and location of, 43; and aims of, 43-44
Uhalberdorde, J. M., 204
Underclass, 9
Unemployment, 14, 127-138, 209, 216, 217
Urban Aid Programme, 16
Urban crisis, 3, 5, 7, 20, 202-218
Urban Development Action Grant, 63
Urban planning, 207-208
Urban politics, 146, 161-166; and urban movements, 161-166
Urban Programme Area, 217
Urban redevelopment, 149-151
Urban Renewal, 20, 27
Urry, J., 18
US House Banking Committee, 149
Vancouver, 121
Vauxhall (area strategy), 52, 54
Voorhees, M., 155
Wachter, S., 204
Walby, S., 120, 125
Walker, A., 113
Walton, J., 145-146, 161
Ward, R., 35, 185, 199
Washington, DC, 146
Waterfront, development of, 48; and in Baltimore, 148-149, 150, 159
Weber, M., 198
Weiskopf, T., 165
Wekerle, G., 112
Werner, B., 113
White, P., 113, 118, 123
Williams, P., 96, 109, 112, 115, 117, 118, 124, 146
Williams, W., 99
Williamson, J., 122

Wilmington, Delaware, 144, 146
Wilson, D., 81, 97
Wilson, W. J., 4
Winchester, H., 113, 118, 123
Wolfe, J. M., 94, 96
Wolman, A., 12
Women, 110; and work; 111-123; and poverty, 112-113; and family, 112-113; and old age, 113
Workplace Nurseries Campaign, 138
Wyckoff, W., 88